Wellbeing of Transnational Muslim Families

This book examines the needs, aspirations, strategies, and challenges of transnational Muslim migrants in Europe with regard to family practices such as marriage, divorce, and parenting. Critically re-conceptualizing 'wellbeing' and unpacking its multiple dimensions in the context of Muslim families, it investigates how migrants make sense of and draw on different norms, laws, and regimes of knowledge as they navigate different aspects of family relations and life in a transnational social space. With attention to issues such as registration of marriage, civil versus religious marriage, spousal roles and rights, polygamy, parenting, child wellbeing, and everyday security, the authors offer national and comparative case studies of Muslim families from different parts of the world, covering different family bonds and relations, within both extended and nuclear families.

Based on empirical research in the Nordic region and further afield, this volume affords a more complete understanding of the practices of transnational migrant families, as well as the processes through which family relations and rights are negotiated between family members and with state institutions and laws, whilst contributing to the growing literature on migrant wellbeing. As such, it will appeal to scholars of sociology and social policy with interests in migration and transnational communities, wellbeing, and the family.

Marja Tiilikainen (PhD, Docent) is Senior Researcher at the Migration Institute of Finland.

Mulki Al-Sharmani (PhD, Docent) is Senior Lecturer of Islamic Theology at the Faculty of Theology, Study of Religions Unit, University of Helsinki, Finland. She is the author of *Gender Justice and Legal Reform in Egypt: Negotiating Muslim Family Law*; the editor of *Feminist Activism, Women's Rights and Legal Reform*; and the co-editor of *Men in Charge? Rethinking Authority in Muslim Legal Tradition*.

Sanna Mustasaari is a postdoctoral researcher at the Faculty of Law, University of Helsinki, Finland.

Studies in Migration and Diaspora

Studies in Migration and Diaspora is a series designed to showcase the interdisciplinary and multidisciplinary nature of research in this important field. Volumes in the series cover local, national and global issues and engage with both historical and contemporary events. The books will appeal to scholars, students and all those engaged in the study of migration and diaspora. Amongst the topics covered are minority ethnic relations, transnational movements and the cultural, social and political implications of moving from 'over there', to 'over here'.

Series Editor: Anne J. Kershen, Queen Mary University of London, UK

Color that Matters
A Comparative Approach to Mixed Race Identity and
Nordic Exceptionalism
Tony Sandset

Lives in Transit
An Ethnographic Study of Refugees' Subjectivity across European Borders
Elena Fontanari

Migration, Work and Home-Making in the City
Dwelling and Belonging among Vietnamese Communities in London
Annabelle Wilkins

Home States and Homeland Politics
Interactions between the Turkish State and its Emigrants in France and the United States
Damla B. Aksel

Undoing Homogeneity in the Nordic Region
Migration, Difference and the Politics of Solidarity
Edited by Suvi Keskinen, Unnur Dís Skaptadóttir and Mari Toivanen

Wellbeing of Transnational Muslim Families
Marriage, Law and Gender
Edited by Marja Tiilikainen, Mulki Al-Sharmani and Sanna Mustasaari

For more information about this series, please visit: https://www.routledge.com/sociology/series/ASHSER1049

Wellbeing of Transnational Muslim Families

Marriage, Law and Gender

Edited by
Marja Tiilikainen, Mulki Al-Sharmani and
Sanna Mustasaari

Routledge
Taylor & Francis Group

LONDON AND NEW YORK

First published 2020
by Routledge
2 Park Square, Milton Park, Abingdon, Oxon OX14 4RN

and by Routledge
52 Vanderbilt Avenue, New York, NY 10017

Routledge is an imprint of the Taylor & Francis Group, an informa business

British Library Cataloguing-in-Publication Data
A catalogue record for this book is available from the British Library

Library of Congress Cataloging-in-Publication Data
A catalog record has been requested for this book

ISBN: 978-1-138-29367-0 (hbk)
ISBN: 978-1-315-23197-6 (ebk)

Typeset in Times New Roman
by Taylor & Francis Books

Contents

Table

Acknowledgements

This book is an outcome of the multidisciplinary research project 'Transnational Muslim Marriages: Wellbeing, Law, and Gender' that was funded by the Academy of Finland for five years from 2013 to 2018 at the Department of Social Research, University of Helsinki, Finland, and directed by Marja Tiilikainen. We owe our gratitude to Professors Ziba Mir-Hosseini, Lynn Welchman, and Ruba Salih, and Dr Samia Bano at the School of Oriental and African Studies (SOAS) as well as to Dr Sara Silvestri at City, University of London, all of whom kindly agreed to serve as members of the scientific advisory board for this book project and shared their insightful comments on the present volume as a whole as well as its individual chapters in two seminars in London in 2014 and 2016. We also want to thank the Centre of Islamic and Middle Eastern Law (CIMEL) at SOAS and the Department of International Politics and Centre for International Policy Studies at City, University of London, for hosting these seminars, which were invaluable for this book to come into being.

This book could not have been written without the contributors of the individual chapters. We want to thank all the authors and participants in the seminars for their patience, commitment, and willingness to work with us. In addition, we want to thank our colleagues Abdirashid Ismail and Linda Hart who worked in our research project and also provided valuable comments on the chapters.

Regarding the role of the book editors, Marja Tiilikainen and Sanna Mustasaari would like to acknowledge Mulki Al-Sharmani's central role, which went well beyond what is usually entailed in being the second editor. Mulki took the lead in conceptualizing the book as well as in writing the proposal and the introduction. She also took the main responsibility for commenting on and editing the individual chapters, of putting together the scientific board, and of identifying and inviting the book contributors from outside the project. Furthermore, she organized two conference panels for the project team members to advance the work on the volume. In addition, Mulki, together with the project director, organized the two seminars in London that facilitated the writing process.

Our thanks are also due to Professor Sarah C. White for theoretical inspiration and giving us permission to quote her draft paper 'But what is Wellbeing? A framework for analysis in social and development policy and practice' from 2008. Dr Robert Whiting from the University of Helsinki has taken care of the language revision – any possibly remaining errors are naturally our responsibility. Finally, we want to thank our Editor Neil Jordan and Editorial Assistant Alice Salt at Routledge for a swift publication process and to express our gratitude to the anonymous reviewers for their invaluable comments on and critiques of the individual chapters.

Marja Tiilikainen, Mulki Al-Sharmani and Sanna Mustasaari

Series Editor's Preface

Wellbeing is a much contested and multi-faceted construct. Each of us aspires to achieve and maintain an acceptable and sustaining life equilibrium – or state of wellbeing. However, there is not just one simple 'fits all' model. Wellbeing within the family is achieved by confronting, challenging and pursuing a range of constituents which include culture, gender, religion, wealth, marital status and sexual orientation. It is a multidimensional, variable, non-static process; one which can be viewed through the prisms of 'multiple laws, norms and value systems'.

The main actors in this book are Muslim migrants many, if not all, of whom wear the mantle of the transnational. Studies of transnationalism have grown in recent years, particularly in the context of Muslim migrants for whom migration, particularly to western countries, has necessitated acclimatisation to different cultures, laws and expectations. Nearly all live some degree of transnational life, or even multi-transnational life; one in which the Muslim migrant maintains economic, familial and social links with more than one country; those 'places' being the current country of residence, their place of origin and other locations where family members are based. Whilst there has been an increasing number of studies of the nature and organisation of transnational lives – those in which the actors maintain an interconnectedness across borders – few, if any, have fused the study of the transnational lives of Muslim migrants with their acquisition and maintenance of a satisfying state of wellbeing in their new lives. This is what this groundbreaking volume achieves.

In this book the contributors examine the 'wellbeing' of their interlocutors within three main perspectives: relational, material and ethical, and it is within these boundaries that the contributions to this volume are focused. The relational elements of wellbeing, those which enable the protagonists to achieve (or not) wellbeing, are in the main through the family; as seen through the lens of both the nuclear and the extended family. The material exists in the tangible elements of everyday life; in the school, the workplace, in interaction with local organisations and communities, whilst the ethical – or moral – element of wellbeing is mainly to be found within the context of the mosque and the teachings of Islam and, particularly for the female interlocutors, is conjoined with the way in which their marriage is enacted and maintained. A strong observance of the Five Pillars of Islam is a characteristic of some female proselytes who often become more devout than their Islamic-born partners. It is interesting to note that at the commencement of structuring a family and, accordingly its wellbeing, a number of female converts to Islam place more importance on a religious marriage than on a civil ceremony, even though this may create problems in the event of an eventual marriage breakdown.

Though geographically this book has strongest ties to the Nordic countries, several of the chapters do extend beyond those boundaries, examining in addition the wellbeing experiences of Muslim transnationals in the Netherlands, the UK and Canada. Some chapters take an abstract as opposed to directly personal approach, while others are more engaged at the grass roots of transnational wellbeing. In each case the reader becomes privy to a variety of attitudes and ambitions of women and children – male actors are in a minority in this volume.

Marriage and wellbeing for the Muslim transnationals is a strong thread throughout this book. However, one aspect which frequently weakens the strength of a marriage is that of the practice of polygamy – almost inevitably on the part of the man. Polygamous marriages exist for a variety of reasons, due to health needs, the 'male only out migration' of the husband, and the constant transnational movements of the husband from over here, to over there – and even in some cases to a second and third 'over there'. Indeed several chapters explore the legal complexities of transnational marriages, particularly when attempting to determine the legitimacy of a marriage when the wife wants a divorce.

The traditional Somali approach to marriage and married life suggests a contrast between wellbeing and married life in Somalia and in the West. This binary, however, is also questioned throughout the volume. The reader is shown how some Somali men maintain the tradition of non-involvement in the domestic side of family life. Instead of remaining close to 'the hearth' and within the family environment, many Somali husbands and fathers choose to sit in local cafés and discuss politics whilst chewing *khat*. An inability to find regular employment in their new place of settlement and the accompanying marginalisation and emasculation caused, frequently results in these 'short-term' absences whilst paternal long-distance travel, and long-term absence, disrupts and undermines family wellbeing. The children have no resident 'father figure' and, particularly in the case of the boy children, lack the control and influence of the male parent; the mother having to provide emotionally and often materially for all. Yet on the positive side Somali culture is strong on family life and parental control and the reader learns that in Sweden, Somali parents are working to retain their traditional authority while permitting their children a level of autonomy as a means of fusing both cultures. In another Nordic country, Finland, a mosque in Helsinki has set up a programme to educate, encourage and enable the integration of Muslim families and hopefully enhance the acquisition of a positive sense of family wellbeing that results in an ethical Finnish Muslim life.

This is a book which not only informs and enlightens, it additionally provides considerable food for thought. How are the constituents of wellbeing to be combined in order to satisfy the diverse migrant groups that now inhabit major metropolises? The response is not simple but this volume provides an important guide as to how this may be achieved and the pitfalls that exist. Whilst it is dedicated to one specific transnational group, Muslim migrants in Europe and North America, it provides a valuable template for other studies which seek to understand how wellbeing can be achieved by transnational migrants in an 'alien' environment.

Anne J Kershen
Queen Mary University of London
Autumn 2019

Contributors

Mulki Al-Sharmani is trained as a cultural anthropologist. From 2013 to 2018, Mulki was Academy of Finland research fellow in the Faculty of Theology, University of Helsinki. She was the principal investigator of the project *Islamic Feminism: Tradition, Authority, and Hermeneutics*; and senior researcher in the project *Transnational Muslim Marriages: Wellbeing, Law, and Gender*. In September 2018, Mulki assumed the post of lecturer of Islamic theology in the same faculty. Mulki researches Somali diasporas, transnational families, Islamic family law and marriage practices in Egypt and Finland, gender in Islamic interpretive tradition, and Islamic feminism. She authored *Gender Justice and Legal Reform in Egypt: Negotiating Muslim Family Law* (2017), and co-edited *Men in Charge? Rethinking Authority in Muslim Legal tradition* (2015). She has also authored "Divorce among Transnational Finnish Somalis: Gender, Religion, and Agency" (*Religion and Gender* 2017), and "Striving against the 'Nafs': Revisiting Somali Muslim Spousal Roles and Rights in Finland" (*Journal of Religion in Europe* 2015). E-mail: mulki.al-sharmani@helsinki.fi.

Rannveig Haga is a researcher affiliated with Södertörn University College. She did her PhD in 2009 in the History of Religions at Uppsala University, Department of Theology, with the title *Tradition as Resource: Somali Women Traders Facing the Realities of Civil War*. It is a qualitative study involving fieldwork in Hargeisa (Somaliland) and in Dubai. Since then she has been the project leader of two extensive research projects on parenting and Islam, based on fieldwork among Somali parents in Sweden and Finland and financed by the Research Council of Sweden and the Baltic Sea Foundation. Her recent publications include "Storytelling as a Way to Reconnect and Co-Create Spiritual Contexts: Conversations with Five Swedish-Somali Mothers" (in V. Reimer, ed., *Angels on Earth: Mothering in Religious and Spiritual Contexts* 2016). E-mail: rannveigjetne@gmail.com.

Betty de Hart is Full Professor of Transnational Families and Migration Law at Vrije Universiteit Amsterdam, in the Amsterdam Centre for Migration and Refugee Law. She received a personal research grant from the Netherlands Organization for Scientific Research (NWO) from 2008 to 2013 for her research project *Transnational Families between Dutch and Islamic Family Law: A study on transnational legal space.* In 2016, she was awarded the ERC Consolidator Grant for the project *Euromix: Regulating mixed intimacies in Europe.* Her research interests include migration and citizenship law, family reunification, intersectionality, and law in everyday life. A specific research interest is how law responds to 'mixed' couples and families in terms of legal status (citizenship or residence), and/or ethnicity or race, and vice versa. E-mail: b.de.hart@vu.nl.

Abdirashid A. Ismail obtained a D.Sc. (econ) from the Hanken School of Economics, Finland, in 2010. The title of his dissertation was *Somali State Failure: Players, Incentives and Institutions.* Ismail works as Senior Researcher at the Migration Institute of Finland and he is also an economics policy fellow with the Heritage Institute for Policy Studies (HIPS) in Somalia. Previously he has worked as a postdoctoral researcher in the Department of Social Research, University of Helsinki. Ismail studies immigration and diaspora, with a focus on Muslims, particularly Somalis, in Europe. His main interest is transnational family and child wellbeing. In addition, his areas of interest include the political economy of conflict, post-conflict state formation, and the political history of Somalia. E-mail: abdirashid.ismail@utu.fi.

Friso Kulk holds an MA in Arabic Studies and an LLM in Dutch Law from the University of Amsterdam. He also studied at the Université Cadi Ayyad in Marrakesh, Morocco and the Netherlands-Flemish Institute in Cairo (NVIC). He obtained his PhD in sociology of law at the Institute for Sociology of Law/Centre for Migration Law, Radboud University, Nijmegen. His research focuses on how legal ties between parents and their children are shaped in transnational contexts. Apart from his research, he has worked as a legal consultant to refugees and written articles on Middle Eastern law aimed at civil registry officials. E-mail: frisokulk@gmail.com.

Anika Liversage (PhD) is Senior Researcher at VIVE – the Danish Center for Social Science Research. Her research interests are immigrant family relations, with particular attention to issues of gender and power. She has studied marital patterns in immigrant families, including the consequences of legislative reform and immigrant divorce, particularly concerning the interplay between, e.g., gender, family networks, and residency status. Another research topic is intergenerational family relations and immigrant aging. She speaks Turkish, having lived four years in the country, and much of her work concerns changes in Turkish immigrant families in Denmark. Recent publications include "Out of Touch – Understanding Post-divorce Relationships between Children and Fathers in Ethnic

Minority Families" (with M.H. Ottosen, *Nordic Journal of Migration Research* 2017) and "Growing Old in Exile – A Longitudinal Study of Migrant Women from Turkey" (with G. Mirdal, *Journal of Ethnic and Migration Studies* 2017). E-mail: ani@vive.dk.

Annelies Moors is Professor of Contemporary Muslim Societies in the Department of Anthropology, University of Amsterdam. She studied Arabic at the University of Damascus and Arabic and anthropology at the University of Amsterdam. She has done extensive fieldwork in the Middle East (especially Palestine and Yemen) and Europe (especially the Nether-lands), and published widely on gendered visibility and multiple belongings (Islamic fashion and anti-fashion; face-veiling), material kinship and material religion (wearing gold; marriage contracts), gendered mobilities and spatialities (migrant domestic labour), and controversies on Islam and Muslims in Europe and beyond (dress and marriage; cultural politics and everyday life). From 2001 to 2008 she was the Amsterdam ISIM Chair, where she directed the programme on Muslim cultural politics. Currently she is the PI of an NWO grant on "Muslim Activism", and of an ERC advanced grant on "Problematizing 'Muslim marriages': Ambiguities and Contestations", which investigates the relation between public debates and everyday life at a global level.

Sanna Mustasaari is a postdoctoral researcher in the Faculty of Law, University of Helsinki. She has conducted research on the legality and recognition of family ties in different normative systems. Her main research interests include religion and family law, human rights law, feminist legal theory, migration law, and transnational family life. Her recent publications include "Best Interests of the Child in Family Reunification – a Citizenship Test Disguised?" (in A. Griffiths, S. Mustasaari, and A. Mäki-Petäjä-Leinonen, eds., *Subjectivity, Citizenship and Belonging in Law: Identities and Intersections* 2017) and "Between 'Official' and 'Unofficial': Discourses and Practices of Muslim Marriage Conclusion in Finland" (with M. Al-Sharmani, *Oxford Journal of Law and Religion* 2018). E-mail: sanna.mustasaari@helsinki.fi.

Ann Phoenix is Professor of Psychosocial Studies in the Thomas Coram Research Unit, Department of Social Sciences, UCL Institute of Education, University of London, and a Fellow of the British Academy. She co-directed the Childhood Wellbeing Research Centre funded by the Department for Education. Her research is mainly about social identities and the ways in which psychological experiences and social processes are linked. It includes work on intersections of racialized and gendered identities and experiences, mixed-parentage, masculinities, consumption, young people and their parents, the transition to motherhood, families, migration, and transnational families. Much of her research draws on mixed methods and includes narrative approaches. From 2016 to 2018 she was the Erkko

Professor at the Helsinki University Collegium for Advanced Studies. E-mail: a.phoenix@ucl.ac.uk.

Iris Sportel is a researcher at the Institute for Sociology of Law/Centre for Migration Law of Radboud University Nijmegen, the Netherlands. She wrote *Transnational Families and Divorce, Marriage, Migration, and Family Law* (Palgrave 2016), on the interactions of transnational families with multiple legal systems in cases of divorce. Her research interests include family, intimate relationships, and law; gender and ethnicity; law in everyday life; and Islamic family law. In 2017 she received a Veni grant from the Netherlands Organisation for Scientific Research to conduct research on the role of ethnicity, culture, and religion in court cases concerning minority parents and children. E-mail: I.Sportel@jur.ru.nl.

Marja Tiilikainen (PhD) is Senior Researcher at the Migration Institute of Finland. She has conducted long-term research on the Somali diaspora and carried out ethnographic research in Finland, Somalia, and Canada. Her main research interests include Muslim minorities, cultural aspects of health and healing, transnational family life, everyday security, and family reunification. She has led several research projects on these themes. Her recent publications include "'Whenever Mom Hands Over the Phone, Then we Talk': Transnational Ties to the Country of Descent among Canadian Somali Youth" (*Migration Letters* 2017) and "Usage of Healthcare Services and Preference for Mental Healthcare among Older Somali Immigrants in Finland" (with M. Mölsä and R.-L. Punamäki, *Ethnicity & Health* 2017). E-mail: marja.tiilikainen@utu.fi.

Vishal Vora is a Research Fellow in the Department of Law and Anthropology at the Max Planck Institute for Social Anthropology in Germany. His postdoctoral research focuses on the new generation of British Hindus, their practice of citizenship, engagement with the law, and relationship to the state. Encompassing the notion of belonging and Britishness, this work examines the politics of racism, theories of multiculturalism, and legal pluralism in practice. The nexus between these three elements is of particular importance in multicultural Britain. Vishal read Human Genetics at University College London prior to his Call to the Bar of England and Wales (Inner Temple) in 2007. In 2010 Vishal began his doctoral research within the School of Law, SOAS, University of London. In 2016 he defended his thesis, entitled *The Islamic Marriage Conundrum: Register or Recognise? The Legal Consequences of the Nikah in England and Wales*. E-mail: vora@eth.mpg.de.

Vanessa Vroon-Najem is an anthropologist, specialized in the field of conversion to Islam in the Netherlands. She obtained a PhD on this subject in 2014 and continued her research at the University of Amsterdam. Together with Professor Annelies Moors, she currently focuses on how converts to Islam in the Netherlands find a partner and conclude their marriage(s), as well as on debates about ('halal') dating, partner choice, and (Islamic) marriages, and the political context in which these debates take place. With visual anthropologist Wendy van Wilgenburg she made a documentary and created an exhibition about her research: *Marrying Before Allah – Personal Stories of Converts* (2017). E-mail: v.e.vroon@uva.nl.

1 Introduction

Wellbeing, family life, and transnational Muslims in the West

Mulki Al-Sharmani, Marja Tiilikainen and Sanna Mustasaari

For an increasing number of migrants in Europe and North America, family life is embedded in a transnational social field (Baldassar and Merla, 2014; Bryceson and Vuorela, 2002). Common to such transnational family lives is organizing and navigating intimate relationships such as marriage, divorce, and parenting through the interplay of multiple norms and laws and through processes and practices cutting across national borders. In the case of transnational Muslim families, this has often meant state scrutiny of their marriage, divorce, and parenting practices since Islam – often being a legal and normative system pertinent to these family practices – becomes the focus of political and cultural contestations in many European public discourses (Razack, 2004; Schmidt, 2011; Rytter, 2012; Charsley, 2013; Grillo, 2015).

There is considerable scholarship in the social sciences on the family practices of Muslims in Europe. Broadly speaking, this literature has tackled marriage and divorce and their transnational dimensions, the generational and gender-based changes in family norms and practices, and state governance of marriage practices (particularly those related to migration) and individuals' and families' strategies in dealing with the challenges and marginalizing effects resulting from state policies (Shaw, 2001; Charsley, 2005; Charsley and Liversage, 2013; Tiilikainen, 2013; Al-Sharmani, 2015; 2017; Tiilikainen, 2015; Vora, 2016; Al-Sharmani and Ismail, 2017; Akhtar, 2018).

A notable gap in this scholarship, however, is multidimensional and multi-sited research on transnational Muslim family practices in the West through the conceptual lens of individual and family **wellbeing**. The aim of this book is to fill this gap. The chapters in the volume investigate how family practices such as marriage, divorce and parenting become part and parcel of (sometimes elusive) pursuits of individual and family wellbeing in diverse national and political contexts in Europe and North America.

By using a processual and multidimensional conceptualization of wellbeing, we seek to capture not only the needs and challenges of individual Muslims and their families as they navigate marriage and family life in a transnational social space, but also their aspirations and their understandings of the material, relational, and ethical dimensions of what constitutes for them a good life. We investigate how individuals and their families in selected contexts make sense of and/or draw on different norms, laws, regimes of knowledge, and values in the course of different family practices, as well as the role of the larger socio-political contexts in these processes. In addition, we examine how law (whether codified or uncodified, religious or secular) functions as a national and transnational site for governance of Muslims' intimate relationships as well as a resource by which individuals − often in differentiated, gendered, and uneven ways − can attend to their family relations and their own needs and aspirations as spouses and/or parents.

Our inquiry into the transnational family practices of Muslims and their families in selected contexts is also part of an effort to contribute to a more robust understanding and use of the concept wellbeing.

As such, our inquiry proceeds from two angles. The first is from the perspectives, experiences, and strategies of individual family members such as spouses, parents, and children. Second, we seek an understanding of the wellbeing of these individuals and their families from the perspectives and practices of institutions that are pertinent to their family lives such as state legal systems regulating marriage and recognition of family relationships, school officials working with Muslim migrant children, mosques carrying out a variety of family welfare activities including marriage solemnization and family dispute resolution, etc. By bringing in these two angles, we wish to highlight the interconnectedness of the private/family life and the public sphere of policy and governance of religious minorities, and we explore the convergences and the divergences among different individual and institutional understandings and pursuits of wellbeing in relation to Muslim family life.

The book draws on research conducted in the Nordic countries of Finland, Sweden, and Denmark that share a Nordic welfare model, but also differ as regards their history of migration. For example, Finland is quite a recent country of immigration compared to its Nordic neighbours. In addition, some of the chapters present research on countries that have a long history of immigration such as the Netherlands, the UK, and Canada.

Wellbeing and Muslim family practices

Theoretical background

Wellbeing has been written about in a number of fields in social sciences (Hall, et al., 2010). However, few conceptual studies have focused on family wellbeing (McKeown and Sweeney, 2001; Zimmerman, 2013). In addition, legal discourses addressing wellbeing have mainly focused on welfare, social justice, and children's rights as well as the different uses of the best interest doctrine in legal fields such as family law, administrative law, and medical law (Nathan, 2010; Herring and Foster, 2012). Relational approaches to wellbeing and rights have also gained ground in legal thinking (Nedelsky, 2011).

On the whole, conceptualizations of wellbeing in social sciences have tended to be both utilitarian and unidimensional. It was only in the first decade of the new millennium that multidimensional conceptualizations of wellbeing emerged. This was also the aim of two interconnected research projects in the United Kingdom. The first project was titled *Measuring Human Well-being* and was conducted by UNU-WIDER. In the context of working on this project, McGillivray (2007) explored multiple dimensions and measurements for the concept of human wellbeing. The second project was titled *Wellbeing in Developing Countries (WeD)*, and was undertaken by the ESRC Research Group at the University of Bath. It is the anthropologist Sarah White at the University of Bath and a leading member of the ESRC research group who is credited with a systematic development of the concept of wellbeing in a series of writings and publications that she has produced since 2008.

Working in the field of social development, White (2008) conceptualized wellbeing as processual, dynamic, and having three dimensions: material, relational, and subjective. The material, according to White, denotes those aspects of wellbeing that are concerned with tangible welfare needs such as education, housing, employment, safe neighbourhood, etc. The relational dimension refers to the personal and social relations in which individuals' pursuit and experiences of wellbeing are embedded. As for the subjective dimension, it is concerned with the individual's values, perceptions, and experiences. In a 2010 article, White modified her conceptualization, classifying the three dimensions of wellbeing as material, social, and human. The first dimension, in this modified model, was still concerned with the individual's practical welfare such as income and assets, whereas the second dimension referred to social relations and access to public services and goods. The third dimension consisted of the individual's capabilities (e.g. education), personal relations (such as family relations), and his/her value systems. Each dimension, White argued, included an objective aspect referring to the indicators listed in this dimension as well as a subjective aspect referring to the individual's perceptions and experiences of this dimension (White, 2010, p.163). In the 2015 volume, which White edited with Chloe Blackmore, the work on wellbeing further evolved into examining how different academic accounts of wellbeing are constructed and the role of the different methodologies that researchers use in these constructions (White and Blackmore, 2015).

In the field of migration, the concept of wellbeing has not been systematically conceptualized or investigated. A number of studies focusing on the issue of care work in migrant families, particularly in relation to children, have presented some cursory definitions and/or explanations of the concept (Abrego, 2009; Heyman, et al., 2009; Graham and Jordan, 2011; Mazzucato and Schans, 2011). In these studies, wellbeing is primarily perceived as outcomes (e.g. psychological, educational, and health in Mazzucato and Schans, 2011) that are achieved or hindered due to a number of factors. These approaches, however, fail to address the role that individual and collective agency plays in creating and maintaining the manifold material and cultural elements of wellbeing. An adequate conceptualization of wellbeing would need to take into account, for instance, how wellbeing happens in reciprocal relations as a process of meaningful engagement with the different structures of one's environment.

Katie Wright (2010; 2012) noted this gap in the literature. She pointed out that while the scholarship in the field highlights the attachments that migrants maintain with people, traditions, and causes in their homeland and beyond, it says little about the goals that migrants set for themselves, their feelings about whether their needs and goals are met, and the strategies that they adopt in different domains of their lives. According to Wright, a more explicit focus on the needs and goals of transnational immigrants and barriers that they themselves identify is necessary. Drawing on the conceptual framework for wellbeing that was developed by the ESRC Research Group (McGregor, 2007; McGregor and Sumner, 2010; White, 2008), Wright proposed the concept of human wellbeing. She used this concept to examine the multidimensional aspects of remittances (i.e. economic, social, etc.) and their impact on migrants and their family relations and lives. Wright's aim was to bring together different dimensions of immigrants' transnational engagements. She argued that

> a human well-being approach has the potential to fill these gaps, first, by focusing on: how migrants' needs and goals are formed and transformed as part of the international migration process; the obstacles to "living well" that migrants identify; and by suggesting that these barriers are linked to a mismatch between aspirations and achievements (Wright, 2010, p.368).

This volume builds on Wright's efforts; we seek to develop a holistic understanding of the wellbeing of transnational Muslim (migrant) families. We draw on (and modify) Sarah White's conceptualization of wellbeing to investigate Muslim migrants' intimate relationships and family life, as they take form through transnational family ties and practices as well as through encounters with multiple laws and norms in transnational space. By employing wellbeing as our key heuristic lens, we seek a holistic and multidimensional understanding of two interrelated issues: **the first** is the politics and lived realities of the family practices and relationships that are the focus of investigation in the different chapters; and **the second** is the meanings ascribed (by different actors) to wellbeing in relation to these family relationships and practices and the ways in which both issues are shaped by the governance of Muslim minorities in the different researched contexts.

Our approach to wellbeing

We envision wellbeing as encompassing three broad dimensions: *material, relational, and ethical*. We propose these three classifications as a simple heuristic tool to enable us to understand and capture needs, aspirations, and challenges pertaining to marriage and family life; relationships both within the family domain and outside it in which individual and family needs, goals, and struggles as well as strategies and choices are embedded; and the normative systems that give meaning to these different aspects of family lives.

In our understanding, *the material dimension* of wellbeing refers to the tangible needs and resources of individuals and families, and the public goods and services that they access or lack, all of which are relevant to their welfare and their families. They include, for instance, individual capabilities such as education and knowledge; resources such as employment and housing; public goods and services such as health care, places of worship, safe neighbourhoods; institutions and mechanisms needed for marriage and divorce; support services for families; and also invisible material structures, such as territorial borders, that affect the mobility of individuals and populations.

The relational dimension refers to the belonging and personal relations and ties, for example with family members, local networks, and religious and cultural communities. This dimension also refers to the individual Muslims' as well as families' interactions and relations with authorities, state officials, service providers, and other actors in the larger society as well as with the hierarchical positioning of different groups in society.

And lastly, *the ethical dimension* is concerned with values, norms, and systems of meanings that are pertinent to people's lives. They include religious beliefs, cultural norms and practices, general attitudes and discourses (e.g. on racialized minorities), laws and regimes of knowledge that shape, influence, or regulate (e.g. through state institutions) people's lives.

We see each of the above dimensions of wellbeing (or ill-being) as involving a subjective aspect that has to do with individuals' feelings and experiences as well as an objective aspect, which is related to the external structures in which experiences (or lack of experiences) of wellbeing are embedded. In this volume, we are interested in capturing the ways in which the three dimensions are interconnected and influence one another in varied, contested, and dynamic ways. We have investigated wellbeing at the level of individual family members, communities, and the state.

Similar to White, we approach wellbeing not as an outcome measured by a list of indicators, but rather **as multidimensional processes** (in this case of transnational Muslims) of strategizing to fulfil needs, confront challenges, and pursue aspirations in the context of family relationships, and through encounters with multiple laws, norms, and value systems that regulate and give meaning to these relationships. The multidimensionality of the needs and aspirations that constitute individual and family wellbeing is emphasized in the various case studies covered in this volume. **Mulki Al-Sharmani**, for example, studies, in chapter 4, a mosque-led programme for Somali Muslim families in Finland. The programme promotes a holistic and multidimensional reform of marriages and spousal and parental roles, aiming at what the mosque calls the 'good of the family', and the 'positive integration' of Somalis into Finnish society. The programme grounds both goals in

Islamic norms. **Iris Sportel, Betty de Hart, and Friso Kulk**, in chapter 6, show how Dutch Moroccan and Dutch Egyptian couples navigate law in the pursuit of material and relational needs in the context of their transnational marriages and family life between Morocco, Egypt, and the Netherlands. Also, **Rannveig Haga**, in chapter 7, examines Somali parents' perspectives on the multidimensional good life that they aspire to for their children. According to the parents, this pursued 'good life' for children encompasses a number of things. It entails securing material resources such as a good education and jobs. It involves cultivating close and interdependent relations between children and other family members. It also necessitates navigating a syncretic system of ethical values and meanings that draws from Islamic teachings, selected Swedish norms on raising children, and certain Somali cultural norms, which together emphasize family solidarity and Islamic ethics while at the same time allow children space for autonomy and claims to multiple identities.

By conceptualizing wellbeing as **processual**, we focus on time and place as factors shaping people's strategies and negotiations within these processes. We highlight and analyse how and why these needs, challenges, and aspirations might change at different junctures in the lives of Muslim family members and according to the multiple contexts in which their lives are situated. Thus, **Marja Tiilikainen**, in chapter 9, tackles the experiences of (in)security among Canadian Somali families and shows how a combination of factors, such as the war on terror, the securitization of Muslims, and the multiple forms of violence that Canadian Somali young men in particular face, influence and change the perspectives of the parents. Mosques, for example, are no longer seen as purely safe places for children, but parents have to monitor and strategize to continue raising their children as Muslims while watching out for the danger of radicalization.

The role of the socio-political context in shaping constructions of individual and family wellbeing (by various relevant actors) is illustrated in the different chapters. In Al-Sharmani's chapter, the multidimensional 'good life' pursued by the mosque is situated in a local Finnish context where the mosque is a registered religious community, partaking in the state's work of producing social cohesion. The mosque's pursuit of family wellbeing by reforming Muslim marriages is also shaped by a transnational Islamic context where the mosque is part of a loose network of religious scholars and institutions in Europe advocating an Islam that is strong, visible, and compatible with living in the West.

Similarly, in Haga's chapter, Somali parents' views and pursuit of their children's wellbeing is shaped by the Swedish context where parents experience silencing and marginalization in their encounters with officials and institutions dealing with their children. Haga shows how these experiences of othering and everyday racism create challenges for parents while at the same time they also influence parents' perspectives on what their children need for their wellbeing and what that entails in terms of how to raise them.

In chapter 3, **Sanna Mustasaari and Vishal Vora** also show how the legal and political specificities of the English and Finnish contexts influence the opportunities and challenges created by the multiplicity of laws and norms that are relevant to the organization of Muslim marriages in the two countries. The authors show that the 'transnational-religious' and 'transnational-foreign' elements of marriages contribute, in different ways, to how the issue of the *nikāḥ* may become framed as a minority issue and consequently how these marriages are seen to comply with the state law. In the English context, the authors argue that some British Muslims are in a disadvantaged position when it comes to marriage formalities and their lack of engagement with the law, as English law often views a non-Christian marriage as a non-marriage rather than a void or voidable marriage. In the Finnish context, issues about the legality of Muslim marriages appear to be of a different kind, having more to do with transnational family situations, limping statuses or precarious residence statuses rather than legal recognition of religious marriages.

The interplay between wellbeing and family practices such as marriage and parenting are not just confined to what family members need or lack or the challenges they encounter. It is also about their aspirations for an ethical life. This central point is illustrated, for instance, in chapter 2. **Annelies Moors and Vanessa Vroon-Najem** examine how converts in the Netherlands opt for only concluding Islamic marriages (rather than conducting civil marriages which are the only unions that are legally recognized by the state) for a variety of reasons that have to do with their different aspirations. For some of these women who are pious Muslims, for instance, it is about attaining their ethical wellbeing by ensuring that their intimate relationships with their partners are Islamically licit at the time when they enter into these unions regardless of whether or not they may decide in the future to conclude civil marriages.

Moors and Vroon-Najem's study also illustrates the opportunities and challenges provided by the multiple laws and norms that are usually at play in the lives of transnational Muslims and their implications for the wellbeing of these individuals. For example, Moors and Vroon-Najem's interlocutors were able to selectively draw on the different laws in their lives in order to exercise agency and strive to fulfil their aspirations. These women chose not to conclude civil marriages; they made use of uncodified Islamic family law which in their diasporic case does not require the involvement of the Dutch state in order to make relationship choices that were suitable for them at particular junctures in their lives. But again, their particular socio-political context also imposed its challenges. The authors highlighted, for instance, how Dutch public discourse and even state policies were increasingly moving towards the criminalization of these unions.

Investigations into different local contexts also highlight the political aspect of accounts of wellbeing. This not only shows how wellbeing, as White (2010) notes, is always a political process but also how wellbeing can be used in political discourses in ways that exclude some individuals and render them non-deserving of wellbeing and security. Transnational families, in particular, often face policies that seek to undermine their possibility of establishing a relationship of belonging and social citizenship with the state (Pellander, 2016; Mustasaari, 2016; Leinonen and Pellander, 2014). Moreover, definitions of wellbeing can be used to govern populations through normalization and division of the population. Feminist studies on family and state, especially research inspired by queer theory, have established a firm link between the legal regulation of the family and normalizing governance (see, e.g., Cadwaller and Riggs, 2012; Meeks and Stein, 2006). These analyses have pointed out that liberal governance based on wellbeing also has its underside. Stemming from the intellectual legacy of Michel Foucault (e.g. Foucault 2003; Rose, 2006), this branch of research investigates biopower and biopolitical aspects of governance that operate through normalization and division of the population into those who deserve rights and privileges and those who do not.

As this division is based on underlying moral ideas of entitlement and responsibility, it is a particularly relevant perspective in research on transnational Muslim families, who have during recent years been constructed as morally suspect families in different public discourses and in different countries. Grillo, for example, argues that the moral order of the minority family is generally believed to be at odds with the one embodied by the European family (Grillo, 2015, p.39). Studying the biopolitics of marriage in an Australian context, Cadwaller and Riggs (2012) note, similarly, that much of the anxiety over the Muslim population is channelled into the governance of family, marriage, and reproduction. In this volume, the complex interplay between wellbeing and state governance of (Muslim) intimate relationships is well illustrated in Moors and Vroon-Najem's study which shows how, in the name of the wellbeing of Muslim women, contracting Islamic marriages is criminalized. Similarly, Mustasaari and Vora's chapter demonstrates how unregistered Islamic marriages in the UK are constructed as an anomaly that does not fit into the country's legal structure governing marriages (with its underlying Christian norms). In addition, Tiilikainen's chapter highlights the vulnerability of black Muslim young men and their parents in the face of the structures of power, in particular the police and justice system. Paradoxically, while official security practices aim at fostering the security of all residents, they lead to the daily marginalization and insecurity of Canadian Somali families.

On the whole, this volume highlights that wellbeing is not a 'thing' that can either be delivered to subjects or simply measured by external standards. Rather, differences and inequalities in how individuals and families are simultaneously positioned in different social categories such as religion, generation, and gender, as well as social class, nation, and ethnicity, are important to how they experience wellbeing. Thus, in an important conceptual and methodological contribution, **Ann Phoenix**, in chapter 10, reminds us that it is important to approach wellbeing from a multidimensional perspective and to stay sensitive to how the subjective and objective aspects of wellbeing are interlinked. Considering the conceptual and methodological issues raised in studying the wellbeing of transnational families, she suggests that analyses of wellbeing should draw on the concept of intersectionality. This may enable the researchers to move the focus away from studying wellbeing as something that people have or do not have towards exploring how accounts of wellbeing are produced and what factors, in specific circumstances, contribute to how people make sense of their life and pursue their goals and what makes them resilient in particular moments of their lifetime. Thus, in chapter 8, **Abdirashid A. Ismail** demonstrates how transnational family practices shape children's wellbeing in complex and mixed ways, and, furthermore, Sportel, de Hart, and Kulk show that it is a confluence of factors and resources that enabled some of their interlocutors to use the law more beneficially than others for different purposes and that these factors shifted. Similarly, in chapter 5, **Anika Liversage** highlights how the practice of polygamy among Pakistani migrants in the UK and Turkish migrants in Denmark becomes part of complex processes in transnational families where different individual and family needs are pursued and challenges are navigated with mixed and uneven impacts on the parties concerned (i.e. polygamous husbands, first and second wives, children).

In short, the chapters of this collection do not aim to apply the proposed heuristic model of wellbeing uniformly and consistently. Rather, our goal is that various studies provide multiple angles from which we can understand the relationship between transnational Muslim families' wellbeing and their experiences, perspectives, and choices regarding marriage and family life. Furthermore, we do not assume that wellbeing of Muslims in the selected contexts is either singular and homogenous, or entirely distinct and different from the experience of wellbeing in general. Instead, through the studies presented in this volume we seek better insights into the meanings of wellbeing as they reveal its specificity as well as diversity and heterogeneity through the practices and experiences of the studied individuals and families.

Why 'Muslim' families?

We chose to focus our inquiry on families of Muslim background for multiple interconnected reasons. There is a long and expanding presence of Muslims from diverse ethnic backgrounds and several generations in Europe and North America. The estimated number of Muslims in Europe was approximately 26 million in 2016, that is 4.9% of the total population (Pew Research Center, 2017). The corresponding figure in the United States is approximately 3.5 million (1.1% of the total population) (Lipka, 2017) and in Canada a bit over 1 million (3.2% of the population) (Statistics Canada, 2018).

Muslim communities in the West are heterogeneous regarding their origins and socioeconomic backgrounds, as some of these Muslims are refugees and migrants, some were born to migrant background families, some are old established ethnic communities, and some are converts to Islam.

Muslims and Islam have been, over the past decades, increasingly ethnicized and politicized in the West, particularly after the 9/11 terrorist attacks in the USA which were carried out by Muslim militants, as well as the more recent terrorist attacks in several European cities. The war on terror and securitization of Muslims (e.g. Wæver, 1995) have had an impact on the everyday experiences of many Muslims in Europe and North America. In addition, 'Muslimness' as a problematic identity marker became evident at the time of the 2015 refugee crisis in Europe when large masses of refugees from the Middle East crossed the borders to Europe fleeing for their lives. In reaction to this mass movement, there were heated state and societal debates across Europe about the presence of these refugees and the perceived danger they pose on different levels (economic, security, religious, cultural). In eastern and southern Europe, attitudes towards refugees and Muslims have been predominantly negative (Wike, Stokes and Simmons, 2016).

This volume aims to problematize the essentializing and othering of Muslims. The case studies show how various European public discourses and policies on the family life and gender relations of migrants create 'Muslimness' as a singular identity and as 'problematic' norms and practices. This is demonstrated, for example, in chapter 2 where Moors and Vroon-Najem show how Dutch public discourses and policies construct Islamic marriages as contravening Dutch values of gender equality and individual freedom and hindering integration of Muslims into the larger society. Yet, the authors highlight the contradictions in this state narrative as it fails to recognize that many Muslim Dutch women who enter into Islamic marriages do so as a way of exercising their rights as Dutch citizens who choose to enter into these unions as a form of cohabiting relationships (albeit religiously licit), knowing that these unions have no legal status according to the state. And yet while Dutch public discourse and policies have no cultural or legal problem with cohabiting relationships between non-Muslim Dutch couples, they are increasingly restricting and almost criminalizing Islamic marriages.

Other case studies in the volume also shed light on the diverse realities of the researched Muslim families and the plurality and dynamism of their understandings of their religious tradition as a source of norms guiding their family relations. In chapter 6, Sportel, de Hart, and Kulk show that it is pragmatism rather than commitment to religious norms which guides how Dutch Moroccan and Dutch Egyptian married and divorcing couples in the Netherlands navigate the legal work needed to carry out their marriage or divorce practices as well as transnational kin work involving children.

For the aforementioned reasons, we believe it is meaningful to employ Muslims and their family lives as a category of analysis to understand the ways in which their intimate relationships become, on one hand, an area of intervention and control with regard to state policies and public discourses and, on the other hand, a domain in which family members negotiate different aspirations, goals, and challenges. In other words, we wish to show the limitations of reifying 'the Muslim experience,' and shed light on how transnational Muslims whether within their families or in different contexts are differentiated by their diverse social locations, resources, gender, and generation, as well as the structures of laws, norms, and policies in which their lives are embedded and hence their varied experiences and voices.

The 'transnational' in Muslim families

In this volume, we do not understand 'transnational' in any fixed sense. Rather, we highlight the layered meanings of the concept as derived organically from the different case studies. Transnational, for example, denotes the material and affective ties and practices linking individuals with family members in different countries, including the country of origin and countries of resettlement where close family and kin reside. These ties shape family and marriage practices, kin work and parenting. In addition, these transnational bonds impact different family members differently. For example, in chapter 8 Ismail discusses diverse transnational practices in which parents partake such as sending financial remittances and visits to Somalia in addition to social activities that, although they take place in Finland, are very much oriented towards Somalia, such as fathers spending time debating Somali politics and/or chewing *khat* (mild narcotic leaves chewed in Somalia). These transnational activities of parents, in particular fathers, are seen to have a negative impact on their children's wellbeing through the lack of time and resources devoted to their parental role. On the other hand, in chapter 9 Tiilikainen shows how parents may rely on transnational family networks when they need support in raising and protecting their children: Canadian Somali children and youth may be sent to family members in the Middle East or the Horn of Africa to stay away from insecure neighbourhoods in Canada and instead spend time in an environment that parents believe to be religiously and culturally secure.

Our understanding of the transnational is further developed by Liversage's study in chapter 5. Liversage examines how transnational migration and mobility shape marriage practices, focusing on polygamy. She shows how the transnationally shaped circumstances and needs of Turkish and Pakistani families in Denmark and the UK and their relatives in the countries of origin lead to the practice of polygamy for diverse purposes. For example, some men enter into new marriages in the UK or Denmark while their first wives are in the country of origin. Other polygamous unions are motivated by the goal of finding a care provider for a sick husband in the country of origin while the first wife cares for the children in the West. Meeting the need of a childless couple to have a child is also another factor leading to polygamy. The impacts of these transnationally shaped practices of polygamy on first wives, second wives, and husbands are heterogeneous and complex, underscoring the need to understand the practice of polygamy (which is typically seen as one of the problematic and patriarchal areas in Islamic law) in a more nuanced way in light of the transnational social spaces inhabited by these individuals and their unequal access to different material and non-material resources that are relevant for their wellbeing.

Transnational in this volume also denotes multiple laws, norms, movements, ideologies, and institutions (state/non-state, religious/non-religious) that guide family relations and practices and extend beyond national boundaries. For example, Sportel, de Hart, and Kulk analyse how Dutch Moroccan and Dutch Egyptian families navigate multiple family laws in transnational contexts and how they engage with often complicated transnational legal work in order to manage ties within family and kin. In another chapter, Al-Sharmani studies a Finnish mosque programme for families that has transnational linkages to a loose network of religious scholars advocating reformist Islamic discourse, as well as to the Federation of Islamic Organizations in Europe, a Brussels-based umbrella organization, inspired by the Muslim Brotherhood's intellectual thought. Tiilikainen in her chapter, on the other hand, describes how parents fear that new transnational militant ideologies and violent radicalized groups influence Muslim youth and may attract them to travel abroad and join the conflict.

Finally, as Phoenix notes in the closing chapter of this book, the term 'transnational' is reactive to what 'nation' is taken to mean. 'Transnational' is thus often socially or legally constructed in contrast to the normative or taken-for-granted 'national'. This observation alerts us to acknowledge that the term is in relation to various different processes of decentralization taking place within and around the socio-cultural construct of 'nation'.

Navigating the plurality of normative systems in transnational family life

Islamic law is present in Western societies in a variety of ways both as a set of legal thought and religious norms and as rules and practices governing interpersonal relations and disputes within religious communities (Ballard, et al., 2009; Bano, 2012; Ahdar and Aroney, 2011; Büchler, 2011; Mehdi and Nielsen, 2011; Shah, 2014; Grillo, 2015). As demonstrated by the example of *nikāḥ*, the Muslim religious marriage, European states differ in their approaches to Islamic norms and legal institutions. As explained in chapters 2 and 3, in the Netherlands it is illegal to marry religiously before a civil marriage, whereas in England such marriage risks being deemed a non-marriage. In yet other countries, such as Finland, Islamic marriages may be included in the legal framework which effectively prevents most cases of non-marriage from arising.

Legal pluralism in today's world means that issues of culture, religion, and law are influenced by accumulated and complex pluralities (Menski, 2010). This diversity is manifest in the analyses offered in the chapters of this volume. For example, in chapter 6, Sportel, de Hart, and Kulk demonstrate how law may become important for transnational families in different situations and how leading a family life across borders requires dealing with multiple laws and bureaucracies. The authors show that people navigate the law, taking legal steps and finding legal information as they go along. Furthermore, law may enable members of transnational families differently, and power relations within families may explain how people mobilize law (Sportel, 2016).

As European states do not incorporate religious laws through a system of personal status laws – Greek Thrace being the only exception to the rule (Shah, 2014; Sezgin, 2017) – the interaction of religious law and state law takes place, on the one hand, within the legal system of one state in a broad range of different practices where questions relating to Islamic norms become invoked. On the other hand, Islamic law can become applicable in a court as the law of a foreign state if there is a connection to a foreign state law that is based on Islamic principles. Whether this foreign law is applied or a foreign decision is recognized, depends on the rules of private international law (also known as conflict of laws). As was demonstrated, for example, in the European Court of Justice in the cases of *Sahyouni v. Mamisch* (C-281/15 and C-372/16) concerning an Islamic, unilateral *talāq* divorce, it is sometimes difficult to identify which norms apply to a case. Yet another aspect influencing the interrelationship between state law and religious law comes from the human rights regime. The provisions of the European Convention on Human Rights concerning the right to property (Article 1 to the 1st Protocol to the Convention) and the right to respect for private and family life (Article 8 ECHR) and the prohibition of discrimination (Article 14 ECHR), for example on the basis of gender, impose certain limitations on how Member States can arrange the recognition of religious law or family statuses (e.g. Rutten, 2010).

Moreover, the unity of state law is in many respects imaginary; state law is a discontinuous, incoherent and plural set of norms. It is organized into different fields, which allows legal power to be exercised according to very different sets of principles in different issues that are analytically constructed as distinct. When these diverse fields of law intertwine, the outcome can be more influenced by the disparate goals of different legal fields than the cultural or religious diversity in people's way of life (see for example de Hart, van Rossum and Sportel, 2013; Mustasaari, 2015). Furthermore, the intersections of different branches of law could place transnational families in positions in which they are impacted more by immigration policies than family policies. For example, the prohibition against circumventing immigration rules might mean that a marriage is not recognized in one legal context while being registered and valid in another legal context (Mustasaari and Al-Sharmani, 2018).

In line with previous research (e.g. Mustasaari and Al-Sharmani, 2018), the chapters in this volume highlight the importance of paying attention to the local legal context within which family relationships are regulated. In chapter 3, Mustasaari and Vora show how the differences between the local contexts and legislative frameworks of England and Finland affect the ways in which Muslim marriages are recognized. The authors note, furthermore, that it is increasingly important to pay attention to the multiple ways in which different laws come together and affect processes in which people engage with the different structures of their environment. This requires approaches that recognize individuals as relational, cultural, gendered, and in many ways differently positioned (e.g. Bano, 2017). Mustasaari and Vora argue that the legal framework should be understood as one that seeks to enhance wellbeing both individually, by creating obligations within the family and, collectively, by levelling the various imbalances prevailing in relations between different groups in society, including minority/majority as well as gender relations.

Gender, marriage, and kin work

The chapters of this edited volume challenge the statist discourse on Muslim patriarchy and oppression of women in relation to Islamic law as well as Muslim family norms and practices. According to the presented case studies, gender roles and relations in Muslim transnational families with regard to marriage and parenting are changing, resulting from the changing lived realities of Muslims in new migratory contexts as well as due to increasing access to religious knowledge and evolving understandings of Islamic law on marriage and family norms. For example, Al-Sharmani shows the mosque's advocacy for companionate marriages and cooperative and non-hierarchical spousal roles is based on the changing needs and lived realities of Somali families in Finland as well as emerging new religious discourse on marriage and gender roles in the family. The author also notes in this chapter and previous research (Al-Sharmani, 2015) how some women have been empowered through the religious knowledge they acquire from diverse sources, including the mosque programmes, resulting in their questioning cultural norms that privilege male dominance. Similarly, parents in Haga's study rely on Islamic teachings to develop their parenting practices and to be able to guide their children to become good members of Swedish society. Haga explains how it is precisely parents' increasing knowledge of Islamic norms on parenting that allows them to revisit and question dominant Somali cultural norms that emphasize parents' absolute authority over their children and limit the children's ability to develop their autonomy and voices vis-à-vis their parents.

The absence of extended family members has added new pressure on the role of a husband and father in the household. In addition to the role of a provider, the father is expected to share care work with his wife and help with raising the children. The absence of fathers, due to transnational engagements, from the everyday life of the children and youth, is often perceived negatively by the rest of the family and is believed to have a negative impact on the wellbeing of the children, as Ismail shows in chapter 8. In addition, Tiilikainen's research (chapter 9) confirms that single parenthood, which mostly means single motherhood, increases the vulnerability of migrant families: mothers in Toronto struggle to raise their racialized sons in insecure neighbourhoods.

Lastly, as Moors and Vroon-Najem show in chapter 2, the strict regulation of Muslim marriages is justified in public discussions with reference to Muslim women's wellbeing, but in reality this rigid approach can effectively endanger the wellbeing of women, who often have sound reasons not to conclude a civil marriage first. Similarly, in chapter 3, Mustasaari and Vora explain how the developing English case law on non-marriage has gender-specific consequences.

Conclusion

In this edited volume we attempt to understand the wellbeing of Muslim families, most of whom have a migrant background, in the context of their transnational family life and relations with multiple laws and norms. The case studies challenge prevalent singular representations of Muslims, which are often based on binaries such as secular versus religious, and legal/rational versus cultural/irrational norms. These kinds of simplifications tend to pathologize Muslim family practices and essentialize Islamic family laws. Instead, the case studies de-essentialize and 'normalize' Muslim families and their family relations and practices in different migratory contexts. These studies highlight bottom-up practices and shifting meanings related to Islam in different places and temporalities. Moreover, the studies highlight variations and negotiations in the use of different legal and normative systems on the part of Muslim families, communities and individuals.

Furthermore, the chapters reveal complex and multidimensional relationships between law, family life, and wellbeing with regard to Muslim (migrant) families and the centrality of gender in this relationship. The three-dimensional model of wellbeing that we have used does not assume that the 'Muslimness', ethnicity, or migrant background define wellbeing or aspects of it in any pre-fixed sense. Rather, it helps us see how different objective and subjective structures, relations, values, and spaces of agency impact the experiences of individuals and families that identify themselves as Muslims or who have been categorized as such.

Additionally, examining wellbeing in legal contexts along the lines suggested by White and Wright and as developed in this volume allows us to get a better grasp of the normalizing impacts of the diverse political and governmental aspects of wellbeing in the context of Muslim family life. First, by focusing on the vast diversity of material – distributive, institutional, and procedural norms – that transnational Muslim families must navigate in diverse contexts, we can begin to grasp the distinct, and often intersectional, impact that the norms have on families and individuals. Second, the relational dimension to wellbeing highlights how people are most often not just individual rights holders, but connected to each other through relations of dependency, duties, and power structures. Third and finally, ethical subjectivity offers means for individuals to resist othering processes taking place in their lives.

Chapter summaries

In the Netherlands, transnational marriages and Islamic marriages concluded prior to a civil marriage are hotly debated in the public domain. These marriages are perceived as not only bringing the 'wrong' kinds of migrants to the Netherlands – those with little education and few skills – or as involving the 'wrong' kind of Muslims, such as the radical or Salafi-oriented, but also as harmful to Muslim women's wellbeing. **Annelies Moors and Vanessa Vroon-Najem** analyse the tensions between how politicians, policy makers, and other state agents in the Netherlands problematize transnational Muslim marriages and how female converts to Islam experience the concluding of such marriages. They show that converts themselves quite regularly opt for concluding an Islamic marriage, which is often simultaneously transnational. These women view an Islamic marriage as important for their ethical, relational, and material wellbeing, and may have good reasons not to conclude a civil marriage first.

The chapter by **Sanna Mustasaari and Vishal Vora** continues with the topic of *nikāḥ*, the religiously valid Muslim marriage, and studies its legal recognition in England and Finland. The authors apply the concept of wellbeing in order to better understand the complex outcomes of law for Muslim couples. English law operates with the concepts of valid and void marriage, but recent case law has introduced the concept of non-marriage, denoting that in divorce the couple have no financial remedies. The authors argue that there is currently a default form of marriage in English law which reflects the Christian form of marriage and results in discrimination against ethnic minority women. Finnish law, in contrast, does not acknowledge the institution of a void or voidable marriage, but religious marriages are usually recognized as legal. Muslim marriages seem to become problematic, particularly in relation to migration and transnational family lives.

Mulki Al-Sharmani examines a mosque programme for Somali Muslim families in Helsinki, Finland. She analyses how the mosque pursues its two stated goals: the 'good of Muslim families', and their 'positive integration' into Finnish society. Locally, the programme is guided by the needs of Somali Muslim families, and it is also enabled by Finnish state policies on governance of religious communities. Transnationally, the mosque programme is part of a loose network of religious institutions and scholars across Europe, educating Muslim families on how to lead a pious, harmonious, and modern family life that facilitates the integration of Muslims into their respective societies. She analyses, in particular, the mosque programme's new discourse on companionate marriage and engaged parenting and reflects on its gender implications.

Anika Liversage investigates polygamous Muslim marriages among immigrants and their descendants living in Denmark and the UK. The data indicates that polygamous marriages take varied forms and are shaped by the transnational social space. Some polygamous marriages arise out of male-only out-migration, others from an effort to meet different family needs related to health and care issues. In such unions, the wellbeing of the husband and the two wives are differently impacted. There are also polygamous marriages which men contract secretly. The first wives often feel betrayed when they find out about the second marriage. Some of them have the resources and options gained through migration to end their unwanted polygamous marriages, while other first wives may be too vulnerable to leave these marriages, engendering considerable ill-being.

Iris Sportel, Betty de Hart and Friso Kulk shed light on how transnational Dutch Moroccan and Dutch Egyptian families relate to multiple family law systems in their everyday lives. With regard to the material aspects of wellbeing, they focus on participants' needs in dealing with legal systems. The findings indicate that it is not that easy for transnational families to translate claims back and forth and strategically use the law across borders, as this requires economic, cultural, and social capital. In the relational dimension, the law is an important aspect of managing transnational family ties. With regard to the ethical dimension, they did not find confirmation of religious or cultural claims as often mentioned in the literature. Rather, family members try to solve normative issues in pragmatic ways. The authors suggest 'navigating' the law as a useful lens through which to study how these family members reconcile the different norms they encounter.

Rannveig Haga studies how Somali parents in Sweden understand and pursue the wellbeing of their children. She focuses on two issues that are pertinent to parents' viewpoints and strategies in relation to their children's wellbeing: namely, navigating Islamic teachings, Somali culture, and Swedish norms and creating family practices and relations that foster strong family ties and support. She situates parents' aspirations for their children in the context of the former's daily experiences of racism and, in particular, their experiences of marginalization (or epistemic injustice) in their encounters with different institutions working with their children, such as schools. She explores how a multidimensional concept of wellbeing can be useful in understanding the interplay between the racial and cultural othering of the parents as knowing and capable child-carers on the one hand and their parenting practices and challenges on the other.

Abdirashid A. Ismail examines the impacts of the transnational engagements of Finnish Somali parents in the diaspora on the wellbeing of their children who are living with them. The findings show that parental transnational practices, such as large remittances sent to relatives, transnational investments, and long-term parental absences as well as *fadhi-ku-dirir* (i.e., sitting in cafés with other Somalis to engage in heated discussions about home-country politics) and *khat* chewing adversely affect family stability and resources, which are central to child wellbeing. These parental transnational practices were found to be gendered, as fathers were mostly the ones who engaged in long-term travel and absences and exclusively in *fadhi-ku-dirir* and *khat* chewing.

Marja Tiilikainen explores Canadian Somali parents' experiences and organization of everyday security that is a central component of individual and family wellbeing. The chapter mostly draws on qualitative interviews with parents in Toronto. The findings show the continuum of violence in the lives of Canadian Somalis who often resettled in insecure low-income neighbourhoods. While national- and municipality-level official security practices aim at fostering the security of all residents, at the same time they marginalize Somali families and contribute to their insecurity especially by framing young black men – many of whom are Muslims – as threats to security. Transnational family connections and (reinterpreted) religious traditions become some of the resources that parents rely on when raising their children. However, Canadian Somali parents are differently resourced and certain groups of parents such as single mothers are particularly vulnerable.

The concepts of 'wellbeing' and 'transnational families' have come into popular usage over the last two decades. Yet, there are relatively few studies that explicitly address the wellbeing of transnational families, particularly from the perspectives of their various members. The final chapter, written by **Ann Phoenix**, makes a contribution to thinking simultaneously about wellbeing and transnational families, focusing particularly on children. It considers contemporary conceptualizations of wellbeing and the conceptual and methodological issues raised in studying the wellbeing of transnational families. In order to do so, it draws on the concept of intersectionality to consider the ways in which family members are multiply positioned. It presents two examples to illuminate these issues and to illustrate some fruitful methodological approaches. The chapter argues for a multidisciplinary perspective in the study of the wellbeing of transnational families that takes into account the viewpoints and experiences of the particular family members involved.

Bibliography

Abrego, L., 2009. Economic well-being in Salvadoran transnational families: How gender affects remittance practices. *Journal of Marriage and Family*, 71, pp.1070–1085.

Ahdar, R. and Aroney, N., 2011. The topography of Shari'a in the western political landscape. In: R. Ahdar and N. Aroney, eds. 2011. *Shari'a in the West*. Oxford: Oxford University Press, pp.1–31.

Akhtar, R.C., 2018. Modern traditions in Muslim marriage practices, exploring English narratives. *Oxford Journal of Law and Religion*, 7(3), pp.427–454.

Al-Sharmani, M., 2015. Striving against the 'Nafs': Revisiting Somali Muslim spousal roles and rights in Finland. *Journal of Religion in Europe*, 8(1), pp.101–120.

Al-Sharmani, M., 2017. Divorce among transnational Finnish Somalis: Gender, religion, and agency. *Religion and Gender*, 7(1), pp.70–87.

Al-Sharmani, M. and Ismail, A.A., 2017. Marriage and transnational family life among Somali migrants in Finland. *Migration Letters*, 14(1), pp.38–49.

Baldassar, L. and Merla, L., eds. 2014. *Transnational Families, Migration and the Circulation of Care: Understanding Mobility and Absence in Family Life*. New York and Abingdon, Oxon: Routledge.

Ballard, R., Ferrari, A., Grillo, R., Hoekema, A.J., Maussen, M. and Shah, P., 2009. Legal practice and cultural diversity: Introduction. In: R. Grillo, R. Ballard, A. Ferrari, A.J. Hoekema, M. Maussen and P. Shah, eds. 2009. *Legal Practice and Cultural Diversity*. Farnham: Ashgate, pp.1–29.

Bano, S., 2012. *Muslim Women and Shari'ah Councils: Transcending the Boundaries of Community and Law*. London: Palgrave MacMillan.

Bano, S., 2017. Agency, autonomy, and rights: Muslim women and alternative dispute resolution in Britain. In: S. Bano, ed. 2017. *Gender and Justice in Family Law Disputes: Women, Mediation, and Religious Arbitration*. Waltham: Brandeis University Press, pp.46–76.

Bryceson, D. and Vuorela, U., eds. 2002. *The Transnational Family: New European Frontiers and Global Networks*. Oxford: Berg.

Büchler, A., 2011. *Islamic Law in Europe? Legal Pluralism and its Limits in European Family Laws*. Farnham: Ashgate.

Cadwaller, J.R. and Riggs, D.W., 2012. The state of the union: Toward a biopolitics of marriage. *M/C Journal*, 15(6). Available at: http://journal.media-culture.org.au/index.php/mcjournal/article/view/585 [Accessed September 22, 2018].

Charsley, K., 2005. Unhappy husbands: Masculinity and migration in transnational Pakistani marriages. *The Journal of the Royal Anthropological Institute*, 11(1), pp.85–105.

Charsley, K., 2013. *Transnational Marriage: New Perspectives from Europe and Beyond*. New York and London: Routledge.

Charsley, K. and Liversage, A., 2013. Transforming polygamy: Migration, transnationalism and multiple marriages among Muslim minorities. *Global Networks*, 13(1), pp.60–78.

Foucault, M., 2003. *Society Must Be Defended: Lectures at the Collège de France 1975–1976*. New York: Picador.

Graham, E. and Jordan, L., 2011. Migrant parents and the psychological well-being of left-behind children in Southeast Asia. *Journal of Marriage and Family*, 73, pp.763–787.

Grillo, R., 2015. *Muslim Families, Politics and the Law: A Legal Industry in Multicultural Britain*. London: Routledge.

Hall, J., Giovannini, E., Morrone, A. and Ranuzzi, G., 2010. *A Framework to Measure the Progress of Societies*. Statistics Directorate Working Paper No 34, OECD.

Hart, B. de, Rossum, W. van and Sportel, I., 2013. *Law in the Everyday Lives of Transnational Families: An Introduction*. Oñati Socio-Legal Series, 3, pp.991–1003. Available at: http://opo.iisj.net/index.php/osls/article/viewFile/338/334 [Accessed September 2, 2018].

Herring, J. and Foster, C., 2012. Welfare means relationality, virtue and altruism. *Legal Studies*, 32, pp.480–498.

Heyman, J., Flores-Macias, F., Hayes, J.A.A., Kenned, M., Lahaie, M. and Earle, A., 2009. The impact of migration on the well-being of transnational families: New data from sending communities in Mexico. *Community, Work, and Family*, 12, pp.91–103.

Leinonen, J. and Pellander, S., 2014. Court decisions over marriage migration in Finland: A problem with transnational family ties. *Journal of Ethnic and Migration Studies*, 40(9), pp.1488–1506.

Lipka, M., 2017. *Muslims and Islam: Key Findings in the U.S. and Around the World*. Washington, DC: Pew Research Center. Available at: http://www.pewresearch.org/fact-tank/2017/08/09/muslims-and-islam-key-findings-in-the-u-s-and-around-the-world/ [Accessed August 13, 2018].

Mazzucato, V. and Schans, D., 2011. Transnational families and the well-being of children: Conceptual and methodological challenges. *Journal of Marriage and Family*, 73, pp.704–712.

McGillivray, M., 2007. Human well-being: Issues, concepts and measures. In: M. McGillivray, ed. 2007. *Human Well-being: Concept and Measurement*. Basingstoke: Palgrave Macmillan, pp.1–22.

McGregor, J.A., 2007. Researching wellbeing: From concepts to methodology. In: I. Gough and J.A. McGregor, eds. 2007. *Wellbeing in Developing Countries: From Theory to Research*. Cambridge: Cambridge University Press, pp.316–350.

McGregor, J.A. and Sumner, A., 2010. Beyond business as usual: What might 3-D wellbeing contribute to MDG momentum? *IDS Bulletin*, 41(1), pp.104–112.

McKeown, K. and Sweeney, J., 2001. *Family Well-being and Family Policy: A Review of Research on Benefits and Costs*. Dublin: Kieran McKeown Limited. Available at:

http://health.gov.ie/wp-content/uploads/2014/03/famrev-report.pdf [Accessed September 25, 2018].

Meeks, C. and Stein, A., 2006. Refiguring the family: Towards a post-queer politics of gay and lesbian marriage. In: D. Richardson, J. McLaughlin and M.E. Casey, eds. 2006. *Intersections Between Feminist and Queer Theory.* New York: Palgrave Macmillan, pp.136–155.

Mehdi, R. and Nielsen, J., eds. 2011. *Embedding Mahr in the European Legal System.* Copenhagen: Djøf Forlag.

Menski, W., 2010. Fuzzy law and the boundaries of secularism. *Potchefstroom Electronic Law Journal*, 13, pp.30–54.

Mustasaari, S., 2015. The 'nuclear family paradigm' as a marker of rights and belonging in transnational families. *Social Identities*, 21, pp.359–372.

Mustasaari, S., 2016. Best interests of the child in family reunification – a citizenship test disguised? In: A. Griffiths, S. Mustasaari and A. Mäki-Petäjä-Leinonen, eds. 2016. *Subjectivity, Citizenship and Belonging in Law: Identities and Intersections.* Abingdon: Routledge, pp.123–145.

Mustasaari, S. and Al-Sharmani, M., 2018. Between 'official' and 'unofficial': Discourses and practices of Muslim marriage conclusion in Finland. *Oxford Journal of Law and Religion.* Available at: https://academic.oup.com/ojlr/advance-article/doi/10.1093/ojlr/rwy029/5067187?guestAccessKey=7a74adcb-e c90-48ee-bb23-b9f3fe419683 [Accessed August 16, 2018].

Nathan, G., 2010. *Social Freedom in a Multicultural State: Towards a Theory of Intercultural Justice.* Basingstoke: Palgrave Macmillan.

Nedelsky, J., 2011. *Law's Relations: A Relational Theory of Self, Autonomy and Law.* New York: Oxford University Press.

Pellander, S., 2016. *Gatekeepers of the Family: Regulating Family Migration to Finland.* Helsinki: University of Helsinki.

Pew Research Center, 2017. *Europe's Growing Muslim Population.* Washington, DC: Pew Research Center. Available at: http://www.pewforum.org/2017/11/29/europes-growing-muslim-population/ [Accessed August 13, 2018].

Razack, S.H., 2004. Imperilled Muslim women, dangerous Muslim men and civilised Europeans: Legal and social responses to forced marriages. *Feminist Legal Studies*, 12, pp.129–174.

Rose, N., 2006. *The Politics of Life Itself: Biomedicine, Power, and Subjectivity in the Twenty-First Century.* Princeton: Princeton University Press.

Rutten, S., 2010. Protection of spouses in informal marriages by human rights. *Utrecht Law Review*, 6(2), pp.77–92.

Rytter, M., 2012. Semi-legal family life: Pakistani couples between the borderland of Sweden and Denmark. *Global Networks*, 2, pp.81–108.

Schmidt, G., 2011. Law and identity: Transnational arranged marriages and the boundaries of Danishness. *Journal of Ethnic and Migration Studies*, 37(2), pp.257–275.

Sezgin, Y., 2017. Reforming Muslim family laws in non-Muslim democracies: Understanding the role of civil courts as agents of social and legal change. In: J. Cesari and J. Casanova, eds. 2017. *Islam, Gender, and Democracy in Comparative Perspective.* Oxford: Oxford University Press, pp.160–187.

Shah, P., 2014. Shari'a in the West: colonial consciousness in a context of normative competition. In: E. Giunchi, ed. 2014. *Muslim Family Law in Western Courts.* Abingdon: Routledge, pp.14–31.

Shaw, A., 2001. Kinship, cultural preference and immigration: Consanguineous marriage among British Pakistanis. *The Journal of the Royal Anthropological Institute*, 7(2), pp.315–334.

Sportel, I., 2016. *Divorce in Transnational Families: Marriage, Migration and Family Law*. London: Palgrave Macmillan.

Statistics Canada, 2018. *Immigration and Ethnocultural Diversity in Canada*. Statistics Canada. Available at: https://www12.statcan.gc.ca/nhs-enm/2011/as-sa/99-010-x/99-010-x2011001-eng.cfm [Accessed August 13, 2018].

Tiilikainen, M., 2013. Illness, healing and everyday Islam: Transnational lives of Somali migrant women. In: N.M. Dessing, N. Jeldtoft, J.S. Nielsen and L. Woodhead, eds. 2013. *Everyday Lived Islam in Europe*. Farnham, Surrey: Ashgate, pp.147–162.

Tiilikainen, M., 2015. Looking for a safe place: Security and transnational Somali Muslim families. *Journal of Religion in Europe*, 8, pp.51–72.

Vora, V., 2016. *The Islamic Marriage Conundrum: Register or Recognize? The Legal Consequences of the Nikah in England and Wales*. PhD. SOAS, University of London.

Wæver, O., 1995. Securitization and desecuritization. In: R.D. Lipschutz, ed. 1995, *On Security*. New York: Columbia University Press, pp.46–86.

White, S.C., 2008. *But What is Wellbeing? A Framework for Analysis in Social and Development Policy and Practice*. Paper for Regeneration and Wellbeing: Research into Practice, University of Bradford, 24–25 April 2008. University of Bath, Centre for Development Studies. Available at: http://staff.bath.ac.uk/ecsscw/But_what_is_Wellbeing.pdf [Accessed September 25, 2018].

White, S.C., 2010. Analysing wellbeing: A framework for development practice. *Development in Practice*, 20(2), pp.158–172.

White, S.C. and Blackmore, C., eds. 2015. *Cultures of Wellbeing: Method, Place, Policy*. Basingstoke: Palgrave Macmillan.

Wike, V., Stokes, B. and Simmons, K., 2016. Europeans fear wave of refugees will mean more terrorism, fewer jobs. Washington, DC: Pew Research Center. Available at: http://www.pewglobal.org/2016/07/11/europeans-fear-wave-of-refugees-will-mean-more-terrorism-fewer-jobs/ [Accessed August 13, 2018].

Wright, K., 2010. 'It's a Limited Kind of Happiness': Barriers to Achieving Human Well-being among Peruvian Migrants in London and Madrid. *Bulletin of Latin American Research*, 29(3), pp.367–383.

Wright, K., 2012. Constructing human wellbeing across spatial boundaries: Negotiating meanings in transnational migration. *Global Networks*, 12(4), pp.467–484.

Zimmerman, S.L., 2013. Conceptualizing family well-being. In: A. Moreno Minguez, ed. 2013. *Family Well-being: European Perspectives*. Dordrecht and New York: Springer, pp.9–26.

2 Converts, marriage, and the Dutch nation-state

Contestations about Muslim women's wellbeing

Annelies Moors and Vanessa Vroon-Najem

Introduction

In the Netherlands, in the course of the previous decades, new legislation has been tabled and older laws have been revived in order to restrict particular kinds of transnational and/or Muslim marriages. An often-used argument in the ensuing public debates is how such restrictions will strengthen Muslim women's position and hence will be beneficial to their wellbeing. This then raises the question of how Muslim women who engage in these marriages evaluate such unions and their impact on them. In line with the introduction of this volume, we focus on wellbeing in a broad sense, that is, including women's ethical, relational, and material wellbeing. In addressing possible tensions between public debate and policy making, on the one hand, and the perspectives of Muslim women, on the other, we focus on one particular category of Muslim women, that is, converts to Islam. We do so as this category is particularly well positioned to highlight the tensions between legal citizenship and national belonging inherent to the hyphenated concept of the secular nation-state. Finally, we analyse the effects of the criminalization of particular forms of marriage and how the notion of the 'freedom to choose whom to marry' is politically instrumentalized to enable and disable particular kinds of marriages.

For this chapter we draw on insights gained from the long-term fieldwork of Vanessa Vroon-Najem on women's conversion to Islam in the Netherlands (Vroon-Najem, 2014) and from Annelies Moors' work on concluding marriages in Muslim majority countries and the Netherlands (Moors, 2013; Moors, 1995). Starting in the autumn of 2014 we engaged in joint fieldwork that focused more explicitly on how converts marry. This included extended conversations with over 35 female converts about how to find a marriage partner and how and when to enter into an Islamic marriage.[1]

The converts we talked with are white Dutch women, as well as women from various migrant backgrounds. Previous research indicates that the former most strongly experience how their conversion produces tensions between juridical citizenship and national belonging. Becoming recognizably Muslim, particularly through wearing a headscarf, puts their *self-evident* belonging to the nation into question and turns them into symbolic migrants. Many of them reported that after their conversion they were asked whether they had 'turned Turk or Moroccan'. Non-white women did not experience such a sharp shift in how the majority society viewed them after conversion, as even prior to their conversion they were already considered as falling outside the national fold (Galonnier, 2015; Özyürek, 2015; Moosavi, 2015; Vroon-Najem, 2014; Jensen, 2008). In this contribution, however, we do not spell out the particular backgrounds of the converts because, for the issue we address, that is, the tensions between the problematization of Muslim marriages and the experiences of converts themselves, our research indicates that it is their positionality as *converts* that affects them most strongly.

In the following we start with an analysis of how transnational and Muslim marriages have become problematized and the lines of argumentation used. We then turn to the converts themselves. After presenting their marriage trajectories, from finding a spouse or turning an already existing relationship into a marriage to decisions regarding how to conclude their marriage and in which order, we analyse how they evaluate such marriages in terms of their ethical, relational, and material wellbeing. Finally, we point to the effects of the criminalization of particular forms of marriage and how the notion of the 'freedom to choose whom to marry' is politically instrumentalized to enable and disable particular kinds of marriages.

Transnational Muslim marriages: regulations and debates

Often the term 'transnational marriages' is used for a particular category of migration marriages that brings together people who have grown up in different countries with which they continue to keep ties (a more precise term would be 'trans-state' marriages). This term is also often used for migration marriages that involve people from the same national or ethnic origin, such as when Moroccan-Dutch men or women marry a partner from Morocco (Hooghiemstra, 2003).

In our research project, we broaden the notion of transnational marriages to also include marriages in which spouses are considered as, or see themselves as, of different national origin, even if they are citizens or long-term residents of the same country, such as when white Dutch men or women marry a partner of Moroccan origin, or when people from a different national origin, say Morocco and Suriname, marry. Such forms of identification are not stable; in due course people may feel more Dutch (or less), in interaction with how they are interpellated by the majority population. In other words, identification and the production of particular forms of subjectivity are always in process.

Using such a broad notion of transnational marriages enables us to address the tensions inherent in the concept of the nation-state between the rights and obligations of juridical citizenship on the one hand and the subjective notion of national belonging on the other (Baumann, 1999, pp.18ff; Hage, 1998, p.52). Focusing on the latter, we foreground in this contribution the subjective element in the hyphenated concept of the nation-state. We use the term 'transnational marriages' then as a floating signifier, as a blurred rather than as a sharply delineated category. Taking subjective feelings into account, marriages are not simply either transnational or not, but they are transnational in different ways, and to a greater or lesser extent.

Our research indicates that marriages of converts to Islam in the Netherlands are often transnational. Some of these converts themselves have a migrant background, and still feel connected to their or their parents' countries of origin. In other cases, their marriages turn out to be transnational because they marry someone who is either a post-migrant or a new migrant from a Muslim majority country. Hence, many converts are not only affected by the discourse on Islamic marriages but also by that on transnational marriages.

Debates and law-making: transnational marriages and Islam

In the Netherlands, both transnational marriages and, more recently, 'Islamic marriages' have, again, become the topic of public debate and law-making.[2] In the 1970s migration marriages were considered as having a negative impact on the wellbeing of white Dutch women who were allegedly tricked into fraudulent marriages by migrant men, while by the 1980s and 1990s post-migrant women were seen as victims of their families, marrying them off for a high dower to men from the country of origin who were eager to migrate and gain residency rights. In the subsequent decades, women who were brought as 'import' brides to the Netherlands from the male (post-)migrants' countries of origin were similarly considered as victims of forced marriages (Bonjour and de Hart, 2013, pp.67–68).

In order to counter migration marriages, policy makers have taken a host of measures, varying from the Act of Prevention of Fraudulent Marriages (1994), increasingly high income and age requirements (starting in the early 2000s), introduction of pre-departure integration requirements (2006), extension to five years of spouse-dependent residency permit (2012), special requirements for consanguineous (cousin) marriages (2014), and the non-recognition of all marriages under 18 years of age (2015). In all of these cases, migrant women's wellbeing (i.e., avoiding 'arranged and forced marriages') has been a strong legitimizing argument, with polygamous marriages, cousin marriages, child marriages, and more generally arranged marriages all considered as an indication of forced marriage (Bonjour and Kraler, 2015; Sterckx, et al., 2014; De Koning, Storms and Bartels, 2014).

Whereas these issues have been extensively discussed in the literature about transnational marriages, one element that has remained undertheorized is how the problematic side of these marriages has increasingly become linked to 'Islam', implicitly or explicitly. This was the case already in the early 1990s when polygamy became a topic of discussion, while the dower (*mahr*) marriages refer to a central element of the Muslim marriage contract. Also, cousin marriages and underage marriages (the former emerging in debates about marriage migration from Turkey and Morocco, and the latter in the case of the recent Syrian refugees) have first and foremost become associated with Muslims.

These debates and policy measures need to be seen in a context in which the presence of labour migrants from Muslim-majority countries has been redefined and problematized in the course of the last 50 years. Already by the 1980s the presence of these migrants and their families was no longer seen as a welcome solution to labour shortages but had become defined as a societal problem. (Post-)migrants from Muslim-majority countries such as Turkey and Morocco, at first labelled as foreign guest workers and then as ethnic minorities, were now increasingly addressed as Muslims, with some also self-defining as such.[3]

By the 1990s, mainstream politicians in the Netherlands had already started to speak about Islam as incompatible with European values, and by the end of the 20th century a populist, neo-nationalist, anti-Islam movement, that claimed to express the emotions and sentiments of 'ordinary autochthonous (white Dutch) people', started to gain ground, arguing that the way of life of the majority population was under threat of Islamization (Geschiere, 2009). The terrorist attacks of 9/11, the murder of Pim Fortuyn in 2002 (by an animal rights activist), and of Theo van Gogh in 2004 (by a Dutch-Moroccan, who claimed to have done so on religious grounds) and the emergence of Wilders' anti-Islam *Party for Freedom* have strongly contributed to an Islam-unfriendly climate.

Dutch policy makers on the right and on the left have increasingly agreed with the position that (post-)migrants will only integrate into Dutch society if the Dutch national identity is more firmly established. This entails that both public debate and policy making have become more explicitly assimilationist, placing increasingly high demands on Muslims in particular to prove their belonging to the nation and their loyalty to the state. With citizenship increasingly defined in terms of shared values rather than with respect to legal rights and obligations, this political discourse produces the differences it seeks to control (Moors, 2009).

Problematizing 'Islamic marriages'

In the above we have argued that transnational marriages as a problem-space have become intimately linked with Islam. In the 2000s, however, we also witness the emergence of 'Islamic marriages' as a topic of debate in itself. The first instance emerged in 2005 in the context of the trial of the members of the Hofstad network (an alleged terrorist organization) when journalists reported about 'Islamic marriages' that were concluded in the circles around this network. These marriages were not preceded by a civil marriage, and they were concluded in a highly informal manner, without the knowledge, let alone the involvement, of the parents of the young women. In early 2006, one of the Dutch security services even published a report asserting that Islamic marriages formed a threat to national security. The main arguments were that these marriages may function as a means of recruiting women for violent jihad, that they can be considered as an indication of a man entering the last phase prior to becoming a martyr in a terrorist attack, and that they may in time be a threat to the democratic rule of law as ultra-orthodox Muslims supposedly refuse to register a civil marriage on ideological grounds (NCTb, 2006, pp.26–27).

In 2008, Islamic marriages again became a topic of extensive public and parliamentary debate. This time the target was imams attached to salafi-oriented mosques; they were accused of concluding Islamic marriages between partners who had not yet performed a civil marriage. Until then the regulation prohibiting religious functionaries from concluding such religious marriages had largely remained dormant. [4] Members of parliament, from the left to the right, played a pivotal role in turning Islamic marriages into a matter of public concern. This time, Islamic marriages were considered as evidence of and as an instrument for the development of a strictly orthodox Islamic 'parallel society' that purposely distanced itself from Dutch society. As had been the case with the newspaper articles in 2005, the arguments presented by members of parliament resonated strongly with those of the reports produced by the Dutch security services (especially AIVD, 2007).

Whereas two different categories of Muslims were the target of these two rounds of media hype, namely violent jihadists and salafi-oriented imams, in both cases the women entering into these marriages were by and large defined as victims. During the first of these, it was argued that the women were recruited by male extremists, who employed 'loverboy-like' practices in order to mobilize them for jihad (NCTb, 2006, p.22). In the case of salafi-oriented imams, the women were considered as the victims of those who wanted to institutionalize *shari'a* with its gender inequality, also enabling polygamous and underage marriages (AIVD, 2007, p.68).

More recently, since 2014, public interest in 'Islamic marriages' has centred on the women travelling to areas held in Syria by ISIS and similar jihadist groups. At first, these women were considered naïve victims of male recruiters, as had been the case with the women in the circles around the Hofstad network. By early 2016, however, the Dutch security services expressed a different point of view (Navest, de Koning and Moors, 2016). Its 2016 report explicitly stated that anyone travelling to ISIS territory consciously chooses to join a group that is involved in terrorist activities, in Europe as well. "In practice this means that both male and female travellers, armed or otherwise, are participants in the struggle of ISIS", the report concluded (AIVD, 2016, p.15).

The most recent focus on 'Islamic marriages' occurred when the right-wing liberal party (VVD) presented a written plea to further criminalize 'Islamic marriages'. Somewhat ironically, the plea starts with the statement that "In the Netherlands you decide for yourself with whom you fall in love, with whom you marry or not, and in which order you choose to do so." The central argument is again that ignoring Dutch civil marriage law is a "rejection of the equality between men and women, the Dutch way of life and the history of emancipation of Dutch marriage law". The plea proposes to further enforce the prohibition against concluding a religious marriage prior to a civil marriage and extend prosecution from the religious functionary involved, "to all parties directly and voluntarily involved in concluding an illegal (religious) marriage" with a maximum sentence of 7 months in prison or a maximum fine of 20,500 euros (Kamerstukken II, 2016/17, 53465–2, p.1).[5]

We have witnessed here a partial shift from attempts to prevent the misuse of civil marriage towards the criminalization and the rendering immoral of 'Islamic marriages'. Policy measures and law-making for transnational marriages sought to limit the access of undesirable migrants to rights of residency and framed these marriages as fraudulent. The argument that naïve Dutch women needed to be protected from foreigners soon gave way to that of post-migrant Muslim women being forced into marriages not of their own choosing. These debates centred on the misuse by Muslim men (husbands, male kin) of *civil* marriages. The more recent discussions about 'Islamic marriages', in contrast, focus on relationships that have become associated with a host of negative characteristics, varying from radicalization to refusal to integrate and to women's subordination.

Muslim marriages and women's wellbeing: the voices of converts

As evident from the above, much literature on transnational Muslim marriages starts from a state-centric point of view, considering such marriage as a threat to the integrity of the nation-state (Bonjour and Kraler, 2015). These marriages are considered fake marriages (only for papers) that bring in the 'wrong' kinds of migrants (poorly educated), and in the case of Muslims, with the wrong values, especially with respect to gender relations. Such marriages then are often framed in terms of current hegemonic discourses on integration and assimilation.

A focus instead on the concept of wellbeing, in its ethical, relational, and material sense, as proposed in the introduction of this edited volume, provides a helpful alternative approach. Whereas policy makers use Muslim women's wellbeing to argue for the restriction of transnational Muslim marriages, listening to how Muslim women themselves voice their needs, aspirations, goals, and strategies with respect to marriage provides a very different perspective.

On the basis of our research, we feel confident in stating that converts often prefer to start with an Islamic marriage prior to a civil marriage. They are aware that religious marriages have no legal consequences but value the existential security such marriages provide, as it helps them adhere to new religious norms such as engaging in sexual relationships only within a marital framework. To highlight their perspectives, we first present the different trajectories towards marriage these women follow and then zone in on their arguments to first conclude an Islamic marriage.

Already in a relationship

In order to understand how women who convert to Islam deal with marriage, their 'point of departure' matters. Some converts are already in a relationship with a Muslim man when they become interested in Islam.[6] Indeed, it is usually their increased familiarity with Muslims more generally that triggers an interest in Islam. This, however, does not mean that women convert for the sake of their partner. On the contrary, narratives often point to the tensions that may well emerge when a non-Muslim woman starts to express her interest in Islam. Some of them actually hide their growing interest from their partner. They first want to figure out for themselves if they want to become Muslim and be certain it is their decision alone, without raising expectations too soon or inviting outside pressure.

Quite regularly such a relationship ends because their partner is not ready for the idea that his non-Muslim girlfriend may convert to Islam. When women become increasingly close to conversion, their partners may feel that they need to consider a more serious commitment that would include introducing her to his family and preparing for a marital relationship, which they may not be ready for. As a young single convert explained:

> For about three years I had a Moroccan[-Dutch] boyfriend. Then I started to read about Islam, he never told me anything about it, really never. He was not interested at all. After I had converted, I told him this with a lot of hesitation. He said something like, "if that is what you want to do, you should do it." But he knew of course that relations [outside of marriage] are not allowed, they all know very well that that is not allowed. He started to feel guilty, he said "you are now engaged in Islam, and I am not". So the relationship came to an end.

Such a response was very common. In other cases, the woman concerned may herself experience that she no longer is able to continue a relationship. A woman who was in her late forties at the time of the interview told us about her relationship, which forms in some ways an interesting contrast to the narrative presented above. When she was still a student she had met a Muslim man and they became involved in a relationship. He was a marginally practising Muslim, observing Ramadan, but also involved in selling non-halal food and alcohol. Once the relationship became more serious, he suggested marrying Islamically, so he could properly introduce her to his parents. Without much ado they quickly married, with an imam and witnesses she would never see again. At the time, such a marriage was a means to an end, a prerequisite in order to be able to meet his parents. Visiting Egypt, and subsequently studying videos and books about Islam on her own, however, she became seriously interested in Islam and started to consider conversion. But once she had done so, this caused a conflict about how her husband was earning his living:

The problem was that he continued to live his life the way he did before. I suggested he sell only halal food, but without consulting me, he bought another store, selling the same items. I realized he didn't take my objections into consideration, and since I wanted to thoroughly rid my life of anything *haram*, and he did not want to come along, I decided we could not go on. Now that I'm older, I realize it might have taken time for him to come around, but back then, I just didn't want that in my life anymore, so we ended the relationship.

In other words, in this case conversion actually meant the end of an Islamic marriage, which had only been concluded for practical reasons, as the woman herself no longer wanted to continue this relationship. Later the very same woman would again conclude an Islamic marriage, but in that case it was out of conviction.

When partners intend to continue their relationship after conversion, there is often a sharp break. Women who convert to Islam, not just for the sake of pleasing their in-laws, but also because they themselves are convinced of the value of becoming a Muslim, quickly realize that a sexual relationship outside of marriage is considered sinful. As conversion in itself is believed to enable them to start with a 'clean slate', with their previous transgressions forgiven, they do not want to start their Muslim life living 'in sin'. The following story of a woman in an Islamic marriage for over a decade and a half, highlights the existential and relational considerations a conversion may entail:

> We aren't married [in accordance with Dutch law]. It was not obligatory [in order for her partner to be eligible for a Dutch residence permit] and it was difficult to obtain the paperwork from Algeria. We both agreed that we don't have to marry [before the Dutch law]. We know we can depend on each other. However, when I became Muslim, I asked [a volunteer of a local Muslim women's group, married to an imam], "What does Islam advise in such a circumstance?" She said that we needed a period of separation. Not as a penance but that way you can be certain in case children are born [who the father is]. Then you are clean when you marry. I liked that very much.

She stayed at her mother's house for two and a half months, and then they got married at the mosque. "He is my husband, you know", she said, "and if we ever get the paperwork in order, then we will marry here [according to Dutch law] too".

Finding a spouse

Women who are not in a relationship when they convert often show a strong interest in marriage. This is so because marriage in itself is considered to be a form of worship ('half the *deen*' meaning 'half the religion'). In addition, new converts may well experience a sense of pressure from fellow Muslims, as they regularly face questions about when they are planning to get married. These women themselves also quickly realize that their appearance as recognizably Muslim (wearing a headscarf) and their changed interests often put existing family relations and friendships in jeopardy. While most of the time they are warmly welcomed by local mosque communities, especially when they publicly convert after Friday prayer, it still takes time to build a new network of Muslim friends. Contrary to their oftentimes high expectations, conversion does not automatically engender a feeling of belonging to and inclusion in a Muslim community. Especially at moments of heightened religious awareness, such as during the month of Ramadan, they may well be overcome by a strong sense of loneliness. For even if their own family accepts their conversion, they will not be able to provide the same forms of sociality as a Muslim family would.

It does not come as a surprise then that converts consider marriage as a solution to the multiple problems they may be facing. They expect that marrying a practising Muslim will enable them to live a more fully Muslim life, with both partners supporting each other in their religious commitment (such as praying and fasting). At the same time, they also hope that such a relationship would provide them with a family of their own, and perhaps even with supportive in-laws.

As many converts take religion quite seriously, they may express considerable hesitation about anything similar to Dutch dating practices, and avoid public dating sites such as bars and discotheques. However, as they do not have a Muslim family that can help them, they may either ask around amongst their friends or at the mosque, or try online Muslim dating platforms such as muslima.com. Whatever the trajectory they opt for, once they find someone they consider a possible partner, they often prefer to only meet a limited number of times, sometimes only in public venues, or/and with others present. It is not simply that they will not have sexual intercourse before marriage, but they also try to avoid other forms of pre-marital intimacies.

This is illustrated in the following narrative of a convert who was in her early twenties when she got acquainted with her husband. This young woman had already been close to Moroccan-Dutch girls while still in school, and when she then went to work in a factory, she joined the women there when they fasted during Ramadan. They could not tell her much about Islam, but one of them had a sister who went to a mosque and she went with her. To her surprise, there were many converts of her own age and within two weeks she said the *shahada*, and quite rapidly started to wear a headscarf and covering dress. Some months later she told a girlfriend that she wanted to marry, who then quickly found a possible husband:

"But I do not know him at all" I said [to my girlfriend]. She said she was going to call him, but I thought it was a joke. But then she did call him and told me, "He'll think it over and he'll call you after Ramadan". And so it happened. We talked for a very long time, mobile to mobile, that must have cost him a mint. But it did not work out. His father is a Berber, very traditional and he said, "There are unmarried cousins in Morocco, it won't work".

I did not really mind, but we kept in contact. He was very active in the mosque and gave me a lot of information, as I was still new in Islam. In the meantime, I had some other marriage offers, but nothing came of that. Then he called me again, "Do you still want to marry?" I thought that he had a candidate. But he asked me to do the *istikhara* prayer [a prayer conducted for the purpose of asking for God's guidance when a Muslim needs to make an important decision and is unsure which path to take] for him. I said, "For you? But your father does not want us to marry". He said, "That is my problem". Three days straight, I prayed and it felt good, so I said, "Go to the imam and arrange it". He was surprised. We had seen each other before on the train when we were both following lessons in another town, but we had not sat together. He asked whether I wanted to meet, in a mosque, because neither of us had family to accompany us, and you cannot be alone as man and woman if you are not married. I said, "For me it is not necessary, I know what you look like and we can talk by phone". We are both God-fearing, we kept it businesslike, talking about all kinds of things, but nothing intimate. Some people say it is not allowed to talk by phone. But I am not going to marry someone I do not know anything about, I have no one I can ask for information about how he is and what he likes, I have to do it myself. I feel we did it as Islamically sound as possible, we kept it decent and we did not fall into sin.

In this case it took the couple about half a year to get married, but we have often encountered far shorter time spans between the first acquaintance and the Islamic marriage. Their reluctance to engage in longer-term dating pushes these converts to marry quickly, as they try to avoid committing the sin of *zina*, that is, engaging in a sexual relationship outside of an Islamic marriage.

Concluding a civil marriage?

Dutch policy makers do not object to people concluding a religious marriage, Islamic or otherwise, but rather insist that such a marriage ought to be preceded by a civil marriage. The question is then, why do the women concerned opt for an Islamic marriage first?

To start with, many converts are not aware of the legal requirement to first conclude a civil marriage. It is true that with the negative publicity about Islamic marriages, there is a growing uncertainty or concern about this issue, yet few converts seem to be aware of this prohibition. A main reason for this is that they find it hard to understand the motivations behind such a prohibition, as they are generally aware of the fact that an Islamic marriage is only a religious act, which does not entail juridical rights and obligations. That is, since their Islamic marriage has no legal effects, their relation is only a form of cohabitation in the eyes of the Dutch law. Thus, why would there be such a prohibition?

For many, concluding a civil marriage right away is impractical for a number of reasons.[7] Some are too young to marry, when they convert as teenagers and want to engage in sexual activity, which is not prohibited in the Netherlands. Some are of legal marital age but still in the midst of completing their education, living at home with their parents or at student facilities, not yet earning enough income to be completely independent. Some converts simply cannot conclude a civil marriage, even if they wanted to. Perhaps their future spouse does not have a legal status (yet) in the Netherlands, or cannot gain access to the documents required (such as a birth certificate). In other cases, the husband is already married. Some converts consider it too dis-advantageous to enter into a civil marriage, as this would mean the loss of particular benefits such as welfare or alimony. Particularly for older converts, who may have accumulated some wealth, for instance owning their own home, it can be too risky as the default option in Dutch marriage law is marriage in community of goods, with spouses sharing assets as well as debts.

Converts may also have emotional considerations for postponing their civil marriage, that is, some do so in order not to alienate their family of origin. Often their parents are not happy with the fact that their daughter is going to marry a 'foreigner' and find it even more problematic if this person is a Muslim. Some converts then either do not mention that they concluded an Islamic marriage or present their husband as a boyfriend or a fiancé. In due course, when their family has started to accept the idea of a lasting relation-ship, they will start preparing them for a civil marriage.

In contrast to what politicians and policy makers often assume, our inter-locutors hardly ever expressed a principled stance against a civil marriage. In the words of a divorced mother of one, in her late twenties, looking for a Muslim husband after her recent conversion:

> What I would consider most important, if I marry again, is that we get the blessing from Allah, and that our union is *halal*. Whether the mar-riage is registered with the state, or how we will work it out financially, or whether we will throw a big party, or not, these are not my priorities. All of that is very unimportant to me. As a matter of speech, tomorrow, I could put on a nice dress, go to the mosque, and marry before the imam. There is no need for hundreds of people to be there, primarily it is something between me and Allah, between him and Allah, and that it is done the right way. ... Civil marriage is important when you want to buy a house, or if you have children. Then, it can be complicated if you are not partners before the law. But for the moment, my priority is an Islamic marriage. Of course, *insha'Allah*, in the future, I would like to make it official with a civil marriage. If you have children [without a civil

marriage], the father has to recognize them, that is impractical and unpleasant, and eventually it would also be fun to adopt his last name, and that it is registered in official documents. Civil marriage is fun, too, but it is the icing on the cake, not a goal in itself.

In other words, these women use the same pragmatic arguments as other cohabiting couples to conclude a civil marriage, at least in those cases where there are no legal impediments. They first opt for an Islamic marriage, which is then comparable to cohabitation, and in due course when there is a good reason to do so, they also conclude a civil marriage. Often when children are born or when property rights in the country of origin or pension rights in the Netherlands are at stake, they decide that the time has come to conclude a civil marriage as that is the fastest and easiest way to arrange these matters. An alternative reason may be that their family of origin has accepted their partner and then considers a civil marriage as an expression of a now desirable commitment.

Wellbeing revisited

Are there no downsides to first, or only, marrying Islamically in the Netherlands? Of course there are. If women envision a life as a housewife, provided for by their husbands, being abandoned after a couple of months of marriage, as does happen sometimes, can be horrifying. Being pregnant or having a newborn baby adds to the hardships some women endure. Similar to cohabiting couples, there are no financial arrangements that can be legally enforced, nor can there be a claim on a rental lease or real estate property owned by their former spouse. In case of disease or death, there are no formal ties with the spouse, and no pension rights can be claimed. For men, it can be difficult to acknowledge children born from such a marriage. Besides the legal reasons, for these reasons too, nowadays imams are wary of performing an Islamic marriage without proof of at least the intention of a civil marriage.

Converts are in some cases also at a disadvantage compared to born Muslims in regard to their knowledge about how to conclude an Islamic marriage. Tracing their marriage trajectories, it is evident that they often lack both Islamic and experiential knowledge about how to go about such a marriage. In the absence of a Muslim family of their own to be of assistance in their path towards marriage, it is often a challenge for converts to properly vet a future spouse. They are frequently unfamiliar with the concept of the *wali* (guardian, ideally the protector of her interests), who will represent her in the marriage ceremony, and hence they easily accept that a close friend or relative of their husband will function as such. They feel uncomfortable about the dower (*mahr*). Instead of considering a substantial sum of money, they quite often only ask for a wedding ring, a Qur'an, or even an uneven number of dates. And most converts are completely unaware of the possibility of inserting conditions in the marital contract.

The point we want to make, however, is that imposing the civil-marriage-first rule causes existential, relational, and material problems for women who cannot, or do not wish to, civilly marry first. Whereas individual converts find themselves in a variety of positions and have different motivations for how and why to marry, common patterns have emerged from our conversations with them. Their decision to conclude an Islamic marriage and to do so quickly, without an extended period of dating, is first and foremost an effect of their ethical aspirations. It is their desire to avoid *zina* that pushes them towards concluding an Islamic marriage. They are generally well aware of the fact that this marriage is not the equivalent of a civil marriage, and consciously opt to start the formalization of their relationship with an Islamic marriage. This means that the ability to conclude an Islamic marriage is crucially important for their ethical wellbeing.

In addition to these ethical considerations, relational aspects also push them towards first concluding a Muslim marriage. In fact, ethical and relational considerations may reinforce each other, with Muslims not only valuing marriage in itself positively, but also considering it a means to further develop their religious commitment. As they often find themselves in an isolated position after conversion, they hope and expect that marriage will provide them with a Muslim family of their own. Simultaneously, they avoid concluding a civil marriage early in the courtship, as they fear that doing so may further alienate their family of origin, who would consider a rapid civil marriage a worrisome development in itself. Moreover, as they often conclude an Islamic marriage quite soon after getting to know each other, they may well feel the need to become more confident of the success of the relationship before signing a legally binding marriage contract.

Material dimensions of wellbeing may also make it attractive for converts to first conclude an Islamic marriage. This is the case because converts tend to be better educated, qualifying for better paying jobs, even though they may face discrimination in the labour market when they wear a headscarf. Entering into a civil marriage may, in fact, put them at risk of exploitation, be it because their spouse only intends the marriage to gain him residency rights or to profit him from the wife's income or assets.

Conclusion: Policy makers versus women converts

As the above indicates, there are strong contrasts between the perspectives of politicians and policy makers and that of converts. Policy makers argue that they try to protect vulnerable women and protect Muslim women's freedom of partner choice by discouraging or prohibiting a wide range of marriages, such as Islamic marriages concluded prior to a civil marriage. Yet converts themselves consider these marriages crucially important for their ethical and relational wellbeing.

One aspect of this misrecognition of problems is that policy makers and politicians tend to automatically consider 'Islamic marriages' as a rejection of Dutch civil marriage and an indication of the desire to 'turn away' from

Dutch society. Yet, one could equally well consider an 'Islamic marriage' as a religiously sanctioned form of cohabitation. After all, converts themselves are generally aware of the fact that concluding an 'Islamic marriage' in the Netherlands is an ethical rather than a juridical act, as it does not provide legally enforceable rights and obligations. Many experience the criminalization of 'Islamic marriages' as a typical case of double standards. The Netherlands has witnessed, from the 1970s onwards, a rapid informalization of marriage, yet when Muslims decide not to conclude a civil marriage, but to engage in a non-state recognized religious ritual, this is turned into evidence of a lack of belonging to the Dutch nation.

The effect of such public debates and policy measures is twofold. It is yet another way in which Muslims are constructed as the other, while simultaneously, only in the case of Muslims, civil marriage becomes idealized and presented as a major mechanism to protect women's rights. This is particularly ironic, as feminists have often pointed out that women may well become entrapped in a marital relationship and that these relationships are a major site of violence against women. Moreover, using the argument of gender equality, the protections that marriage has offered women have also become increasingly eroded. In the case of converts, a civil marriage may actually put them at risk of exploitation, either materially (in the standard case of marriage in community of goods) or for the sake of acquiring residency rights (combined with automatic guardianship over children). And these risks are greater if the couple aspires to marry quickly for ethical reasons.

Criminalizing 'Islamic marriages' not only makes it harder for converts to live an ethical life, but also further contributes to a climate in which distrust of Muslims and Muslim institutions is encouraged. The risk is that converts will find themselves more isolated from their family and their previous circle of friends, which, in turn, places them in a more vulnerable position. An increasingly Muslim-unfriendly climate also makes it harder to engage with the real problems these women may experience. In hindsight, they regularly complain that they entered too quickly into an 'Islamic marriage', did not sufficiently check on their partner, and were unaware of the possibilities that the Islamic marriage contract offers.[8] In some cases they feel taken advantage of sexually, as their partner was only interested in a quick sexual relationship, but not in a longer-term stable relationship, or they may get stuck in their marriage as their partner refuses a divorce. Some of these problems may be prevented through a greater awareness of the possibilities that the Islamic marriage offers, such as a well-chosen *wali* who may support them, the registration of a dower (*mahr*), or the insertion of conditions in the marriage contract that may help to protect them from 'marital captivity'.

In short, policy makers' strong stance against Islamic marriages may well be harmful for the wellbeing of converts, as it makes it more difficult for them to live an ethical life. It also puts them more at risk because it contributes to a general anti-Islam climate which may further converts' social isolation (and rapid marriage) and it makes it harder to have an open discussion about the possibilities that an Islamic marriage contract offers women. Moreover, idealizing civil marriage disregards the possibility that entering rapidly into such a marriage may increase rather than decrease the risk of exploitation.

Notes

1 This is part of a larger project for which we also interviewed male converts, imams, and men acting as *wali* (marriage guardian) on women's behalf, attended (mosque) lectures, seminars, and courses about the topic of (concluding a) marriage, and looked at online efforts and initiatives in the field of match-making and of providing guidance and advice to converts about how to find a suitable spouse. Research for this project is funded by the ERC advanced grant on 'Problematizing "Muslim marriages": Ambiguities and contestations' (Grant number: 2013-AdG-324180).
2 In the Netherlands, policy documents far more often use the term migration marriages than transnational marriages (Sterckx, et al., 2014, p.12). Discussions about transnational marriages in the broad sense are not new. For debates about such marriages in colonial times, see de Hart (2015) and Stoler (1992).
3 By then, Islamic revivalist movements had emerged on a global scale. This was soon after the Netherlands witnessed a late, yet very rapid, process of deconfessionalization.
4 According to the Dutch Civil Code, 'religious functionaries' are only allowed to conclude a religious marriage after a civil marriage has been concluded (Article 68 Book 1 Civil Code). This regulation emerged in the course of contestations between state authorities and the Roman Catholic Church in the early 19th century. See van der Leun and Leupen (2009, p.8ff) for debates in the field of law about the relation between civil and religious marriages.
5 Simultaneously the TV programme *Undercover*! exposed an imam in the act of concluding such an Islamic polygamous marriage. https://zoek.officielebekendma kingen.nl/dossier/34565/kst-34565-2?resultIndex=1&sorttype=1&sortorder=4
6 As evident from earlier research, conversion is a process, rather than a sharply defined moment (Vroon-Najem, 2014).
7 See also Moors, 2013. Many of these motivations are not only valid for converts, but also for born Muslims.
8 It is in this context that sometimes the value of a civil marriage was mentioned. As it is more difficult to conclude, it may be an indication of a more serious commitment.

Bibliography

AIVD, 2007. *Radicale da'wa, de opkomst van het neo-radicalisme in Nederland* [Radical da'wa, the emergence of neo-radicalism in the Netherlands] Available at: https://www. rijksoverheid.nl/documenten/rapporten/2007/10/09/aivd-rapport-radicale-dawa-in-vera ndering-de-opkomst-van-islamitisch-neoradicalisme-in-nederland [Accessed June 13, 2017].

AIVD, 2016. *Leven bij ISIS, de mythe ontrafeld* [Life under ISIS, the myth unravelled] Available at: https://www.rijksoverheid.nl/documenten/publicaties/2016/01/12/publicatie-leven-bij-isis-de-mythe-ontrafeld [Accessed June 13, 2017].

Baumann, G., 1999. *The Multicultural Riddle: Rethinking National, Ethnic, and Religious Identities.* London: Routledge.

Bonjour, S. and Hart, B.de, 2013. A proper wife, a proper marriage: Constructions of 'us' and 'them 'in Dutch family migration policy. *European Journal of Women's Studies*, 20(1), pp.61–76.

Bonjour, S. and Kraler, A., 2015. Introduction: Family migration as an integration issue? Policy perspectives and academic insights. *Journal of Family Issues*, 36(11), pp.1407–1432.

Hart, B.de, 2015. *Unlikely Couples: Regulating Mixed Sex and Marriage from the Dutch Colonies to European Migration Law*. Amsterdam: Amsterdam Centre for European Law and Governance.

Koning, M.de, Storms, O. and Bartels, E., 2014. Legal "ban" on transnational cousin-marriages: Citizen debate in the Netherlands. *Transnational Social Review*, 4(2–3), pp.226–241.

Galonnier, J., 2015. The racialization of Muslims in France and the United States: Some insights from white converts to Islam. *Social Compass*, 62(4), pp.570–583.

Geschiere, P., 2009. *The Perils of Belonging: Autochthony, Citizenship, and Exclusion in Africa and Europe*. Chicago: University of Chicago Press.

Hage, G. 1998. *White Nation: Fantasies of White Supremacy in a Multicultural Society*. Annandale: Pluto Press and Comerford and Miller.

Hooghiemstra, E., 2003. *Trouwen over de grens: Achtergronden van partnerkeuze van Turken en Marokkanen in Nederland* [Marriage across the border: Backgrounds of partner choice of Turks and Moroccans in the Netherlands] Den Haag: Sociaal en Cultureel Planbureau.

Jensen, T., 2008. To be 'Danish', becoming 'Muslim': Contestations of national identity? *Journal of Ethnic and Migration Studies*, 34(3), pp.389–409.

Kamerstukken II, 2016/17, 34565–34562, published 6 October 2016 Available at: http s://zoek.officielebekendmakingen.nl/kst-34565-2.html [Accessed July 13, 2017].

Leun, J.van der and Leupen, A., 2009. *Informele huwelijken in Nederland; een explor-atieve studie* [Informal marriages in the Netherlands: An explorative study]. Leiden: Universiteit Leiden, Faculteit der Rechtsgeleerdheid.

Moors, A., 1995. *Women, Property and Islam: Palestinian Experiences, 1920–1990*. Cambridge: Cambridge University Press.

Moors, A., 2009. The Dutch and the face veil: The politics of discomfort. *Social Anthropology*, 17(4), pp.393–408.

Moors, A., 2013. Unregistered Islamic marriages: Anxieties about sexuality and Islam. In: M.S. Berger, ed. 2013. *Applying Shari'a in the West: Facts, Fears and the Future of Islamic Rules on Family Relations in the West*. Leiden: Leiden University Press, pp.141–164.

Moosavi, L., 2015. The racialization of Muslim converts in Britain and their experiences of Islamophobia. *Critical Sociology*, 41(1), pp.41–56.

Navest, A., Koning, M.de and Moors, A., 2016. Chatting about marriage with female migrants to Syria. *Anthropology Today*, 32(2), pp.22–25.

NCTb, 2006. *Informele islamitische huwelijken:. Het verschijnsel en de (veiligheids) risico's* [Informal Islamic marriages:; The phenomenon and the (security) risks]. Den Haag: NCTb.

Özyürek, E., 2015. *Being German, Becoming Muslim: Race, Religion, and Conversion in the New Europe*. Princeton and Oxford: Princeton University Press.

Sterckx, L., Dagevos, J., Huijnk, W. and Lisdonk, J.van, 2014. *Huwelijksmigratie in Nederland: Achtergronden en Leefsituatie van Huwelijksmigranten* [Marriage migration in the Netherlands: Backgrounds and living conditions of marriage migrants]. Den Haag: Sociaal-Cultureel Planbureau.

Stoler, A.L., 1992. Sexual affronts and racial frontiers: European identities and the cultural politics of exclusion in colonial Southeast Asia. *Comparative Studies in Society and History*, 34(3), pp.514–551.

Vroon-Najem, V., 2014. *Sisters in Islam. Women's Conversion and the Politics of Belonging: A Dutch Case Study*. PhD, University of Amsterdam.

3   Wellbeing, law, and marriage

Recognition of *Nikāh* in multicultural
Britain and the Finnish welfare state

Sanna Mustasaari[1] and Vishal Vora

Introduction

Enhancing the wellbeing of individuals is currently understood as a central
concern of contemporary family law in liberal European states (see e.g.
Eekelaar, 2013). Previous studies on Muslim marriages and law (see e.g. Jänterä-Jareborg, 2014b; Liversage, 2014; Bredal and Wærstad, 2014; Grillo,
2015; Vora, 2016a) took place within the broader framework of legal engineering in a welfare state. In this chapter we examine the legal recognition of
nikāh, the religiously valid Muslim marriage, from the perspective of wellbeing – a concept which has received only scant attention in socio-legal literature. We study *nikāh* in England and Finland and draw on our earlier
work on the legal recognition of *nikāh* in these two local contexts. We explore,
in particular, if and how a multidimensional understanding of wellbeing –
such as the heuristic model developed in this volume following White's (2009;
2010; 2015) approach – might help us better understand and map the complex outcomes of law for transnational Muslim families.

The marriages discussed in this chapter are 'transnational' to a varying
extent and in different senses. On the one hand, the *nikāh,* an Islamic
marriage, can be understood as a transnational institution in the sense that
it is shaped by laws, norms, and cultural practices that transcend one
nation-state (Bowen, 2004; Lecoyer, 2017). On the other hand, some – but
not all – of the marriages that our analysis draws on are transnational in
the sense that they were solemnized abroad or the spouses live in different
states, which, depending on the particulars of the case, either results in a
more straightforward recognition of the *nikāh* or in a more complex
situation (Al-Sharmani, Tiilikainen and Mustasaari, 2017). The 'transnational-religious' and 'transnational-foreign' elements of these marriages
contribute, in different ways, to how the issue of the *nikāh* comes to be
framed as a minority issue.

We begin by introducing the research context and background informing
our analysis. Then we describe the legal recognition of *nikāh* in England and
Finland. These two contexts offer interesting insights as their family law systems have some significant differences regarding what happens if the legal

norms of the jurisdiction are not followed when a marriage is solemnized. In some jurisdictions failure to comply with the legal norms renders the marriage non-existent, whereas in others such a failure has the effect of a void marriage.

English law has traditionally operated with the concepts of valid and void marriage, and the concept of non-marriage has only begun to emerge in the case law since 1997. While a conceptual difference is difficult to draw between a void and a non-marriage, the difference is significant in terms of consequences (Probert, 2013). When a marriage is declared void, financial orders available are the same as in a case of divorce, whereas holding the relationship to be a non-marriage means that no financial remedies can be used; the marriage simply never existed in legal terms. We focus on the concept of non-marriage as developed in the English case law and argue, based on Vora's extensive research in the field, that following the new case law there is currently a default form of marriage which reflects the Christian form of marriage and results in discrimination against ethnic minority women.

Finnish law, on the contrary, does not acknowledge the institution of a void or voidable marriage. A marriage either exists or does not; a failure to comply with the norms considered constitutive of the marriage render it non-existent. After looking at the legal framework in which Muslim marriages are solemnized in Finland, we note that issues concerning the validity of Muslim marriages are yet to emerge in Finnish courts. However, previous research (Mustasaari and Al-Sharmani, 2018) indicates possible hidden problems connected with legal recognition of Muslim marriages. Muslim marriages seem to appear in Finnish legal proceedings particularly in relation to migration and transnational family lives.

By putting together our findings from these two local contexts, we examine the wellbeing concerns that arise from the contemporary legislation in the two countries. The comparative approach we adopt in this chapter will enable us to see how the broader local legal context affects and shapes the ways in which legal norms can contribute to the wellbeing of families who belong to minority religions and transnational families. In the final part of the chapter we examine the concept of wellbeing and the relationship between recognition and civic inclusion. We conclude that the real quest is making the legal system inclusive to the extent that all citizens would feel it as relevant to their lives and identities.

Research context and background

We both have studied Muslim marriages in our own local contexts using slightly different approaches and collecting different kinds of research material. In this chapter we draw on these studies, acknowledging, however, the differences between our materials. Vora's previous research focused on examining the conundrum of Muslim unregistered marriages in England and why some citizens are getting married outside the legal framework (Vora, 2016a).

The study was a pluralistic investigation of English law, using the case study of marriages of Muslims from the Indian subcontinent. This research was one of the first detailed investigations concerning non-legal marriages, and although the study was not intended to be exhaustive, it marked an important beginning in what is a difficult area to study. Despite the small size of the interviewed sample (ten women), the study produced insightful findings regarding why such marital arrangements are entered into, but also how and why they come about. Overall, Vora's study shed light on the wider socio-legal reality of British Muslim women in unregistered marriages.

Mustasaari has studied how state law deals with the plurality of normative systems and cultural practices, examining Muslim marriage practices in Finland as well as the regulation of transnational families in the intersecting fields of family law, private international law, and migration law (Mustasaari and Al-Sharmani, 2018; Mustasaari, 2017). In the context of this study, Mustasaari and Al-Sharmani have been conducting collaborative research on marriage practices and registration of marriage among Finnish Muslims from the interrelated perspectives of mosques, individuals, and the state (Mustasaari and Al-Sharmani, 2018). In this collaborative study various sets of data were collected, including: interviews with imams and their assistants in eight Helsinki-based mosques, interviews with state officials at the local registration office, and decisions and documents concerning the recognition of marriage in local register offices and courts. In addition, selected Muslim women and men were interviewed.[2]

In the English context, Vora collected material directly from women in non-legal marriages, and the data collected focused very much on the personal experiences of the ten respondents with regard to the difficulties they faced as a consequence of their non-legal marriages. In the Finnish context, Mustasaari aimed to map the different ways in which legality of marriage becomes constructed in the discourses of different actors.

While both Finland and England are examples of Western-European welfare states and are to a large extent bound to the same international and regional treaties, such as the European Convention on Human Rights, these local contexts also differ in many respects. Muslim populations in these two countries are different with respect to size, history, and the communities' ethno-cultural backgrounds. Moreover, important differences exist between the two countries regarding both the welfare model and the legal system. The United Kingdom is often considered as an example of a liberal welfare state, whereas Finland represents a social democratic model of a welfare state (Esping-Andersen, 1990). In terms of the legal system, the UK follows a common law legal tradition and Finland belongs to the civil law tradition, and at the level of specific laws and policies, such as the regulation of intimate relationships, even more variation between the two countries can be found, such as the stark difference in the ways in which Finnish and English law deal with the conceptual distinctions between valid, void, and non-existing marriages. Thus, our comparative observations highlight how the challenges and solutions in the two contexts are different.

Muslim marriages in English law

Changing marriage practices and evolving case law

Marriage is an important milestone in one's life. Moreover, some communities continue to hold marriage as a mandatory requirement, despite the increasing trend of cohabitation in wider British society.[3] For example, in order for a British Muslim couple of South Asian background to live together and be accepted by their community, they must marry; cohabitation is not permitted by their faith beliefs. It is not acceptable religiously and socially, at least in a public and open form. However, many of the British Muslim women who are married according to their religious beliefs may be unaware of the fact that their marriage may lack legal recognition in the jurisdiction of England and Wales.[4] In such cases, in the event of marital breakdown, there would be no financial remedy available for these women as the law would treat the couple as mere cohabitees and English law provides no cohabitee rights. Reasons for the current situation are twofold. On the one hand, it seems that the marriage practices among British Muslims of South Asian background have changed (Vora, 2016a). On the other hand, the English marriage law is outdated and in recent case law Muslim marriages have often been classified as *non-marriages*.

For the first-generation British Muslims of South Asian background, their marriages and migration to the UK were often interconnected processes. They were thus keen to secure the legality of their marriages through obtaining the necessary documentary evidence. However, for the subsequent British-born generations this need to comply with the law has faded, as marriage, for them, is no longer connected to migration. Instead, young Muslim couples want to use the opportunity of marriage to celebrate their inherited culture by remembering and reaffirming traditions and beliefs from 'home' (Macfarlane, 2012, p.40) and as such, getting married in a traditional ceremony is much more meaningful to them than simply signing a functionary piece of paper in a civil ceremony of marriage. In addition, the analysis of interview data in Vora's doctoral research (Vora, 2016a) revealed that among the young people of South Asian descent marriages were being entered into without necessarily understanding or appreciating the perils of failing to comply with the required formalities of marriage.

Cultural and religious diversity of marriage practices is a fact in contemporary British society. The English marriage law, which was first put on the statute books in 1753 and which in its current form is from 1949, was never envisaged to deal with the increased levels of cultural diversity present in society today. The current Marriage Act of 1949 regulates how to marry: for example, it is important for the state, through their agent – the superintendent registrar – to ensure that those parties wishing to marry are legally entitled to do so and that the marriage will result in a legally binding union. The Marriage Act 1949 sets out the formalities required to effect a marriage according to the rites of the Church of England and the formalities required to effect a marriage otherwise. It allows for several routes to marriage such as marrying in a register office, in a 'registered building' (for religious worship), and on 'approved premises' (hotels, restaurants and the like for civil ceremonies). The current Act is the result of a series of consolidating amendments, on a piecemeal basis; it is reactive in nature, designed to cope with the stresses of the time. As a result, the current Marriage Act is complex and sometimes tricky to navigate, which is compounded by changes in customary practices of minority ethnic groups such as the British Muslims.

According to English law, to effect a valid marriage, the formalities as set out by the Marriage Act 1949 must be followed. The law has another category, *void*, for marriages that do not comply with the legal requirements as set out in the Matrimonial Causes Act 1973, Section 11. While the categories of valid and void were the only ones that were thought to be needed, what some Muslim couples are facing today is the classification of their marriage as not existing; instead of being deemed void, a *nikāh* marriage that does not meet the requirements of the law risks being deemed a non-marriage. This can have quite severe consequences. Should a marriage fail to be recognized by the law and deemed a non-marriage, the parties are excluded from making any applications for financial remedies, for example, those dealing with the matrimonial home and other assets such as savings, pensions, and whether spousal support (alimony) will be paid. This is unlike the case for parties to a void marriage who are entitled to apply to the court for financial relief. Although the exact difference between a voidable or void marriage and a non-marriage is far from clear, the conceptual difference can be located in the elements that are considered constitutive of a marriage (Jackson, 1969). For example, according to Joseph Jackson (1969, p.86), "private and secret declaration of consent does not create any kind of marriage, even a void one".

There is no mention of 'non-marriage' in the Marriage Act 1949. The concept is a court-developed one, which is why it has been criticized for not having been approved by the Supreme Court, placing doubt on its existence (Le Grice, 2013, p.1278). The category of non-marriage gives the court the power to exercise its discretion and declare a particular ceremony of marriage a non-existent marriage. Some argue the law remains unclear (Law Commission, 1973, paragraph 120; also quoted in the seminal case of *MA v. JA* and the Attorney General 2012, paragraph 86); however, based on recent case law it would appear to be the opposite. When an Islamic ceremony of marriage is conducted without the corresponding civil registration it often amounts to a non-existing marriage, not even an invalid one that might be later ruled to be void. While it is right that the state should have a hand in regulating relationships (both validating and denying), as they result in financial and other obligations, legal cases show that the current usage of non-marriage is being stretched far beyond what the concept was originally intended to cover.

Two reported legal cases illuminate the potentially discriminatory impact of current legal constructions of marriage. The first case, Gereis v. Yagoub (1997), concerned a religious ceremony of marriage that took place in a Coptic Christian Orthodox church that was not registered for the solemnization of marriages and the priest who conducted the marriage was not authorized to do so. This case was the first to set out the fact that external appearances of a marriage ceremony are deemed very important by the English law when marriages in contravention of the Marriage Act 1949 are conducted. There was much emphasis on the form of marriage in this case, it being Christian and therefore more recognizable than other forms of marriage.

The priest advised both parties to have a corresponding civil ceremony of marriage, which they failed to do. The marriage broke down after 14 months at which point the wife presented a petition for dissolution. This was met with the answer that no lawful marriage existed for the court to dissolve. The matter got to the High Court and it was found that the ceremony was within the provisions of the Marriage Act 1949, but that the marriage was void. This was because both parties had 'knowingly and wilfully' married under the provisions of Part III of the Act without complying with the required formalities. The marriage was dissolved by way of nullity.

In this case a distinction was drawn between void marriages and cases where there was no marriage at all (Gereis v. Yagoub, 1997, p.857). An example of the latter could arise when two parties undergo a ceremony of engagement or when a marriage conducted in Britain was polygamous. It was held that the marriage in question was neither of these examples as it was a valid marriage according to the religion of the parties and

> as it was an ordinary Christian marriage, it was something that this court could recognise as being something that the court could consider, even though, because the requirements of the Marriage Act had not been complied with, it was a void marriage (Gereis v. Yagoub, 1997).

In particular, the marriage was considered by the presiding judge to have hallmarks of a Christian marriage in that it was one that was intended to be monogamous and for life. The judge, furthermore, commented on the couple's behaviour post marriage; they cohabited after the ceremony whereas they had not before and they engaged in sexual intercourse, which they had not before. The judge said:

> I am satisfied that those who attended the ceremony clearly assumed that they were attending an ordinary Christian marriage … and that what happened gave all the appearance of and had the hallmarks of a marriage that would be recognised as a marriage but for the requirements of the Marriage Act (Gereis v. Yagoub, 1997, p.858).

The decision in this case has been criticized for being "a value judgement as to what an English ceremony of marriage entails and how closely the disputed ceremony resembles it" (Probert, 2002, p.403). The next case contrasts the position taken in Gereis, as it demonstrates that the outward and Christian-like appearance of marriage continues to be an important element of escaping the classification of non-marriage.

The case of Dukali v. Lamrani (2012) concerned a Moroccan couple, both Muslims, who entered into what they both believed to be a valid and legal civil ceremony of marriage at the Moroccan Consulate in London. A Moroccan notary conducted their marriage, as they specifically wanted a legal marriage and not a religious one. The marriage was celebrated with close family and friends, in the usual manner. Following the marriage, a property, the matrimonial home, was purchased in the husband's name. The couple had a child shortly after marriage and the relationship broke down about seven years later, causing the wife to petition for divorce. This prompted the husband to issue a parallel petition for divorce in Morocco. The Moroccan divorce made a very modest financial provision for the wife. The wife argued that she had a right to apply for financial relief following an overseas divorce under Part III of the Matrimonial and Family Proceedings Act 1984.

The husband opposed her application on two grounds, first because there was no marriage suitable for recognition in England and Wales to dissolve, and secondly because he said the Moroccan divorce should not be recognized in this jurisdiction. The High Court gave judgement and had to decide if the wife could establish there had been a marriage within the wording of section 12(1)(a) of the 1984 Act and, if so, was the Moroccan divorce recognizable in England and Wales as required by s12(1)(b)?

The judge found the marriage was not valid due to the wholesale failure to comply with the formal requirements of English law. In other words, since the marriage was not recognized under the Marriage Act 1949, it was declared to be a non-marriage. Furthermore, the judge was not persuaded to apply a presumption of marriage as he was not shown any authority where the presumption had been applied after the parties lived together as man and wife for a period anywhere near as long or as short as seven or eight years. He was unwilling to suggest how long parties need to have cohabited before such a presumption may apply but considered that a longer period than seven or eight years was needed. Accordingly, the marriage was judged to be a non-marriage, and the wife was enjoined from applying for any financial orders under Part III of the 1984 Act.

The two cases discussed above demonstrate that currently legal authorities remain inconsistent as to how marriages are deemed either void or non-existent. It is clear that the marriage in the case of Dukali does not fit into the definition of a non-marriage as given by Joseph Jackson. In fact, it is more in line with marriage than is the case of Gereis in terms of hallmarks of marriage: the couple, the official, and the guests all assumed they were attending and witnessing a marriage.

Towards more inclusive recognition through cohabitation law?

Disregarding religiously valid marriages and giving them absolutely no legal effect is a form of disrespect and currently constitutes a form of discrimination. Divorcing ethnic minority women feel the negative consequences the most as the case law indicates that a non-Christian ceremony of marriage is much more likely to be declared non-marriage than a Christian one. This is because non-Christian ceremonies of marriage are unlikely to bear enough hallmarks of what English law considers to be a valid form of marriage (see further Bevan, 2013). The problems relating to non-recognition of *nikāḥ* in English law represent a typical welfare concern; instead of simply relying on the doctrinal construction of marriage as a legal status, addressing this concern requires that the impact of the law on the wellbeing of individuals belonging to minorities is paid due respect. It seems that English law, for the moment, is unwilling to accept that a Muslim ceremony of marriage provides enough evidence to avoid the pitfalls of at least void marriage. Prior to the application of non-marriage such incomplete marriages would have been classified as simply void, and yet would have carried the same financial obligations as a valid marriage. Strikingly, half of the respondents featured in Vora's doctoral research (Vora, 2016a) entered *nikāḥ* marriages without informed consent concerning their legal validity.

As parties to unregistered marriages are considered cohabitees from a legal perspective, a starting solution might be found in the law of cohabitation (Vora, 2016a; 2016b; 2016c). In any case, regulation of the rights of cohabiting couples currently requires a reform of the law, as, contrary to the prevalent belief, English law does not provide cohabiting couples rights comparable to marriage.[5] A Law Commission report from 2007 on the subject of cohabitation rights made recommendations to provide financial remedies to cohabitants on relationship breakdown, redressing the economic differences incurred during the course of the relationship.[6] Calls for the law to cater to a wider variety of relationships have also been made in the Supreme Court.[7] More nuanced cohabitation provisions would help provide British Muslims in unregistered marriages, especially wives, with the protective framework they need. While the status of cohabitation would presumably be unsatisfactory in principle for many Muslim couples, those in potential or actual non-marriages might still benefit from the legal recognition that could then be afforded to their relationship.

At present, all cohabiting relationships that are not marriages (or same sex civil partnerships) are considered to be cohabitation. Such a single form of classification is crude, as it fails to take into account the circumstances and background of the couples. Based on the research findings on British Muslims in unregistered marriages, Vora (2016b) proposed a model of cohabitation that would include those persons who have entered religiously valid marriages that are not legally recognized. Vora's tiered model of cohabitation focuses on creating different categories of cohabitees in line with the realities of present day society (Vora, 2016a; Vora, 2016b, p.97). It seems unlikely that a young couple who have been cohabiting for 18 months are in the same position as another couple with children who have been cohabiting for the past 15 years. Furthermore, there are those parties who may have married without completing all the formalities of marriage who may not consider themselves as cohabitees at all. And if a consenting Muslim couple wished to opt out and forego the automatic protections that come with marriage, such a provision should be made available to them, as long as such a decision was made with a comprehensive awareness of the consequences.

A tiered model of cohabitation allows for relationships to be better classified on the basis of circumstances and facts. Introducing such a tiered model (Vora, 2016a) is a starting point for discussion and it is appreciated that such bright-line indicators will not resolve all cases: there will of course be those that fall in between the proposed tiers. However, it is argued that, if the status of cohabitees was recognized within a relatively short period of time, the recurrence of unregistered Muslim marriages would be greatly reduced. At the very least, the number of such marriages being deemed non-marriages would fall because the financial incentives not to legalize would no longer be attractive to husbands or wives. Furthermore, the finding of non-marriage would also decline and revert back to its originally intended limited application.

Reforming the law on cohabitation with a view to cultural and religious pluralism would address one aspect of British Muslim couples', especially women's, wellbeing – that is, the material concerns relating to divorce. Should cohabitation reform occur in England and Wales, the due marital obligations for British Muslims in unregistered marriages will be forthcoming, or at the very least, enforceable by the courts. However, as a solution cohabitation rights alone are insufficient. Such a mechanism still results in not accepting what is a religiously valid form of marriage, the *nikāḥ,* as being legally binding and this denial seems to be based on elements of the marriage ceremony that are not adjustable to the external appearances.

Human beings are culturally embedded, and they place a great deal of value on their cultural identity (Parekh, 2005). Viewed through the lens of marriage, culture for many is inescapable, and as such, a value judgement should not be made. South Asian identity formation, generally speaking, has become increasingly ethno-religious in character (Modood, 2017, p.187), and getting married in a non-religious ceremony can prove to be meaningless for the parties. Social recognition is central to identity (Taylor, 1994). The social recognition of marriage practices, that is, allowing citizens to get married in a way that is meaningful to them, is essential to the experience of wellbeing particularly in the relational and normative dimensions. Ultimately, while citizenship is about rights, these rights can only be used by citizens when they feel as if they belong, and are welcomed and accepted. Speaking especially of the British context, the multi-dimensional concept of wellbeing could counter the narrow race-oriented definition of what it means to be British in which 'everyone is British but some are more British than others'.

The reform of cohabitation rights discussed above is a step towards allowing such a purpose to come into view, although we appreciate that, with respect to unregistered Muslim marriages in the English and Welsh context, it merely seeks to provide an interim solution. A real challenge is to consider the fundamental question of whether the current English law on marriage allows people in our culturally diverse society to form relationships that are meaningful to them, while still in compliance with the statutory framework.

The legal case of Dukali discussed earlier certainly seems to be making a value judgement on what can and cannot be called a marriage. In balancing the functional over form, a middle ground needs to be found, or even created, that allows *all* citizens equality concerning relationships. A fuller solution under the rubric of wellbeing lies in focusing on relationships, with all their diversity. This means reforms both in the Marriage Act and cohabitation rights.

Muslim marriages in Finnish law

Marriage as a case of joint governance

Contrary to the British context, cases concerning disputes about the legal validity of a Muslim marriage (or some other religious marriage) solemnized in Finland have not been reported in the courts. Presumably the reasons for this are many, starting with the demographic fact that the Muslim community in Finland is rather small and heterogeneous. The estimated number of Muslims in Finland is around 80,000. Generally speaking, the Muslim population is socioeconomically disadvantaged compared to the majority of Finns as many of them arrived as asylum seekers and refugees. It is possible that their divorce-related disputes merely have not reached courts because in only a few cases is the economic interest involved considerable enough to make a legal dispute worthwhile. Comparative observations from Sweden, where the number of Muslims is significantly higher, indicate, however, that the size of the community is not the only relevant factor explaining why these legal disputes have not emerged in courts – perhaps not even the most significant.

Despite the large numbers of Muslims in Sweden, there are no cases in which the legal recognition of *nikāḥ* has been disputed in a court. By contrast, other types of cases involving Islamic family law, for example, disputes about Islamic dower, *mahr*, have emerged in Swedish (but not in Finnish) courts. This suggests that legal and institutional factors are important. What is common between Sweden and Finland is their legal framework regarding both the solemnization of marriage and the elements considered constitutive for marriage. Furthermore, both countries have exhaustive population register systems, and their welfare systems are similar.

Unlike in several other European states (see for example Grillo, 2015; Moors and Vroom-Najem in this volume), neither Swedish nor Finnish law includes provisions that would somehow penalize religious-only marriages or, for example, require that a civil marriage be concluded prior to a religious one. Marriages are, rather, governed through a system of *joint governance*; both certain state officials and religious communities can solemnize legally valid marriages, either in religious or civil ceremonies.

Marriage is the most important legally recognized relationship form, as it provides the couple with extensive rights and obligations towards each other, including the right and obligation to maintenance during the marriage and remedies in the event of its dissolution. A marriage is conducted with an act of solemnization, which is a legally regulated procedure involving the couple, witnesses and a third person who has the legal competence to conduct the formula of the marriage. The 1929 Marriage Act (234/1929) lays down the basic requirements concerning the solemnization of marriage as well as the process of divorce and financial implications of marriage and divorce.[8] Historically, only Christian churches were in a position to solemnize marriages; the mandate was given to state and other religious communities only in the early 20th century. The 1929 Marriage Act gave all religious communities the right to solemnize marriages, provided that they had been granted a permit for this from the government. Following the constitutional reform in 2000 and the generally increased awareness that the legal framework concerning any delegation of public authority to private actors had to be established with detailed regulations and supervision in place, a specific law was passed in 2008 on the Performing of Marriage Ceremonies (*Laki vihkimisoikeudesta*, 2008/571). In the 2008 Act, the mandate or licence to solemnize marriages was made personal and attached to membership in a religious community that needs to be registered according to the 2003 Freedom of Religion Act (*Uskonnonvapauslaki* 453/2003). The local register office is the state authority responsible for granting, upon request, a licence to solemnize marriages, as well as for supervising that this mandate is used in accordance with the law.

A marriage solemnized by a licensed person is immediately legally valid without further acts of registration, although the marriage certificate needs to be presented to the local register office so that it can be entered into the population register. According to the statistics, in each of the 17 registered Muslim religious communities, one or more members are currently licensed to solemnize marriages (Maistraatti, 2017). The fact that the legal validity of the marriage is attached to the competence of the person conducting the marriage seems to work against claims of alleged non-marriages. It also offers a form of recognition of religious identity by recognizing the significant role of religious communities in the solemnization of marriages, which contributes to an inclusive understanding of citizenship which embraces religious belonging (see also Al-Sharmani in this volume).

A hidden issue of non-marriage?

Compared to the legal framework of England and Wales, Finnish law deals with the legality and validity of marriage differently. The institution of void marriage does not exist in Finnish law. According to Finnish law, elements constitutive of a marriage are: 1) that it is solemnized by a person with a competence to solemnize marriages, 2) that both of the spouses-to-be are present simultaneously at the ceremony, and 3) that the person solemnizing the marriage asks consent to the marriage directly on that occasion and individually from each spouse-to-be.[9] In principle, a failure to comply with these provisions will render a marriage non-existent. In comparison, a failure to follow other legal requirements, such as statutory impediments to marriage, do not render the marriage non-existent.[10]

Marriage customs followed by some Muslims may be potentially problematic from the perspective of legal validity (Mustasaari and Al-Sharmani, 2018). According to the majority schools of Islamic jurisprudence, the marriage contract is concluded through the following constitutive elements: the consent of both parties actualized through the act of the bride's offer (*ijāb*) to enter into the marriage and the groom's acceptance (*qubūl*), and the presence of the bride's guardian (father), the two witnesses, and the agreed upon dower. In some Muslim communities the custom is that the bride delegates her role in the ceremony to her guardian and hence is not physically present during the officiation of the marriage contract. This is problematic in the legal view; in order to effect a legally valid marriage, both partners are required to be simultaneously present to express their consent to the marriage before being declared married. While cases in which these marriages have been claimed to be non-marriages have not been reported in courts, the concern is real and has also been voiced in the Swedish context (Jänterä-Jareborg, 2014a, p.98).

The registration of the marriage and the question of its legal validity are, in principle, separate issues. On the one hand, even an unregistered but properly solemnized marriage is a legally valid marriage. On the other hand, the registration of the marriage alone does not guarantee that it is legally valid. With no precedents, it is difficult to predict how claims of non-existence of the marriage would in actual fact turn out in Finnish courts. The registration entries concerning the couple in the Finnish population register would, however, be the starting point.

The Finnish population register is an exhaustive database including a variety of personal data, such as civil status, permanent residence, and family relations. The Finnish state collects information for the population register at several sites, and the registration of information is based on statutory notifications made by both private individuals and public authorities. Any non-compliance with the register concerning the marriage status is likely to be noted by individuals themselves or by officials, as the information in the population register system is used throughout Finnish society's information services, governance, and public administration, for example, in taxation and judicial administration. The information contained in the population register is considered publicly reliable, so anyone claiming that the registration entry in the population register is incorrect will need to provide strong evidence. The exhaustive population register and its extensive use by nearly all public authorities might be what in practice prevents non-marriages most efficiently, as it increases awareness of the legal status and effectively limits disputes over it.

Couples sometimes try to register Islamic marriage certificates that lack the constitutive formal requirements of the law. For example, the marriage certificate may have been issued by an imam who does not hold a licence to solemnize marriages (Mustasaari and Al-Sharmani, 2018). Problems could potentially arise if the registration of the marriage is delayed or if one of the spouses mistakenly assumes the marriage is registered.

Even though the legal validity of Muslim or other religious marriages has not emerged as a burning legal issue in courts, three types of potential problems can be connected to legal recognition and regulation of some Muslim marriages (Mustasaari and Al-Sharmani, 2018). The first type, explained above, is about the validity and legal existence of a marriage conducted according to cultural norms and customs that do not comply with the provisions of the Marriage Act. As a result, the marriage may, in theory, be declared non-existent in spite of its being properly registered. The other two issues have less to do with cultural or religious plurality and more with the transnational element of family life.

Since most Muslim families in Finland currently have a recent history of migration, the issues relevant to migrant marriages often overlap with Muslim marriages, emphasizing the complex nature of the intersection of religious law and family relationships. In the Finnish context, Muslim marriages typically become contested not so much because they are religious or Muslim marriages but because there is a transnational element involved in these cases (Mustasaari and Al-Sharmani, 2018). A marriage has legal implications in several different contexts, such as financial relations between partners, immigration law, and the legal relations between parents and children. A marriage, particularly a marriage conducted abroad, may be recognized or have legal implications in one context but be refused in another. Thus, the second problem regarding marriage practices has to do with these 'limping statuses' and whether or not people actually are aware of the contested status of these relationships.

One of these contexts where marriage has significant legal implications is the process of establishing the paternity of a child because of the statutory link between the marital status of the mother and the establishment of paternity. A review of paternity cases and files in the local register offices and courts showed that there were cases in which the mother had been in a transnational marriage which had not been dissolved legally, although the individuals had obviously thought that the marriage had ended. In these cases, the mother had remarried in a religious ceremony, although the marriage was not solemnized by a state-licensed member of a religious community. The legal non-recognition of the marriage only became an issue after a child was born in the new marriage. Since the previous marriage was still legally in force, the previous husband was automatically registered as the *de jure* father of the child.

For example, typical of the Somali cases was that the mother of the child had married a man abroad, but the husband had not been based in Finland for years. Later the mother had divorced and remarried religiously but this new marriage was unofficial. The previous marriage thus existed in the register. The new, religiously married husband and biological father of the child could only be registered as the father after the *de jure* paternity of the previous husband was annulled. The process of annulment of paternity and divorce in these cases was often a complex process. From the perspective of Muslim marriages, the question the study raises is why these individuals had left their divorces and new marriages unregistered. Was it because they were not aware of the 'limping' legal statuses of the previous marriage and the new religious marriage, or did they feel that state law on marriage had little relevance to their lives? This points out an important research gap relating to Muslim families, religious plurality, and transnational family lives in contemporary Finnish society.

The third problem is the limited access to marriage of a particular group of transnational migrants. The right to marry can be extremely restricted for those with precarious residence statuses and restricted access to legal documents from their countries of origin. Several interlocutors in the study by Mustasaari and Al-Sharmani (2018), both in mosques and local register offices, spoke of asylum seekers often not being able to access legally valid and recognized marriages due to problems with obtaining the required legalized documents which prove that the person has the right to marry. If these documents were not available for some reason, for example because the person could not contact the state authorities of his or her country of origin, the only way to conduct a marriage was in a religious ceremony. Thus a religious-only marriage was in fact the only form of marriage available to them (Mustasaari and Al-Sharmani, 2018). It seems unfair that these marriages lack any form of legal recognition.

From the outset it seems that Finnish law is rather responsive to the wellbeing of culturally and religiously diverse families. The legal system embraces religious belonging by legally recognizing religious solemnization of marriages, which enhances material protection within the relationship, and supports relationships by providing public recognition. Furthermore, the legal system supports the normative dimension of wellbeing by ensuring that a marriage can be solemnized and celebrated in a meaningful way according to the cultural and religious norms of the couple. Despite these positive aspects, research indicates that the wellbeing and needs of some families are excluded. From the wellbeing perspective it is pivotal that these experiences are not perceived as marginal and isolated from the general issues in family policy.

Scholars have noted the need to find alternatives to the model which attaches the legal implications, rights, and duties almost exclusively to the status of marriage (e.g. Pylkkänen, 2012) as well as the need to move from formal status norms towards relationship recognition (e.g. Hart, 2016). The introduction of cohabitation rights in 2011, as modest as these rights may be, does reflect the changing family forms in Finnish society as well as the attempts of the legislature to secure the interests of vulnerable individuals who live in unregistered relationships (Lötjönen, 2010).[11] The next step in cohabitation law might well be towards better recognition of diversity of relationships, cultural and religious identities, and individual situations. In this context, the differentiated model of cohabitation as suggested by Vora (2016b; 2016c) offers an interesting point for reflection, as it would allow different obligations being attached to different forms of family life. Vora's model could, in particular, offer tools to address concerns relating to relationship recognition in a transnational context.[12]

Conclusion: Rethinking the nexus between legal recognition of Muslim marriages and wellbeing

In the prevailing theory of liberal individualism, legal subjects are viewed as self-sufficient persons whose culture is legally speaking irrelevant, and prescriptive ideas about free agency and equal bargaining power are attached to legal rules concerning marriage and other relationships. As White (2015) notes, underlying ontologies, such as assumptions about personhood, are important to how accounts of wellbeing are produced. To look at 'wellbeing' first and foremost as a relational concept requires a relational approach to law (e.g. Nedelsky, 2011). Rather than looking at wellbeing as something that law delivers, we should look at how law, in different ways, affects processes in which people engage with the different structures of their environment (introduction in this volume). The focus on wellbeing highlights the inadequacies of applying a general framework of contract to intimate relationships, which leads to the privatizing of whatever harm individuals suffer due to power imbalances in their intimate relationships.

Enhancing wellbeing, which modern family law increasingly claims to do, requires viewing individuals as relational, cultural, gendered, and in many ways differently positioned. This echoes a multicultural position in terms of recognizing identities (Parekh, 2005; Estin, 2008; Taylor, 1994). In accordance with this view, the legal framework should be understood as one that seeks to enhance wellbeing both individually, by creating obligations within the family, and collectively, by levelling the different imbalances prevailing in relations between different groups in society, including minority–majority as well as gender relations.

Our analysis suggests that promoting wellbeing as the main justification for family law requires that, while formalities continue to be necessary for a marriage to happen, we should also develop other means of recognizing relationships. We noted that the 'transnational-religious' and 'transnational-foreign' elements of the studied marriages contributed, in different ways, to how the issue of the *nikāḥ* came to be framed as a minority issue.

In the UK, in earlier decades virtually all *nikāḥ* marriages were transnational involving cross-border mobility and migration. The strict requirements of the law were met as these marriages were considered valid foreign marriages. With subsequent British-born generations, the marriages are decreasingly transnational in the traditional cross-border sense. Instead, these marriages are transnational as regulated by transnational religious norms and laws that are not recognized by the courts. We highlighted the disadvantageous position in which some British citizens find themselves compared to others when it comes to marriage formalities and their lack of engagement with the law.

English law under the current legislative framework views non-Christian marriage in a way that can be considered discriminatory. As such it fails to deliver wellbeing at the material and relational levels to some citizens who think their marriages are recognized by the law and that they can rely on its protective mechanisms. To view other religious marriages, not only Islamic ceremonies, as less real than Christian marriages implies that some religious ethics are excluded while others are seen as complying with the law. This signals a failure to enhance wellbeing even in the ethical dimension of the concept. Moreover, the harsh consequences of non-recognition are primarily experienced by minority women in the most vulnerable positions. This makes little sense, especially given that it is the vulnerable whose wellbeing is the official justification for interfering with relations in the private sphere.

At best, religious marriages should be considered void instead of non-existent. Public policy guidance (Law Commission, 1984) has dictated the preservation of the institution of marriage. This means recognizing the rights of citizens making up our plural society without altering the concept of what marriage is. This need not mean that the concept of non-marriage is completely abandoned. There will be situations where the category of non-marriage will be required, but it needs to be reserved for those cases where significant public concerns demand that the relationship is not recognized as existing in any form (even as void) – namely marriages in fiction and ceremonies between very young children. After all, this was what the concept originally intended.

In the Finnish context, non-marriage is not a burning legal issue, although it is possible that there are some hidden cases of non-marriage. We identified other concerns, which often had to do with transnational family situations, limping statuses, or precarious residence statuses. In the Finnish context then, it was the 'transnational-foreign' element in relationships that posed problems to how marriages, but also other relationships, became problematized in different legal discourses. Given the increasing plurality of normative frameworks, marriage customs and ceremonies, it is possible that courts or the legislature will increasingly be faced with questions about the validity or existence of Muslim marriages. The actors in the field, the legislature, courts and legal scholars, might be wise to reconsider the requirements considered constitutive of marriage in a contemporary culturally plural society.

While the material dimensions of wellbeing are connected with redistribution, the claims for due recognition of identities are essentially connected with the relational and ethical dimensions. The relational dimension of wellbeing is focal for intimate citizenship (Roseneil, 2010), which includes the freedom and ability to live selfhood in a wide range of close relationships with respect and recognition from state and community. Furthermore, the ethical dimension of wellbeing is also central to intimate citizenship, which is shaped by the laws, policies, and cultures that prescribe and regulate intimate life in ways that are impacted by other hierarchies and social norms (ibid.).

We need much more knowledge of how people actually understand and negotiate the different meanings of marriage. The question we need to address in future research, in English as well as Finnish societies, is why some citizens do not use the law to validate their relationships, even when it seems quite straightforward to do so. What else is at play?

Notes

1 Authors' names appear in alphabetical order to indicate equal contribution.
2 In the Finnish context, Mustasaari and Al-Sharmani conducted eight tape-recorded interviews with imams and other individuals affiliated with mosques and four tape-recorded interviews with individual Muslim women. Five tape-recorded interviews were conducted with staff at local register offices. The analysis is also informed by unrecorded interviews and informal discussions with lawyers at the public legal aid service, child supervisors, and NGOs. Furthermore, cases and documents were investigated in four local register offices and three district courts. For a detailed description of the data, see Mustasaari, 2017.
3 The cohabiting couple family is currently the second largest family type in the UK (Office of National Statistics, 2017).
4 Finding precise figures for the incidence of unregistered Muslim marriage is difficult. However, the most recent large-scale survey (of 901 respondents) in the UK conducted by Channel 4 (Hall, 2017) put the total number of unregistered marriages at 16.8%. This figure represents those British Muslim women who are married in accordance with their religious beliefs but not within the parameters of English marriage law.
5 According to the myth of 'common law marriage', an unmarried cohabiting couple will, through the passage of time, acquire legal marriage-like rights. This misbelief is presumably traceable to the 1970s media usage of the term (Probert, 2008, p.22).
6 An opt-out provision was also proposed, giving couples the ability not to be bound by the proposals. On the face of it, the scheme appeared a little complex in terms of determining what exactly would be a qualifying contribution, as couples rarely keep accounts of such matters in the real world. In providing a comprehensive mechanism that was based on the economic impact of cohabitation, the Law Commission sought to make the financial consequences of ending a cohabitation relationship vastly different from that of a marriage (Law Commission, 2007).
7 In the Supreme Court case of Gow v. Grant (2012) which concerned a mature Scottish couple's finances on separation, Lady Hale (now Head of the Supreme

Court), agreeing with the lead judgement of Lord Hope, proceeded to give several important lessons that England and Wales may benefit from. She remarked there is a need for such remedies in England and Wales as the law at present is uncertain, which can result in injustices.

8 The 1929 Marriage Act replaced the 1734 law on marriage and thus modernized Finnish relationship regulation, introducing, for example, legal equality between husband and wife. The Act has been reformed on several occasions. For example, the no-fault divorce was introduced in 1988 and same-sex marriage in 2017.

9 However, using the Finnish language in the ceremony is not considered constitutive for the marriage. The Swedish interpretation, for example, is that the official part of the ceremony needs to be in Swedish in order for the marriage to be properly legally solemnized.

10 For example, a marriage may have been solemnized despite one of the spouses being already married. In this case, the latter marriage exists as a valid marriage but may have the consequence of divorce; if the spouses do not file for divorce on their own initiative, the public prosecutor will initiate divorce proceedings.

11 The Act on the Dissolution of the Household of Cohabiting Partners (26/2011) improved the protection of cohabiting partners by providing the cohabiting partners with the right to initiate legal proceedings in which the property of the couple is separated (S 4); establishing a presumption of co-ownership according to which a moveable object is considered jointly owned unless it can be shown otherwise (S 6); and giving the partners the right to compensation for their contributions to the shared household (S 8). A relationship is a 'cohabiting partnership' when the partners live in a relationship (cohabiting partnership) in a shared household; and they either have lived in a shared household for at least five years or have a joint child or joint parental responsibility for a child. In the debates over the new law it was considered important that a distinction was maintained between marriage and cohabiting partnership and that the property rights of individuals were not interfered with by the new law. As a result, cohabiting partnership grants partners only limited rights compared to marriage.

12 For example, a religious marriage conducted by an asylum seeker could result in a legally recognizable relationship with marriage-like obligations, such as maintenance, being binding *inter partes*, between the spouses. Or a religious marriage recognized as spousal cohabitation could be taken into account in paternity proceedings as overruling the *pater est* presumption at least in cases where the whereabouts of the mother's registered husband are unknown.

Bibliography

Al-Sharmani, M., Tiilikainen, M. and Mustasaari, S., 2017. Transnational migrant families: Navigating marriage, generation and gender in multiple spheres. *Migration Letters*, 14(1), pp.1–10.

Bevan, C., 2013. The role of intention in non-marriage cases post Hudson v Leigh. *Child and Family Law Quarterly*, 25(1), pp.80–95.

Bowen, J.R., 2004. Beyond migration: Islam as a transnational public space. *Journal of Ethnic and Migration Studies*, 30(5), pp.879–894.

Bredal, Anja and Wærstad, T., 2014. *Gift men Ugift: Om utenomrettslige religiøse vigsler*. Oslo: Institutt for samfunnsforskning.

Eekelaar, J., 2013. Then and now: Family law's direction of travel. *Journal of Social Welfare and Family Law* 35(4), pp.415–425.

Esping-Andersen, G., 1990. *The Three Worlds of Welfare Capitalism*. Princeton, NJ: Princeton University Press.

Estin, A.L., 2008. *The Multi-Cultural Family*. Aldershot: Ashgate.

Grillo, R., 2015. *Muslim Families, Politics and the Law: A Legal Industry in Multicultural Britain*. London: Routledge.

Hall, A., 2017. The truth about Muslim marriage. Available at: https://truevisiontv. com/films/details/295/the-truth-about-muslim-marriage [Accessed March 6, 2018].

Hart, L., 2016. *Relational Subjects: Family Relations, Law and Gender in the European Court of Human Rights*. Helsinki: University of Helsinki. Available at: https://helda. helsinki.fi/bitstream/handle/10138/161283/RELATION.pdf?sequence=1 [Accessed July 30, 2018].

Jackson, J., 1969. *The Formation and Annulment of Marriage*. 2nd ed. London: Butterworths.

Jänterä-Jareborg, M., 2014a. On the cooperation between religious and state institutions in family matters: Nordic experiences. In: P. Shah with M. Foblets and M. Rohe, eds. 2014. *Family, Religion and Law: Cultural Encounters in Europe*. Farnham: Ashgate, pp.79–101.

Jänterä-Jareborg, M., 2014b. Cross-border family cases and religious diversity: What can judges do? In: P. Shah with M. Foblets and M. Rohe, eds. 2014. *Family, Religion and Law: Cultural Encounters in Europe*. Farnham: Ashgate, pp.143–163.

Law Commission, 1973. *Report on Solemnisation of Marriage in England and Wales*. Available at: http://www.bailii.org/ew/other/EWLC/1973/53.pdf [Accessed July 30, 2018].

Law Commission, 1984. *Family Law: Declarations in Family Matters*. Available at: http://www.bailii.org/ew/other/EWLC/1984/132.pdf [Accessed July 30, 2018].

Law Commission, 2007. *Cohabitation: The Financial Consequences of Relationship*. Available at: http://www.bailii.org/ew/other/EWLC/2007/307.pdf [Accessed July 30, 2018].

Lecoyer, K., 2017. Marriage conclusion in Belgian Muslim families: Navigating transnational social spaces of normativity. *Migration Letters*, 14(1), pp.11–24.

Le Grice, V., 2013. A critique of non-marriage. *Family Law*, 43(10), pp.1278–1285.

Liversage, A., 2014. Secrets and lies: When ethnic minority youth have a nikah. In: P. Shah with M. Foblets and M. Rohe, eds. 2013. *Family, Religion and Law: Cultural Encounters in Europe*. Farnham: Ashgate, pp.165–179.

Lötjönen, S., 2010. Yhteistalouden purkaminen avoliitossa [The Dissolution of the household of cohabiting partners]. *Lakimies*, 7–8, pp.1326–1346.

Macfarlane, J., 2012. *Islamic Divorce in North America: A Shari'a Path in a Secular Society*. Oxford and New York: Oxford University Press.

Maistraatti, 2017. Open data and statistics. Available at: http://www.maistraatti.fi/Pa lvelut/Mare/ [Accessed July 30, 2018].

Modood, T., 2017. Multicultural citizenship and new migrations. In: A. Triandafyllidou, ed. 2017. *Multicultural Governance in a Mobile World*. Edinburgh: Edinburgh University Press..

Mustasaari, S., 2017. *Rethinking Recognition: Transnational Families and Belonging in Law*. Helsinki: University of Helsinki.

Mustasaari, S. and Al-Sharmani, M., 2018. Between 'official' and 'unofficial': Discourses and practices of Muslim marriage conclusion in Finland. *Oxford Journal of Law and Religion*. Published online 6 August 2018. Available at: https://academic. oup.com/ojlr/advance-article/doi/10.1093/ojlr/rwy029/5067187?guestAccessKey=7a 74adcb-ec90-48ee-bb23-b9f3fe419683 [Accessed August 16, 2018].

Nedelsky, J., 2011. *Law's Relations: A Relational Theory of Self, Autonomy, and Law*. New York: Oxford University Press.

Office of National Statistics, 2017. *Families and Households in the UK: 2017*. Statistical bulletin, 8 November 2017. Available at: https://www.ons.gov.uk/releases/familiesa ndhouseholdsintheuk2017 [Accessed July 30, 2018].

Parekh, B., 2005. *Rethinking Multiculturalism: Cultural Diversity and Political Theory*. 2nd ed. Basingstoke and New York: Palgrave.

Probert, R., 2002. When are we married? Void, non-existent and presumed marriages. *Legal Studies*, 22(3), pp.398–419.

Probert, R., 2008. Common-law marriage: Myths and misunderstandings. *Child and Family Law Quarterly*, 20(1), pp.1–22.

Probert, R., 2013. The evolving concept of non-marriage. *Child and Family Law Quarterly*, 25(3), pp.314–335.

Pylkkänen, A., 2012. *Vaihtoehto avioliitolle* [An alternative to marriage]. Tampere: Vastapaino.

Roseneil, S., 2010. Intimate citizenship: A pragmatic, yet radical, proposal for a politics of personal life. *European Journal of Women's Studies*, 17(1), pp.77–82.

Taylor, C., 1994. The politics of recognition. In: A. Gutmann, ed. 1994. *Multiculturalism: Examining the Politics of Recognition*. Princeton, NJ: Princeton University Press, pp.25–73.

Vora, V., 2016a. *The Islamic Marriage Conundrum: Register or Recognize? The Legal Consequences of the Nikah in England and Wales*. PhD. SOAS, University of London.

Vora, V., 2016b. The problem of unregistered Muslim marriage: Questions and solutions. *Family Law*, 46(1), pp.95–98.

Vora, V., 2016c. Unregistered Muslim marriages in England and Wales: The issue of discrimination through 'non-marriage' declaration. In: Y. Suleiman and P. Anderson, eds. 2016. *Muslims in the UK and Europe II*. Cambridge: Cambridge University Press, pp.129–141. Available at: http://www.cis.cam.ac.uk/publications/m uslims-in-the-uk-and-europe-ii/ [Accessed July 30, 2018].

White, S.C., 2009. *Analyzing Wellbeing: A Framework for Development Practice*. Working Paper. Bath: University of Bath/Wellbeing in Developing Countries Research Group. Available at: http://opus.bath.ac.uk/13944/1/WeDWP_09_44.pdf [Accessed July 30, 2018].

White, S.C., 2010. Analysing wellbeing: A framework for development practice. *Development in Practice*, 20(2), pp.158–172.

White, S.C., 2015. *Relational Wellbeing: A Theoretical and Operational Approach*. Working Paper No 43, Bath: The Centre for Development Studies, University of Bath. Available at: http://www.bath.ac.uk/cds/publications/bpd43.pdf [Accessed July 30, 2018].

Cases

Dukali v. Lamrani (Attorney General Intervening), EWHC 1748 (Fam) (2012).
Gereis v. Yagoub, 1 FLR 854 (1997).
Gow v. Grant, UKSC 29 (2012).
MA v JA and the Attorney General, EWHC 2219 (Fam) (2012).

4 A mosque programme for the wellbeing of Muslim families

Mulki Al-Sharmani

Somalis say they know religion, but they only know to pray, and go to mosques, they do not know to work on marriages and families.

A mosque imam and a key organizer of the mosque programme for Muslim families.

Introduction

The quotation above alludes to the concerns of a Helsinki mosque programme regarding Finnish Somalis' religious understandings and family practices and their impact on their wellbeing. This chapter tackles how Muslim religious institutions in Finland understand and play a role in the pursuit of family wellbeing. I focus on the work of one mosque programme, which was established in 2011 and predominantly serves Somali families. I examine the programme's two stated goals: the 'good of Muslim families', and their 'positive integration' into Finnish society. How are these two goals understood, interconnected, and pursued by programme organizers? And how can the concept of wellbeing (White, 2008; 2010; 2016) help us understand the programme's vision and work?

I trace both the local and transnational contexts shaping the work of the mosque programme. As Finland is increasingly becoming multicultural and multi-religious through immigration, family wellbeing becomes ever more intertwined with the issue of integration and empowering membership in the society. Somalis, the largest Muslim black immigrant community in Finland, confront multidimensional challenges such as economic marginalization, educational and employment challenges, limited social mobility, and racism (OSF, 2013). I examine how the goals of the mosque programme are driven by tackling the impact of these challenges on marriage relationships and parent–children relations. Also relevant to the programme is the Finnish state governance of religious communities. Recent scholarship argues that changes in the welfare state after the 1990s have resulted in a new form of governance where third sector associations and civil society partake (with the state) in the work of family welfare and identity-making (Mårtensson, 2014; Martikainen,

2014). As part of this new governance, new laws and policies have been passed which create more legal and public space for religious institutions from minority communities. I shed light on how the researched programme is enabled by these state policies.

Additionally, I highlight how the vision and language of the mosque programme are also shaped by its being part of a loose network of Islamic institutions and individual religious scholars across Europe. This network works towards promoting modern and harmonious Muslim families who are grounded in Islamic norms while at the same empowered and active members of their respective societies. I examine, in particular, the mosque's discourse on companionate marriage and engaged parenting. I analyse the Islamic arguments and language used in this discourse, reflecting on their gender implications.

Research background

This chapter is part of a larger study on Muslim marriage norms and practices in Finland.[1] I conducted the ethnographic research on the selected mosque from 2013 to 2017. I collected data through: participant observation, interviews, life history interviews, informal discussions, and content analysis.[2] I conducted participant observation of family seminars, usually held once every four to six weeks for six hours each time. I also attended two annual conferences organized in 2015 and 2016.

I conducted a series of individual and group interviews with nine key interlocutors (four men and five women) who were organizing and assisting with programme work. I also interviewed and had informal discussions with programme participants. My access to female participants was better than the male for several reasons. More women than men attended the activities. Also, because women and men sit separately on parallel sides of the room during programme events, I was often in the company of women rather than men. Hence, I conducted group interviews with eight female participants as well as individual life-history interviews with three of these participants. I also had many informal discussions with the women. While I did not get to interview individual male participants, I had informal discussions with some of them. All interviews and discussions were conducted in Somali. In addition, I analysed programme pamphlets, seminar PowerPoint presentations, and videotaped lectures.

Two final points regarding research ethics are noteworthy. To ensure that this research does no harm to my interlocutors, I discussed with them the issue of anonymity and confidentiality. It was their decision that while the name of their mosque would not be disclosed, accurate and sufficient information would be provided about the programme to help with their advocacy for its goals. Programme organizers, furthermore, read several drafts of this chapter and approved its accuracy and its adherence to our agreement.

Cognizant of the vexing question of power and knowledge in anthropology and feminism as fields of knowledge, I have also reflected on my own positionality as a researcher (Abu-Lughod, 1990). I share with my inter-locutors the same religious and Somali diasporic background although as an immigrant I grew up elsewhere. This shared background, on the one hand, facilitated my access and ability to do the research. On the other hand, it made me more aware and reflective of power relations in my research and its potential consequences for my interlocutors. I discussed candidly with my interlocutors a common perception among the Somalis in Finland that they have been over-researched because of their visibility as the largest Muslim black community, yet this research has often been perceived to have benefitted the researchers more than the immigrants themselves. My interlocutors and I agreed that one way to partially redress this issue in this study is that I undertake volunteer work that would directly benefit them. Upon the request of the women, I committed to teaching them English once a week in the mosque, and the class has been open to women and girls from the community at large. This volunteer work since then has become – for me – part of a larger personal/political engagement that goes beyond the scope of this research.

Religious communities in Finland

The Lutheran Church of Finland is the official church of the country with a long history of close relationship with the state (Sakaranaho, 2013). The Orthodox Church also has similar official status. The largest religious com-munities belong to the Lutheran Church with 80.6% of the total population, the latter being approximately 5.5 million (Statistics Finland, 2016). Muslims, whose number is roughly 60,000–65,000, constitute 1% of the total popula-tion. Muslims in Finland have diverse backgrounds. In addition to some 600 Finnish Tatars who are also the oldest Muslim community, there are Muslim communities from: the Horn of Africa, North Africa and the Middle East, Sub-Saharan Africa, South East Asia, and the Indian subcontinent, as well as Finnish converts. The majority of the Muslim communities are of refugee background. The Somalis comprise the largest Muslim and African commu-nity, with a total number of 19,059 in 2016 (Statistics Finland, 2016).

In the 20th century, as Finland was increasingly becoming multi-religious, there was a need to recognize this religious diversity and affirm the equality of all citizens. Therefore, in 1923 the Freedom of Religion Act was introduced. This law affirms the separation of the state and church, cementing the autonomy of the church which had begun in the late 19th century (Kää-riäinen, 2011, p.157). The law also safeguards the freedom of citizens to pro-fess and practise religion freely, and to form religious communities. The right to freedom of religion was also enshrined in Finland's 1919 constitution at the time. In 2003, a new Freedom of Religion Act was introduced. This new law introduced the notion of 'positive freedom of religion'. (Kääriäinen, 2011, p.158). It was now the state's responsibility not only to safeguard against religious discrimination but also to create an environment where citizens can practise their religion – the latter now being seen as part of 'community tradition' to be nurtured (Kääriäinen, 2011, p.158). The country's new constitution, which was passed in 2000, also affirms the state's double role as protector of religious equality and nourisher of citizens' and communities' religious identities (Kääriäinen, 2011, p.157). Like its predecessor, the new Freedom of Religion Act stipulates that a minimum of 20 individuals can establish a religious community. Religious communities can register with the state either under the Freedom of Religion Act or under the Association Act of 1989. Communities registered under the former have to meet more rigid criteria than those registered under the latter law, but they enjoy more rights such as the legal authority to conclude marriages and the right to religious education (Kääriäinen, 2011, p.158). Registered religious communities are entitled to receive annual financial assistance from the state if they have at least 200 registered members.

In the early 1990s, there were a handful of mosques[3] in Finland. But by the 2010s the total number had reached 50 as many made use of the new state laws to register as religious communities (Ketola, Martikainen and Salomäki, 2014). In earlier eras, most of these mosques were ethnically divided, whereas nowadays there is a combination of multi-ethnic and ethnically divided mosques. For example, there are three main mosques in Helsinki managed and frequented by Somalis, including the researched mosque. There are also mosques in Helsinki predominantly frequented by South Asians, English speaking Muslims, Finnish converts, and the Shi'a community. Most mosques provide religious and social services such as conducting daily and Friday communal prayers, Ramadan and Eid prayers, weekly religious classes for children and adults, and burial rites. In addition, mosques usually conclude marriages and divorces,[4] as well as undertake family dispute resolution.

The researched mosque is part of a non-profit Islamic umbrella organization that was first established in 1986. It was the second Islamic organization in the country after the Tatar Islamic organization and mosque, which were established in the first half of the 20th century. The total number of the mosque's registered members is between 1700 and 1800, with 600 to 800 members paying annual donations. The majority of members are Somalis, but some come from other ethnic backgrounds. The members of the advisory council overseeing the umbrella organization are of diverse ethnic background, but those running mosque activities are predominantly Somalis. The umbrella organization consists of eight associations covering Qur'anic education and recitation, media, children's day care, women, youth, Islamic relief, endowments, and family wellbeing. It is this latter association that manages the researched programme. The mosque is registered according to the 2003 Freedom of Religion Act, while the associations comprising the umbrella organization are registered according to the Association Act of 1989.

Al-Usra al Muslima: A mosque programme for families

The 'good of the family' and 'positive integration': seeking wellbeing?

The mosque programme is well structured with a clear vision and goals. It was established in February 2011 and is called Muslim Families of Finland, or simply *al-Usra* (the Arabic word for the family). *Al-Usra* provides mediation and arbitration for family disputes. It also holds regular seminars for families, promoting knowledge and skills that enhance the 'good' of the family. The programme, furthermore, holds lectures for youth, which cover Islamic family law, foundations for good Muslim marriages, Finnish family laws, the place of love in marriage, etc. Since late 2016, the programme has also begun training workshops for parents and newlyweds. These workshops, however, have not been regular. Once a year, the programme also hosts an international conference bringing together Muslim religious scholars and community activists mostly from Europe but on some occasions from North America and Somalia as well. The programme conducts all its activities (with the exception of family dispute resolution work) in Somali and targets Somali Muslim families. But the organizers are planning to extend this work to non-Somali Muslim families, once they have recruited enough volunteers from other ethnic backgrounds.

The programme is organized by five board members (three men and two women). The men are first-generation immigrants who are in their forties, while the women are in their mid-thirties and moved to Finland in their teens. Two of the male board members are also the mosque imams and members of the dispute resolution committee. One of these imams had a previous career in a professional field but was also mentored in Islamic religious sciences first by mosque imams in Somalia and then in Finland. The other imam was also mentored in Somalia and was at the time of the research pursuing a long-distance degree in Islamic religious sciences from a private institution in Europe. The other three board members are: a male member who teaches Islam in public schools and had a previous career in a business-related field, and two female members who work in the fields of health and social work. The three male board members are the ones who normally lecture on Islamic teachings in the seminars and workshops. The female board members, on the other hand, give presentations on health-related issues, invite speakers from different Finnish organizations, and advertise activities.

These board members are assisted by four interlocutors (one man and three women). These helpers are in their late twenties and moved to Finland when they were young children. The male interlocutor is also pursuing a long-distance degree in Islamic religious sciences. The three women also work in the health sector. While the women interlocutors do not have formal expertise in religious knowledge, they are all diligently pursuing religious knowledge from multiple sources (e.g. classes at the mosque, independent studies from books and online lectures, etc.).

The scholar Sarah White (2008; 2010; 2016) produced a series of important writings engaging with the concept of wellbeing and developing it as a layered and useful analytical tool in social sciences. Drawing on White's work, I understand wellbeing to be *not* simply an outcome but rather a **holistic process** that encompasses material, relational, and ethical dimensions. The material dimension covers resources needed for daily lives such as education, jobs, housing, health, physical safety, places of worship, legal mechanisms of marriage and divorce, etc. The relational dimension has to do with the social relations in which people's lives are embedded in the family, community, or larger society. And the ethical dimension is related to the systems of norms, laws, and values that shape people's decisions, actions, and claims. The three dimensions are organically linked, and the process of seeking and experiencing wellbeing is shaped by the specific temporalities and localities of the people concerned.

This conceptualization of wellbeing, I contend, is a useful tool to understand the *al-Usra* programme. The organizers often describe their work as having two intertwined goals: the 'good of Muslim families', and their 'positive integration'. That is, the pursuit of both goals, in the programme's vision, is very much akin to the notion of seeking multidimensional wellbeing encompassing its material, relational, and ethical aspects. Realizing both goals, furthermore, necessitates two interconnected pathways: first, programme participants are to acquire good knowledge of Islamic norms on marriage and parenting, knowledge of the distinction between Islamic and Somali cultural norms, knowledge of modern ideas and concepts in psychology and communication so as to acquire the skills needed to have healthy family relationships, and knowledge of laws and norms of the larger society so as to claim and experience empowering membership in the society. Secondly, participants are to apply this knowledge to establish harmonious and cooperative relationships with family members and the larger society.

The attainment of the good of the family, on one level, has to do with fulfilling their material needs such as education, employment, and housing as well as knowledge of relevant policies and institutions for family welfare. On a relational level, it is concerned with reforming participants' relationships with their spouses and children. Additionally, the 'good of the family' includes an ethical dimension which entails acquiring the 'correct' understanding of religious norms on marriage and family relations, reflecting critically on Somali cultural norms that are seen to justify male dominance in marriage and gendered parenting roles, and navigating Islamic family law and Finnish state codes.

Positive integration, according to the programme organizers, is a distinct kind of engaged and empowered membership in the society while maintaining one's Islamic norms and identity. Similar to the first goal, 'positive integration' is also a process that has material, relational, and ethical dimensions. Again, on the material level, it means acquiring knowledge of the policies and services of state and third sector organizations concerned with participants' family life such as the health sector, schools, law enforcement, child protection agencies, community centres providing leisure activities, registrar offices recording marriages, etc. On a relational level, it involves interacting with these institutions from a position of knowledge, agency, and cooperation. Ethically, positive integration means navigating successfully the multiple norms and laws that regulate or impact participants' family life.

Programme organizers repeatedly emphasize the intertwining of the good of the family and its positive integration. One cannot happen without the other and vice versa. To provide better care for one's children and become a better spouse and parent, one needs to have the knowledge of state and third sector policies and services that impact family wellbeing. One also needs to reach out to relevant institutions, not as a marginalized immigrant but as a right-bearing and engaged citizen. The connection between the two goals is captured by a female programme organizer in the following quotation, as she explains why she is doing this work:

> I was very eager to work in this programme. Muslim families have a lot of problems here, but we Somalis, especially, have a problem. The state provides housing, education, health, and many things. But people do not have knowledge, people keep to themselves. There is fear, we have been living here for many years, but mothers are afraid, they do not use state services, they do not interact with them, they are afraid their children will be taken, they do not join the society. And some people think this is a *gaal* (non-Muslim) society and so they keep to themselves. And Somali fathers, those who are physically here and those who are not, they are all the same, they are not doing their part. When I listened to the seminar of … [the co-founder of the programme], I felt this is exactly what we need. Our goal is a Finnish, Somali, Muslim identity, and to build this for the young generation. How can Somali families living here build this identity? This is our goal.

The following ethnographic vignette, furthermore, sheds light on the programme's promotion of multifaceted family wellbeing:

> In a family seminar, the mosque imam began the event with Islamic teachings on how to prepare oneself spiritually for the month of Ramadan as the blessed month was approaching. Then another programme organizer, a trained nurse, presented health advice on how participants could take care of their physical wellbeing while fasting (e.g., how women and men could take care of their skin). This was followed by a presentation by an invited medical expert on recent changes in state laws regarding access to health care for young children. Then another programme organizer presented statistical information on how immigrant students, and in particular Somalis, were performing in high school and their challenges in pursuing higher education. Next was a presentation by the

mosque imam on marital relations and the challenges of conflating Somali cultural norms with Islamic teachings, leading to hierarchical and male-dominated marriage relationships that are detrimental to the wellbeing of the family. Finally, there was a general discussion and participants were asked to reflect on the issues, share their personal experiences, and identify specific challenges to tackle and propose solutions.

The seminar described above reflects the programme's holistic multidimensional approach towards family wellbeing. Each seminar consists of several components that focus on the material, relational, and ethical needs and aspirations of couples and parents, and which are also linked to their place and experiences in the larger society. This holistic approach towards family wellbeing has an affinity with White's argument that wellbeing goes beyond meeting needs or overcoming problems to the pursuit of a meaningful and fulfilling life. Similarly, the programme's vision also highlights an endeavour to promote a well-rounded, fulfilling, and meaningful life. One of the key organizers explains its holistic vision as follows:

> We adopt the approach of *shumūlīya* [Arabic for holistic and comprehensive], we do not focus on only one part of Islam, we have to cover more than one aspect, for example, we have problems with youth, we have problems with our relationships with government, we have to work with other organizations, how to deal with media, with academia. *Our approach is broad.* (My emphasis)

The use of the term *shumūlīya* by the interlocutor in the quotation above is meant to denote an Islamic reformist approach which emphasizes that seeking and enacting Muslim piety is not confined to religious rituals but has to permeate all aspects of one's life including social relations and interactions in the larger society. The interlocutor explains further that the role of the programme goes beyond '*da'wa*' (promoting the faith and teaching its tenants and rituals). It involves tackling in his words "integration, education, health, civilization". He also sees their holistic approach as setting them apart from other mosques in the city since the latter, according to him, do not have the same level of systematic, regular, and goal-focused support for families as the researched mosque does.

In short, the programme organizers see the wellbeing of Somali Muslim families as being multidimensional (material, relational, and ethical) and its realization as taking place through an organic link between one's private family life and membership and active participation in the larger society. Moreover, these religious actors see their institution as playing a crucial role in the pursuit of this goal.

The *al-Usra* programme: local and transnational

Local challenges

Al-Usra, on one level, is shaped by its local context. It is driven by the challenges facing Muslim minorities in Finland, and more specifically the problems confronted by Somali families. Research shows that Muslim immigrants face a number of socioeconomic challenges such as unemployment, limited possibilities for higher education, and racism (EU-MIDIS, 2009; Kilpi, 2010; Shayan, 2013). In particular, the scholarship on Somalis reports that they face a host of problems such as low educational attainment (especially higher education), high unemployment rate, increasing number of female-headed families, and considerable discrimination and racism (OSF, 2013). The state's welfare policies and discourse emphasizing gender equality and women's autonomy have also added to the marginalization of men, who are often unemployed or underemployed (Peltola, 2016).

These problems, according to many in the Somali communities, have had an adverse impact on family relations. In this diasporic context, women may not need a male provider due to their either receiving welfare provisions or earning their own income, particularly among the younger generation who are reported to do better (than the men) in school and to have job opportunities, particularly in the health sector. Instead, it is the sharing of childcare and housework that becomes needed and more meaningful in marriage (Al-Sharmani, 2015). Lacking the support of the extended family which they had in the home country, women have to shoulder childcare work, especially in a context where their children's wellbeing becomes complex and entangled with state policies and discourses on child welfare on the one hand, and marginalization and racialization of immigrant (Muslim) families on the other (Pösö, 2015). Fathers often do not help with care work either because they are physically away on prolonged transnational trips or divorced from the mothers or are present but feel disempowered and marginalized both by their limited economic opportunities and by the state public policy and discourse on gender equality (see Ismail, this volume). These challenges, in addition to the pressures arising from couples' obligations towards their transnational families, contribute to marital disputes (Al-Sharmani, 2017; Al-Sharmani and Ismail, 2017). Furthermore, women, becoming more religiously knowledgeable about their marital rights as well as espousing modern ideas about companionate marriages, are increasingly resisting patriarchal marriages (Al-Sharmani, 2015; Al-Sharmani, 2017). Mosque imams witness these problems first hand through their work as mediators and arbiters in family disputes (Al-Sharmani, Mustasaari and Ismail, 2017). It is within this context that programme organizers see their mosque as having a significant role to play in helping families tackle these problems and attain a well-rounded, thriving life by promoting a pious, modern, and harmonious Muslim family life where spouses share companionate marriages and partake together in engaged parenting.

The mosque programme's vision is also shaped by Finnish state policies on the governance of religious communities and its discourse on the shared responsibility of state and non-state institutions towards family welfare. Tuomas Martikainen (2014) highlights that, with the 1990s, Finland witnessed socio-political and economic changes, the most notable of which are: increase in the volume of immigration, economic recession, adoption of neo-liberal policies that promote efficient public management through privatization of social welfare work and project-based governance, as well as the country's new commitments to EU and global treaties which privilege such policies. Martikainen notes that these changes have led to what he calls a 'de-secularization' of Finland, i.e., shifts in the nature of the traditional role of the Finnish welfare state as the sole caretaker and the new expectation that different actors in civil society – such as immigrant associations and religious communities – also share the work of providing "services and goods", and creating "social cohesion" (Martikainen, 2014, p.85). In the case of Muslims, this means the state's relationship with religious communities has changed from a "neutral and marginal" to "an active one" (Martikainen 2014, p.98). For instance, the registration of Muslim religious communities (as well as immigrant associations) has increased significantly since the 1990s. The new visibility of Muslim associations and religious communities has also been enhanced by the establishment of broader organizations concerned with the rights of minorities such as the Ombudsman Office for Minorities in 2002, and the national and regional board for ethnic minorities (ETNO). More specifically the Islamic Council of Finland was also founded, an umbrella organization bringing together different Muslim religious communities.

In the aftermath of 9/11 and with the increasingly hegemonic discourse of the 'war on terror' a global environment of Islamophobia and pathologization of Muslims became ever more visible (Morgan and Poynting, 2012). Notwithstanding these challenges (and partly because of them) the role of mosques in the governance of Finnish Muslims continues to be emphasized in the statist discourse (Martikainen, 2014, p.96).

Programme organizers explicitly frame their work and goals within this state discourse. This is reflected in the organizers' coupling of the good of the family and its positive integration. It is also manifested in how they incorporate into their seminars knowledge about different relevant state and non-state institutions and policies, and encourage participants to interact with these different actors. However, these interlocutors also emphasize that their goal, as an Islamic institution, is to promote a distinct form of integration for Muslim families, one that is underpinned by Islamic values and norms.

The mosque, furthermore, makes use of the legal space created by policies regulating the role and work of religious communities. The programme draws on state resources and agencies – albeit severely insufficient – to conduct some of its work. For example, some of the programme's work has been funded by the small annual membership grant that the mosque receives from the state although this grant is primarily intended for the mosque and the associations comprising the mosque's umbrella organization (such as *al-Usra*) are expected to raise their own funds. Furthermore, in 2016, *al-Usra* secured professional grants from Helsinki municipality to enrol three of its organizers at the Open University, to study social psychology and organizational management. The interlocutors who took these courses drew on their acquired knowledge in programme seminars and workshops. Still the support that the programme receives from the state (whether financial, professional development, or mechanisms for coordination) remains highly inadequate. Also, organizers undertake the time-consuming work of the programme on a voluntary basis. These challenges, which are encountered by other mosques as well, greatly limit the scope of the mosque programme and its reach (Al-Sharmani, Mustasaari and Ismail, 2017).

The transnational context

The programme's vision and approach also speak to a larger transnational context. For one thing, the idea of the programme was born in 2009 when the Brussels-based Federation of Islamic Organizations in Europe (FIOE) held a conference in Belgium on the theme of Muslim marital life. FIOE, a Muslim Brotherhood inspired umbrella organization, was founded in 1989 and has hundreds of member organizations across 28 European states. FIOE lists on its website 12 objectives for its mission, the first being, "introducing Islam and its values and shaping Islamic culture in accordance with the requirements of the age and the unique features of the current status of Europe" (FIOE, 2018).

The main purpose of the FIOE 2009 conference, which was attended by one of the key interlocutors in this research, was to promote initiatives that strengthen Muslim marriages and contribute to the stability and wellbeing of Muslim families. The conference proposed a campaign of 100 goals and called on participating organizations to adopt some of these goals. This interlocutor and others in the mosque, in fact, have been part of a loose network of religious scholars and institutions such as FIOE that have been meeting at various Islamic conferences since 2000 and organizing semi-regularly towards the collective goal of educating Muslim families in their respective societies on how to live a modern life that embodies Islamic norms and values while also facilitating their successful integration. In addition to FIOE, diverse Islamic organizations in Europe (including Nordic countries) have also espoused similar Islamic discourse (Maréchal, 2008). Notably, this vision of promoting a modern, tolerant, and pious Muslim way of life is taking place in a context where many diverse Muslim immigrant communities in Europe are facing challenges of multiple forms of marginalization, racialization, and increasing Islamophobia, all of which are also exacerbated by the radicalization of some Muslims and the terrorist acts committed by some militant armed Muslim groups both within Western countries and in the Middle East and Africa.

It is in this transnational context that the key interlocutor in the researched mosque, after returning from the 2009 FIOE conference, together with others in the mosque, decided to establish the mosque programme for Muslim families to address the specific challenges of Somali Muslim families in Finland and link it to this larger transnational endeavour to reform European Muslim families. This interplay between the transnational and local is observable in the language used by programme organizers to describe their approach as well as the transnational actors with whom they collaborate. For example, programme organizers, drawing on FIOE language, repeatedly emphasize *wastīya* (moderation) as their key approach in understanding and promoting the role of Islamic teachings in the lives of Muslim families. Similarly, in the programme's 2015 conference titled 'This is Our Islam', the centrality of moderation as an Islamic value drawn from the Qur'an and the Prophetic tradition was stressed by the key speakers. One of these speakers was Khaled Hanafi, an Egyptian religious scholar and member of the FIOE affiliated organization, the European Council for Fatwa and Research (ECFR). Hanafi argued that European Muslims' enactment of the Islamic value of moderation entailed embracing the culture of citizenship and setting roots in their settled countries. Furthermore, he added, embodying the Islamic virtue of *wastīya* also meant living gender relations free from male dominance and discrimination against women. This leads me to the question of gender in the work of the mosque programme, which I address in the next subsection.

Reforming gender roles

Companionate marriages and engaged parenting: an Islamic discourse

In the vision of the programme, a good family life requires companionate marriages based on affectionate and cooperative spousal relations as well as involved and informed parenting. Both can be attained by acquiring good knowledge of religious norms on marriage and parenting and applying this knowledge to one's family life. This process also entails reflecting critically on Somali cultural norms, some of which privilege male dominance and gendered spousal and parental roles, to the detriment of women who shoulder all care work and children who may not receive the kind of parental care that they need, particularly from their fathers. Somali marriage customs, the speakers in the seminars would frequently argue, discourage couples from expressing affection to each other and fathers from getting involved in childcare. But Islamic marriage is based on *mawada* and *raḥma* (affection and compassion) as instructed by the Qur'an and attested by the example of the Prophet Muhammad and his followers.[5] In a 2015 seminar, for instance, the mosque imam told the audience about the example of 'Abdullah ibn 'Abbas, the Prophet's companion and an erudite religious scholar, who would dress up nicely for his wife, as an expression of his affection for her. The speaker contrasted ibn 'Abbas' example to that of Somali men who find it unbecoming to express their affection to their wives. In another seminar, the speaker, a Somali religious preacher and motivational speaker from the UK, talked about love as a core Islamic value. The speaker noted that love was mentioned 70 times in the sacred text, an indication of its centrality in the Qur'anic norms. He encouraged participants to be affectionate spouses who communicate with one another, spend time together, and share housework and childcare.

The companionate Islamic marriage being promoted by the programme is also one where spouses cooperatively and flexibly negotiate their spousal and parental roles in light of their lived realities. For instance, in one of the seminars the mosque imam criticized men's understanding of *qiwāmah* – a principle in Islamic jurisprudence that obligates husbands to provide for and protect their wives. The imam pointed out that husbands often erroneously understood and practised *qiwāmah* as a male prerogative and authority, rather than a responsibility. These problematized religious understandings were attributed to uncritical espousal of Somali cultural norms, which were seen as incongruent with the spirit of Islam and particularly harmful to family wellbeing in the context of migration.

Lena Larson (2015) has similarly written about how the shifting realities of Muslim minority communities in Europe impact religious discourse on gender roles and rights, as constructed by religious actors such as the renowned mufti the late Syed Mutawalli ad-Darsh in the UK and established transnational Islamic institutions such as the European Council for Fatwa and Research (ECFR). Larson shows how these muftis, in light of the new realities of Muslim families in Europe, similar to the religious actors in this researched mosque, have been navigating the process of arriving at nuanced understandings of *qiwāmah* and spousal roles, which foreground husbands' roles as caretakers and involved parents rather than their role as providers.

According to programme organizers, involved and informed parenting is another key component of good Muslim family life. Participants are frequently asked to reflect on why they are having children. Parents are told that children need not only material things such as a good school, adequate housing, clothes, and food, but also nurturing and supportive relationships with their parents. Parents are trained in how to spend quality time with their children, communicate positively with them, guide them towards productive and fulfilling leisure time activities, etc. Again, participants are taught to separate what is 'cultural' from what is 'Islamic' as they relearn how to parent their children. For example, the mosque imam would often note that in Somalia childcare was primarily the role of mothers, whereas fathers were only expected to provide. But he would add that in the diaspora it is not only the changing realities of Somali families that demand revisiting these parental roles but also the goal of relearning Islam and living a pious Muslim family life.

In promoting a new Islamic discourse on marriage and parenting, the programme organizers use a mode of argument that posits 'harmful' Somali cultural norms and 'religiously uninformed' family practices of older generations against the 'new piety' being promoted and which emphasizes pursuit of reflective religious learning and embodied Islamic virtues. Similar modes of argument (with their complex and mixed implications for the notion of a gendered Muslim self) have also been reported in scholarship on piety and generational differences among various Muslim immigrant groups in Europe (Amir-Moazami and Salvatore, 2003; Jouili, 2011; Jacobsen, 2011). These modes of argument seem to invoke the language of oppositional binaries (culture versus religion, past versus modern). They also seem to invoke modern registers of individual reasoning and autonomy, and the pursuit of a fulfilling life. Nonetheless, it is misleading to understand the programme's new discourse merely or primarily through the lens of a liberal modernist framework. That is, the underpinning goals of this discourse, while concerned with reform of gender relations, are neither about gender equality nor the attainment of an assimilationist modern life where Islamic norms have little or no presence in participants' lives. In the following subsection, I elaborate on this point through an analysis of the programme's discourse on marriage in relation to modern professional counselling.

Professional marriage counselling and gender reform?

The programme's discourse on marriage invokes the language of modern professional marriage counselling. Marriage is depicted as 'work' to be undertaken by the spouses to create marital harmony and happiness (Celello, 2009; Davis, 2010). A big part of this work is psychological: organizers, like professional marriage counsellors, advise spouses to know themselves, to choose their marriage partners wisely. Do they have similar interests (e.g., in religion, volunteer work, educational and career goals)? Do they agree on how to manage their resources and navigate their responsibilities towards their transnational relatives? Participants are advised to depart from the old ways in Somalia where, as one organizer put it, "people did not think much about why they were getting married, they just got married." Instead they are to think rationally as they do the 'work' of finding a suitable spouse and creating happy marriages. Kristen Celello (2009) notes how the modernist language and ideology of creating happy marriages has become, in the context of post-World War II America, part of the governance of families towards the goal of a stable thriving nation. In this mosque programme, the reform of marriages is also linked to the goal of the thriving of the Somali Muslim community in the larger Finnish society. But the work of reforming marriages, in this case, is also part of the spiritual striving of individual participants towards the goal of a closer relationship with their divine creator. In other words, this work, as one of the mosque imams tells participants, is seen to be as much about participants' 'afterworld', as it is about their 'happiness in this world'.

Also writing about the American context, Rebecca Davis (2010) notes the importance of religious actors in the work of marriage counselling. She highlights how these actors have begun to draw on the field of psychology as they work with their congregations on marriage counselling, driven by the goals of staying relevant in work with families, and by the fact that some of these religious actors have themselves espoused these new ideas and language. In the context of the mosque programme, religious language is also continually mixed with gendered ideas and concepts from modern popular psychology. For instance, participants are told to be cognizant of the different ways in which men and women are socialized and which impact their expectations and behaviour towards their spouses. Husbands are encouraged to listen to their wives, ask them about their day, give them foot massages, compliment them, and show them affection, etc. And wives are encouraged to understand the distinct ways in which men may express their love, not to bombard them with demands and complaints, communicate their needs in a positive blame-free manner, and praise their husbands when the latter do pleasing things, etc.

But does the mosque's work address the question of gender equality? Both Celello and Davis argue that modern marriage counselling has not necessarily created space for gender equality. In some ways it may have even reproduced hierarchical gender norms, as women are frequently socialized to work hard at saving their marriages. In this mosque programme, the revisiting of spousal and parental roles is not based on an agenda of realizing the goal of gender equality. For instance, some of the unequal spousal and parental rights in Islamic jurisprudence are not questioned. Men, not women, are still believed to have the religious duty to provide for their families. Unlike women, men have the right to unilateral repudiation, and can enter into polygamous marriages. But through its activities, the programme is increasingly foregrounding an ethically oriented reading of Islamic law which is based on the lived realities of participants. This interestingly leads to revisiting these male privileges. Thus, programme organizers admonish belligerent men who refuse to divorce their wives when the latter want to exit the marriages, depicting the behaviour of such men as un-Islamic. They also advise against the practices of men who enter into polygamous marriages to the detriment of their wives and children. This ethical reading of Islamic law and the centring of families' lived realities results in men becoming the focus of this reform work. That is, traditional Somali understandings of privileged masculinity and male rights are revisited and problematized as part of a larger effort to promote a new Islamic viewpoint of gender roles in marriage and parenting.

Still, the lack of explicit and coherent commitment to gender equality as a programme goal is reflected in the contestations that take place at some of the events. For example, in the 2015 conference, a female participant asked one of the speakers about the right of women to insert stipulations in their marriage contracts against polygamy. The answer of this speaker, a well-known Somali religious scholar who is based in the UK, was that while couples could agree on stipulations in the marriage contract, polygamy was permissible in Islam. This scholar, in other words, was reluctant to categorically endorse the practice of writing stipulations against polygamy, as it contradicted his understanding of polygamy as a male prerogative sanctioned by the sacred text. Yet, in another seminar, one of the mosque imams while not explicitly encouraging the use of stipulations against polygamy talked about the importance of following the Prophet's example in spousal relations and pointed out that men often – because of either poor religious knowledge or lack of piety – erroneously justified their practice of polygamy on religious grounds, while failing to emulate the Prophet in his affectionate and respectful relationships with his spouses. These varying positions towards restricting men's right to polygamy are to be juxtaposed with the mosque's strong encouragement of women and men to become more knowledgeable about their religious tradition and to use this knowledge to reform their marriages. This has subsequently led to more women seeking religious education, and as a result in recent years there began an increasing trend of women (particularly the younger generation) inserting stipulations in their marriage contracts against polygamy, and some of these women were even formulating very nuanced religious arguments that made it spiritually imperative for them to reject polygamy (Al-Sharmani, 2015).

Additionally, pathways of empowerment for some women have been enabled through their involvement in the mosque and participation in the programme activities. Some women who help with the programme work, for example, have been able to lobby for the inclusion of their concerns in the activities. In one case, two members of the women's association in the mosque proposed 'love in Islam' as the theme of one of the seminars and invited two speakers from the UK, a mosque imam and his wife, both of whom are well-known Islamic motivational speakers in the Somali diaspora. Also, with the help of the network of people established through the programme and the knowledge gained from its activities, one of the female participants has been able to seek opportunities for higher education and employment. Furthermore, she established, with another friend, a small women's association in her neighbourhood, where they hold family seminars and after-school activities for children in coordination with the mosque.

Conclusion

This case study shows the significance of wellbeing as a conceptual tool to understand the multi-layered needs, challenges, and aspirations of Finnish Somali families from the perspective of a religious institution. The mosque programme makes the case that the pursuit of an all-round meaningful life requires a holistic processual reform that attends to different dimensions of participants' family lives and links this reform to the attainment of empowered membership in the larger society. It shows how religion and involvement in mosque activities can be a pathway towards the pursued transformative change. Furthermore, by promoting an Islamically oriented family wellbeing and integration, the mosque is exhibiting its agency vis-à-vis the state as a significant actor in the governance of Muslim Finnish citizens, and which entails both working for their welfare and partaking in their identity building.

However, the mosque programme's efforts are focused on spouses, parents, and youth. Its underlying message seems to be that individual family members can and should be the main agents of change through a multi-dimensional self-reform process that combines acquisition of multidimensional knowledge and embodiment of Islamic virtues in the family and larger society. Does this focus on individual family members conceal the role of state institutions as well as ethnic and religious communities in enabling or hindering the pursued positive change? One could argue that the mosque's programme is inadvertently concealing the structural problems that preclude the wellbeing and integration of Finnish Somali Muslim families, i.e., economic, social, and racial barriers to their full participation in different domains of Finnish society. White (2016) cautions against such an understanding of wellbeing, which may focus too much on the individual and not enough on the role of institutional actors and structural factors. But one could also counter-argue that the programme, with its efforts to contest hierarchical and gendered spousal and parental roles and its sought goal of empowering Muslim families in the larger society, can be said to have elements that could potentially facilitate the needed structural changes.

Still, to what extent is the programme reforming hierarchical gender norms and relations in Muslim Somali families? This needs further research. The programme activities target women, men, and youth. It is predominantly women who attend and take part in the activities, while men's (especially married men's and fathers') attendance is still not large. This, on the one hand, limits the impact of this programme on changing men's behaviour. On the other hand, both young men and women actively participate in the youth seminars and this could, in the long run, be one mechanism through which change is affected in gender relations.

Lastly, while other mosques also work with families, what is distinct about this mosque programme is its systematic and coherent vision. It is also noteworthy that its work is enabled by a number of factors: the organizers' espousal of a distinct Islamic discourse on how Muslims can lead a pious and fulfilling life in Finland and more broadly in Europe; their ties with diverse networks of individual and institutional religious actors on the continent who are undertaking crisscrossing reform efforts; the long-term involvement of young women and men in the mosque's reform efforts. Still further longitudinal research is needed on this programme, and possible motivations and avenues for collaboration between the various mosques in the country to pursue broader organized efforts for the wellbeing of Muslim families of different ethnicities.

Notes

1 This chapter is part of a study titled *Transnational Somali Muslim Families in Finland: The Lived Realities and Discourses of Marriage* designed and directed by the author. It is part of a larger Academy of Finland research project titled *Transnational Muslim Marriages: Wellbeing, Law, and Gender* (2013–2018).
2 I extend my thanks to all the interlocutors who graciously and generously took part in this study.
3 With the exception of the oldest mosque, built by the Tatar community, all other mosques are housed in buildings that are intended for other use.
4 Mosques need to be licensed by the registrar office to conclude legally recognized and registered marriages. Most mosques that conclude marriages are licensed. The divorces concluded by mosques are strictly religious and are not recognized by the state. See Al-Sharmani, Mustasaari and Ismail (2017).
5 Qur'an 30:21.

Bibliography

Abu-Lughod, L., 1990. Can there be a feminist ethnography? *Women and Performance: A Journal of Feminist Theory*, 5(1), pp.7–27.

Al-Sharmani, M., 2015. Striving against the 'Nafs': Revisiting Somali Muslim spousal roles and rights in Finland. *Journal of Religion in Europe*, 8(1), pp.101–120.

Al-Sharmani, M., 2017. Divorce among transnational Finnish Somalis: Gender, religion, and agency. *Religion and Gender*, 7(1), pp.70–87.

Al-Sharmani, M. and Ismail, A.A., 2017. Marriage and transnational family life among Somali migrants in Finland. *Migration Letters*, 14(1), pp.38–49.

Al-Sharmani, M., Mustasaari, S. and Ismail, A.A., 2017. Faith-based family dispute resolution in Finnish mosques: Unfolding roles and evolving practices. In: S. Bano, ed. 2017. *Gender and Justice in Family Law Disputes: Women, Mediation and Religious Arbitration*. Waltham, MA: Brandeis University Press, pp.270–291.

Amir-Moazami, S. and Salvatore, A., 2003. Gender, generation, and the reform of tradition: From Muslim majority societies to Western Europe. In: S. Allievi and J. Nielsen, eds. 2003. *Muslim Networks and Transnational Communities in and Across Europe*. Boston and Leiden: Brill, pp.52–77.

Celello, K., 2009. *Making Marriage Work: A History of Marriage and Divorce in the Twentieth Century United States*. Chapel Hill, NC: University of North Carolina Press.

Davis, R.L., 2010. *More Perfect Unions: The American Search for Marital Bliss*. Cambridge, MA: Harvard University Press.

EU-MIDIS, 2009. *European Union Minorities and Discrimination Survey: Main Results Report*. Vienna: European Union Agency for Fundamental Rights. Available at: http://fra.europa.eu/sites/default/files/fra_uploads/663-fra-2011_eu_midis_en.pdf [Accessed January 12, 2018].

Federation of Islamic Organizations in Europe (FIOE), 2018. Objectives. Available at: http://fioe.org/node/173 [Accessed July 28, 2018].

Jacobsen, C., 2011. Troublesome threesome: Feminism, anthropology, and Muslim women's piety. *Feminist Review*, 98, pp.65–82.

Jouili, J., 2011. Beyond emancipation: Subjectivities and ethics among women in Europe's Islamic revival communities. *Feminist Review*, 98, pp.47–64.

Kääriäinen, K., 2011. Religion and state in Finland. *Nordic Journal of Religion and Society*, 24(2), pp.155–171.

Ketola, K., Martikainen, T. and Salomäki, H., 2014. New communities of worship: Continuities and mutations among religious organizations in Finland. *Social Compass* 61(2), pp.153–171.

Kilpi, E., 2010. *The Education of Children of Immigrants in Finland*. PhD. University of Oxford. Available at: http://citeseerx.ist.psu.edu/viewdoc/download?doi=10.1.1.696.1088&rep=rep1&type=pdf [Accessed January 10, 2018].

Larson, L., 2015. 'Men are the protectors and maintainers of women…' Three fatwas on spousal roles and rights. In: Z. Mir-Hosseini, M. Al-Sharmani and J. Rumminger, eds. 2015. *Men in Charge? Rethinking Authority in Muslim Legal Tradition*. Oxford: OneWorld, pp.197–218.

Maréchal, B., 2008. *The Muslim Brothers in Europe: Roots and Discourse*. Leiden: Brill.

Martikainen, T., 2014. Muslim immigrants, public religion, and developments towards a post-secular Finnish welfare state. *Tidsskrift for Islamforskning, The Nordic Welfare State*, 8(1), pp.78–105.

Morgan, G. and Poynting, S., eds. 2012. *Global Islamophobia: Muslims and the Moral Panic in the West*. Farnham: Ashgate.

Mårtensson, U., 2014. Introduction – 'public Islam' and the Nordic welfare state: Changing realities? *Tidsskrift for Islamforskning, The Nordic Welfare State*, 8(1), pp.4–55.

OSF, 2013. *Somalis in Helsinki*. New York and London: Open Society Foundations. Available at: https://www.opensocietyfoundations.org/sites/default/files/somalis-helsinki-20131121.pdf [Accessed January 2, 2018].

Peltola, M., 2016. Respectable families: Discourses on family life, ethnic hierarchies and social positioning. *Ethnicities*, 16(1), pp.22–39.

Pösö, T., 2015. How the Finnish child protection system meets the needs of migrant families and children. In: M. Skivenes, R. Barn, K. Kriz and T. Pösö, eds. 2015. *Child Welfare Systems and Migrant Children: A Cross Country Study of Policies and Practices*. Oxford: Oxford University Press, pp.19–38.

Sakaranaho, T., 2013. Religious education in Finland. *Temenos*, 49(2), pp.225–254.

Shayan, F., 2013. Ontological anxiety among Shii Muslims in Finland: A case study of first generation immigrants in the city of Tampere. *Islamic Perspective: Journal of the Islamic Studies and Humanities*, 9, pp.91–106.

Statistics Finland, 2016. Population structure. Language according to age and sex by region in 1990 to 2016. Available at: http://pxnet2.stat.fi/PXWeb/pxweb/en/StatFin/StatFin__vrm__vaerak/statfin_vaerak_pxt_010.px/?rxid=40252902-b370-44ea-8183-d2fc305596e6 [Accessed January 2, 2018].

White, S.C., 2008. *But What is Wellbeing? A Framework for Analysis in Social and Development Policy and Practice*. Paper for Regeneration and Wellbeing: Research into Practice, University of Bradford, 24–25 April 2008. University of Bath, Centre for Development Studies. Available at: http://staff.bath.ac.uk/ecsscw/But_what_is_Wellbeing.pdf [Accessed January 2, 2018].

White, S.C., 2010. Analysing wellbeing: A framework for development practice. *Development in Practice* 20(2), pp.158–172.

White, S.C., 2016. The many faces of wellbeing. In: S.C. White and C. Blackmore, eds. 2016. *Cultures of Wellbeing: Method, Place, and Policy*. Basingstoke: Palgrave Macmillan, pp.1–46.

5 Polygamy, wellbeing, and ill-being amongst ethnic Muslim minorities

Anika Liversage

Introduction

Polygamy "is not a single syndrome but is produced by diverse strategies under a range of different conditions and comprises different systems of meaning and function" (White, 1988, p.558). Two main forms of polygamy exist, with polygyny (one husband and two or more wives) being far more common than polyandry (one wife and multiple husbands). Polygamous marriages can be found in Europe, North America, Africa, Asia, the Middle East, and Oceania (Altman and Ginat, 1996), and are most common in West African countries such as Mali. While such marriages exist in many predominantly Muslim countries worldwide, they are generally much less common than their monogamous counterparts (Charsley and Liversage, 2013). In this chapter, the focus is on polygamous (primarily polygynous) marriages among Muslim ethnic minorities in northwest Europe, with family backgrounds in the Middle East, North Africa, and South Asia.[1]

For Muslims, men's ability to take multiple wives is attributed to the Qur'an, which says:

> And if you have reason to fear that you might not act equitably towards orphans, then marry from among [other] women such as are lawful to you – [even] two, or three, or four: but if you have reason to fear that you might not be able to treat them with equal fairness, then [only] one – or [from among] those whom you rightfully possess. This will make it more likely that you will not deviate from the right course (Qur'an 4:3, translated Asad, 1980).

As the religious prerogative to treat all wives "with equal fairness", may be considered impossible to fulfil in practice, whether Islam should be considered as sanctioning polygamous marriage in practice is a matter of debate (Abbott, 1962; Mashhour, 2005). The legality of polygamous marriages in the Muslim world also varies; in some countries – such as Syria, Iraq, and Jordan – it is restricted through legal provisions such as court approval, notification of the first wife, etc. In countries such as Turkey and Tunisia it is illegal (Welchman, 2007).

In earlier work with Katharine Charsley, I have investigated how processes of migration may not only bring practices of polygamy from one part of the world into another, but also lead to the development of new forms of polygamy (Charsley and Liversage, 2013). New forms may arise due to factors such as changes in gendered and generational hierarchies, secrecy enabled by long distance, and the co-existence of different types of marriage and divorce under civil and religious codes. Based on qualitative interviews with ethnic Muslim minorities in Denmark and the UK, this chapter extends the work in Charsley and Liversage (2013), investigating the links between polygamous marriages, transnational social spaces, and the wellbeing of different family members. As described earlier in this volume, the wellbeing perspective evolved not within migration research but in developmental studies. This perspective conceptualizes wellbeing as dependent on the resources that individuals are able to command and on what they are able to achieve with these resources. Hence, the approach is actor-oriented, focusing on both what needs and goals individuals are able to meet and the meanings they attribute to these needs and goals (White, 2008; 2010). Drawing on White's understanding of wellbeing as a three-dimensional concept, wellbeing in this volume is understood as comprising three interrelated dimensions: the *material*, the *relational*, and the *ethical*.

Another central concept in White's wellbeing approach is 'aspirations' – what individuals strive for. While aspirations may be deeply individual, such aspirations are also embedded in cultural frameworks, conditioning what people aspire towards. As Pierre Bourdieu argued, "the level of aspiration of individuals is essentially determined by the probability (judged intuitively by means of previous successes or failures) of achieving the desired goal" (Bourdieu, 1977, p.111). Thus, social structures and unequal power dynamics condition individual aspirations, and these aspirations – whether or not they are achieved – are central to understanding migrant family wellbeing.

While wellbeing is an inherently positive concept, White (2010) also points out that inequalities at various levels may prevent both individuals and communities from shaping their lives in the desired positive ways. Feminist researchers have long emphasized that the imagery of the family home as a 'haven' in a heartless world is typically a male construction, and that women more often than men may experience hard work and even repression and violence within the home (Mallett, 2004). Changes in the last half of the 20th century, such as female entry into the labour market and access to abortion and contraception, have contributed to what has been termed "the crisis of the patriarchal family" (Castels, 1997). Nonetheless, men still often hold more power than women, and "being a man" often entails "claiming privilege [and] eliciting deference" (Schrock and Schwalbe, 2009, p.281). Inequalities in gendered power relations are often stronger in traditional breadwinner/homemaker families where women are economically dependent on men. When the aspirations of such wives do not correspond to their husbands' views, they may not easily be fulfilled. Furthermore, particularly where norms against divorce combine with an ideology of female 'sacrifice' and endurance within marriage, women may remain in marriages that seriously undermine their wellbeing. In such cases, individual 'ill-being' rather than 'wellbeing' may be at stake (White, 2008; Qureshi, 2013). Adopting the wellbeing approach proposed by White and elaborated on in this volume's introduction, this chapter addresses the following question: *How are polygamous practices among Muslim ethnic minorities in Denmark and the UK associated with individual aspirations towards wellbeing in transnational social spaces?*

The chapter is structured as follows: First, it sketches some of the findings from studies on polygamy and its relation to wellbeing. Second, it explains the underlying empirical material and analytical approach. Third, it presents different motivations for polygamous marriages among the interlocutors connected to male-only out-migration, family needs such as having children and providing care for a sick family member, and men's secret desires for additional or alternative female company while still adhering to a cultural and religious prohibition against sex outside of marriage. The analysis shows how these polygamous marriages are enabled by migration and the transnational lives of the involved parties. In particular, I shed light on the ways in which such unions may impact the wellbeing of the women and men in these relationships and how they reinforce or reshape gendered power structures.

Polygamy and wellbeing in global context

In 1967, George Murdock estimated that while 85% of world societies permitted polygamy, the global incidence of the practice was low (Zeitzen, 2008, p.14). Commonly associated with Islam (Chamie, 1986), polygamous marriage has its highest occurrence in Sub-Saharan Africa. A narrow definition of polygamy involves simultaneous legally sanctioned marriages to more than one spouse, valid according to a given state authority. A broader definition would also include marriages contracted under different systems, whether under the laws of different states or without the implication of a state authority but sanctioned by, for example, religious authorities in given communities. A yet broader definition includes also 'marriage-like' domestic arrangements (Zeitzen, 2008, p.17), even when these do not involve legally or religiously sanctioned marriages. In this study, I take a broad approach, including the three above-mentioned definitions of polygamous marriages.

Some literature exists on connections between polygamy and wellbeing. One review, concerned with family members' psychological, social, and family functioning, concludes that "the current state of the research reveals with moderate confidence, a more significant prevalence of mental-health issues in polygynous women as compared to monogamous women" (Shepard, 2013, p.47). While this statement may imply that polygyny promotes the interests of men over those of women, a separate review has suggested that levels of wellbeing in polygamous marriages are also lower for children and husbands (Elbedour, et al., 2002). Indeed, Slonim-Nevo and Al-Krenawi's (2006) qualitative research on polygamy among Bedouins in Israel, including an exploration of husbands' views of multiple marriages, reveals that some men enter second marriages reluctantly. When a man dies, for example, his brother may be under family pressure to marry the widow to keep her children within their father's family. Other men in the same study regretted having acted on an infatuation that engendered a conflictual family life, with tensions between their two wives.

According to the literature, reasons for lower levels of wellbeing in polygamous marriages include strains on resources (due to more family members) and conflicts between co-wives – both of which may lead to family dissolution (Elbedour, et al., 2002). Life in a polygamous marriage may be particularly hard on first wives, who often experience their husbands' second marriages as traumatic (Hassouneh-Phillips, 2001; Ozkan, 2006). Children of first wives may receive less attention from their fathers, to the detriment of their wellbeing (Al-Krenawi and Graham, 1999). Overall, occurrences of polygamous marriages must thus be understood within unequal gender structures in which women's economic survival is often intricately tied to their positions as wives (Bao, 2008).

The literature also shows that the wellbeing consequences of living in polygamous marriages may vary, depending on both intra-familial and societal processes. Polygamous marriages tend to fare better when husbands consult with first wives before marrying a second time. Other factors enhancing outcomes include families having sufficient resources, resources being shared equally, and co-wives having separate accommodations (Bao, 2008; Elbedour, et al., 2002). Debra Majeed's work with the small minority of African American Muslims who are polygamously married also documents some co-wives' efforts to "rearticulate multiple-wife marriage as a liberating rather than abusive structure" (Majeed, 2016, p.86).

A central point is that life in polygamous marriages also depends on the socio-cultural context, particularly with regard to whether such marriages are attributed positive value or not (Anderson, 2000; Slonim-Nevo and Al-Krenawi, 2006). As Chamie (1986, pp.65–66) posits, in societies where women are strongly dependent on men for survival, "women prefer to marry as additional wives rather than remain childless, divorced or as widows". The economic function of polygamous marriages may also depend on the surrounding societal context. In a study of polygamous marriages in South Africa, polygamously married women supported the institution, primarily due to the need for a male breadwinner but also because of the economic benefits of a co-wife, who could be central in generating household income by taking care of all the household's children, enabling another wife to earn money outside the home (Anderson, 2000).

Empirical material and analytical approach

The analysis in this chapter is based on qualitative research on Muslim minorities in Denmark and the United Kingdom. From Denmark, the cases were drawn from the author's work with ethnic minorities from a range of different studies (Charsley and Liversage, 2015; Liversage, 2012a; 2012b; 2012c; 2014; Liversage and Ottosen, 2014; Liversage and Rytter, 2015). From the UK, the cases were drawn from Katharine Charsley's research on Pakistani families, both from our previous collaboration on polygamy (Charsley and Liversage, 2013), and her independently published work (Charsley, 2006; 2013). Hence, this chapter builds on a broad body of empirical material, which mostly was not, however, collected with the specific topic of investigating polygamous marriages (for details on Charsley's data, see Charsley, 2013). As a substantial share of the material underlying this analysis focused on the topic of divorce, the analysis draws more on conflictual marital relations than on harmonious ones.

As to the interview data, the author located interviewees through different channels such as language schools, immigrant organizations, and personal or network contacts. Interviewees were both male and female (with the latter predominating), and individuals were of varied age groups, educational level, migration history (i.e., arrived in Denmark as migrants or had been born and/ or raised there). While a substantial number of interviewees were of Turkish origin, others came from (or had parents who had come from) other countries in the Middle East, Northeast Africa, and Southeast Asia. Interviews were mainly conducted in a life story interview format. Such interviews, which were very open, began with a request that interviewees 'tell their life story'. Much of the subsequent questioning covered various issues that interviewees themselves brought up when constructing their life story narrative (Liversage, 2009). In a small number of the interviews, interviewees recounted experiences of polygamy. Such experiences were drawn together in the present analysis.

One must bear in mind that polygamous marriages arise out of a process: they are not constituted through a single wedding ceremony, with two (or more) brides. Instead, a monogamous marriage – which may have lasted for years – becomes polygamous when the husband marries for a second time. In my analysis, I focus both on the *aspirations* that this second union is intended to fulfil, i.e., the motivations behind its creation, and the *consequences for wellbeing* for the parties involved.

Transnational dynamics of polygamy

Polygamous marriages among immigrants are often shaped by the transnational social field inhabited by the involved parties. In what follows, I will present three kinds of polygamous marriages found in the research data that take place in such transnational social spaces. I will examine how these marriages impacted, in various ways, the wellbeing of the first and second wives, the husbands, and in some cases the children as well.

Male-only out-migration and polygamy

One type of polygamous marriage that has been commonly reported in the literature is that contracted by married men who migrate alone. These male immigrants, having left their first wives behind in the countries of origin, would take second wives in the host countries. For example, a study reports that Hong Kong factory managers in the Guangdong province in China form 'second families' with female factory workers while still returning regularly to their established families in Hong Kong (Lang and Smart, 2002). In Senegal, rural-to-urban migrant men may jokingly refer to having a *femme de cour* (farm wife) in the rural homestead, and a *femme de cœur* (love wife) in town (Zeitzen, 2008, p.153). A similar pattern of men forming new families after emigrating is documented in the Pakistani immigration to Britain (Shaw, 2000). These polygamous marriages often arise from male aspirations (e.g., for female company or a caretaker). However, these unions have also been found to have a negative impact on the wellbeing of both wives. For instance, with polygamy not permitted in Europe, relationships with second wives – if solemnized in Europe in marriages recognized by the state – could effectively block the immigration prospects of the first wife. Equally, second wives – particularly if not legally married (as was often the case) – could fear that their relationships had little future. In our data, one first wife, Esma, relates the following about the situation years ago, after her husband left Turkey to go to Denmark:

> He was here [in Denmark] for some years. I was in Turkey with three children. I heard that he lived with a woman – a Danish one. I got very sad. I didn't want that – it was as if he was not going to be with us. ... But they didn't get along, thank God, otherwise, he might have left us. But he didn't leave us – he came back for us, and brought us to Denmark.

Overall, this type of 'polygamy' appears to be mostly a transitory phenomenon during settlement and often to be brought to an end by the reunification of the original couple. Shaw (2000), for example, reports how some female migration in the mid-1960s was triggered by concerns over husbands possibly having married or formed relationships in the UK. One such woman arrived to find her fears confirmed, and had to live in the same house as the English wife for a year, until the latter departed (Shaw, 2000, p.55). Similar cases are reported in the initial male Turkish labour immigration to Europe (Brouwer and Priester, 1983). In other words, these kinds of cases of polygamy are embedded in particular historical periods and patterns of migration.

Negotiated polygamous marriages to meet different family needs

With the settlement and growth of Muslim immigrant communities in Europe, polygamous marriages motivated by new and diverse factors emerge. One kind has been polygamous marriages that are contracted as part of a family effort to address specific needs and challenges encountered by the involved parties. These kinds of unions underscore that the understanding of a polygamous marriage and how acceptable such a marital arrangement is for the different parties involved are strongly tied to the surrounding value context. Hence, such family arrangements may be considered a fully acceptable way of living in some milieus and an established way of fulfilling the familial aspirations of the parties involved. The data again shows that the transnational lives of the immigrants and their families also create the conditions that make such unions possible. The following Turkish and Pakistani cases illustrate polygamous marriages of this kind.

The Pakistani couple, Hafeeza and her husband, resided in the UK with their children until Hafeeza's husband became ill and had to return to Pakistan. Hafeeza could not follow him, as the children needed to stay in the UK for school. In Pakistan the husband, however, needed a female caretaker, and hiring a 'live-in-maid' would have challenged propriety norms. Thus, entering into a second marriage enabled him to have a caretaker in Pakistan, while the needs of the children were also met in the UK. The distance between the wives reduced possible conflicts, and although the resources of the family were stretched, the arrangement provided a livelihood for the second wife in Pakistan.

In the case of Dudu and her husband, a Turkish couple residing in Denmark, the motivation behind the second marriage was Dudu's inability to have children. However, the couple did not want to divorce. Thus the husband married the second wife in Turkey and had children. The children were then brought to Denmark to live with Dudu and their father and pursue their education. By raising the children, Dudu was indirectly able to fulfil her aspiration to be a mother. However, the second wife, who had to remain in Turkey due to immigration rules, was separated from her children. Again resources in the polygamous household were stretched, but the second wife benefitted from the husband's remittances from Denmark.

In these two cases, the polygamous marriages were long lasting and stable though embedded in complicated family circumstances. Taken as a whole, the polygamous marriages of both Hafeeza and Dudu could be seen as fulfilling needs for care, propriety, bearing children, or all three. The Turkish case was propelled by the central importance generally attributed to having children in Turkish families (Ataca, Kagitcibasi and Diri, 2005). While infertility might lead Turkish men to divorce and remarry (van Rooij, van Balen and Hermanns, 2009), strong norms against divorce (Liversage, 2012c) could motivate husbands to take second wives (see Shaw, 2000, on British Pakistanis). The Pakistani case was propelled by different needs for care: the man's children need to remain in the UK for both their education and a better material future. As the children needed female care, the first wife could not accompany her husband back to Pakistan. The husband's need for (female) care in Pakistan (where the climate would benefit his health) led him to marry a second time, as only marriage can make the care arrangement socially acceptable and hence avoid gossip.

Thus these marriages were strongly gendered and tied to norms and practices from their countries of origin. Furthermore, these unions arose in the context of migration. Accordingly, they were affected by distances and differences across transnational space where some of the involved individuals may be geographically separated, while at the same time their marriage experiences bring into contact societies with different levels of economic development and different norms, practices, and expectations. The spatial separation of the co-wives' households minimized conflict, while the arrival of second wives stretched family resources. The second marriages also provided needed female 'family services', which the first wives, for different reasons, were unable to provide.

While the interview data does not allow a thorough assessment of the impact of the second marriage on the wellbeing of all individuals involved, a few observations can be noted. Both cases, for instance, raise concerns about the wellbeing of the second wives. In the Turkish case, the second wife eventually lived alone in Turkey while her young children lived with their father and his first wife in Denmark. In the Pakistani case, the second wife cared for an older infirm man. At the same time both cases suggest that the material wellbeing of the two second wives may have improved thanks to the husband's European income. Both women's motivations (and/or that of their families) for entering the marriages may also be important, as women sometimes accept the role of second wife when their other marital options are limited. Where women's social position depends significantly on marriage, polygamy can offer a pathway out of an undesirable single status. The economic function of marriage is also central. Chamie's (1986) observations that polygamous marriages may be better for some women than the alternative of, for example, remaining unwed may also hold true in these cases. Moreover, in a global context, that the men had income from affluent Europe may have made them more attractive marriage partners (despite the presence of a pre-existing spouse) than they would otherwise have been.

Second marriages contracted secretly by mobile immigrant men

Some cases of polygamy involve immigrant men contracting a second marriage without the knowledge of their first wife. These men were already settled immigrants who were also engaged in relatively frequent travelling. Such polygamous cases were plentiful in the empirical data and the second marriage was often, from the perspective of the first wife, an act of betrayal on the part of the husband. Generally, the first wives had no knowledge of the second marriage and sometimes divorced their husbands upon their finding out about it. In some cases, the second wives were also unaware that the men they married already had a first wife. The examples of Dilek and Sumera below illustrate such unions.

While one of the women interviewed (Dilek) was a second wife, and the other (Sumera) a first wife, the dynamics of their marriages are similar. Men's independent mobility (within or across national borders) made them encounter women other than their first wives. Such encounters could also occur as part of family arrangements. With cultural and religious prohibitions against sex outside of marriage, these men did not simply take the 'other' women as mistresses. Instead, they married them as second wives but apparently sought to keep the first and second wives secret from one another. When one of the wives found out that there was another woman, feelings of anger and betrayal ensued, albeit leading to different conclusions.

In the first case, Dilek (a Danish woman of Turkish heritage) was divorced from her first husband and lived a rather isolated life as a single mother stigmatized in the local Turkish community (Akpinar, 2003; Liversage, 2012c). She then met a man of Turkish descent who told her that he was also divorced. They grew to like one another and had a religious marriage (*nikah*) to solemnize their relationship. While Dilek had expected that they would start living together, the husband kept putting it off. He was also away frequently telling her that he was traveling for work. Dilek learned about his deception in the following way:

> One winter, he went on a pilgrimage [to Mecca] … I hear through the grapevine that he has gone there with his wife. That they are still married! So when he comes back, I pack his things and throw him out. … [Calling the first wife …] I tell her that I am married to [husband]. She tells me that that cannot be true, because they never divorced, they are still together. I just feel SO deceived. But it made it easier to leave the relationship because I had good reason. … I suspect that he chose me because I was an easy target: divorced and with children and entering into something for the second time. That makes it a bit more difficult to get out again, because you lose face.

In the second case, British Pakistani Sumera married a husband, Tariq, in Pakistan, and he came to join her in the UK. The marriage became conflictual early on, and Tariq disliked the amount of time Sumera spent with her natal family (Charsley, 2013). After some years, Tariq went on holiday to Pakistan alone. Sumera's cousin was in Pakistan at the same time, attending a family wedding. When the cousin was sent to pick up the wedding video, the photographer mentioned that he had also filmed Tariq's recent marriage, a piece of information that the cousin passed on to Sumera in the UK. Discovering Tariq's polygamy in this way, Sumera initially wanted to divorce Tariq but was advised against doing so by other women on the grounds that such a divorce would benefit Tariq by enabling him to bring the second wife to the UK. Tariq and Sumera subsequently reconciled, while the second wife – whom Sumera considered an innocent party – was left living with Tariq's family in Pakistan receiving money that he sent for her support. After the reconciliation the polygamous marriage became polygamous in name only, not in practice.

In these two cases, marriages became polygamous when the husbands secretly married for a second time. After a period of successful concealment, the secrets were discovered by one of their wives, leading to considerable anger and resentment from the women interviewed – and most likely from the other involved women as well. The two cases also illustrate gendered power structures where men had greater scope for agency than women. Because of the religious right to polygamy (Bao, 2008), men had the ability to contract second marriages and made use of their mobility to enter into such unions. The existence of these gendered power structures was central in shaping men's aspirations and actions leading to the formation of polygamous marriages, to the later demise of some such marriages, and to consequences for the well- or ill-being of those involved. Dilek, for example, divorced her husband. Such a divorce calls attention to the relatively strong position of some ethnic minority women in Europe. Often having better access to wage work, social security measures, and gender-equal legislation than women in the parental countries of origin, such women had the resources to leave their unwanted marriages (Liversage and Ottosen, 2015). Indeed, of all the parties involved in these two cases, the Pakistani woman left behind with her in-laws in Pakistan could arguably be the one to whom the ill-fated polygamous marriages had caused the greatest harm.

But not all women, however, have resources and choices that enable them to exercise agency and exit polygamous marriages which undermine their wellbeing. In fact, some circumstances in the transnational context may render women particularly vulnerable to the harm of polygamous marriage and leave them with few means of escaping it. Domestic violence, for example, may render the abused wife unable to leave the violent partner. There are also other reasons that contribute to making women subordinate and unable to end unwanted marriages. Saida's case is a good example. She had migrated to Denmark as a result of a short and childless marriage to a majority ethnic Danish man who turned out to be psychologically unstable. The couple divorced, and Saida – who had neither formal educational nor Danish language skills – was left socially isolated. She then found a job in a Turkish-owned company, where her somewhat older boss started to court her. After a period, the following occurred:

> I couldn't say 'no' to my boss, and he said that he wanted to marry me and that he would give me a really good life. ... [The marriage] is one giant theatre show: We have the wedding dress, we have pictures taken, we go to a restaurant ... and I quickly become pregnant. And then he is gone. ... [While pregnant] I meet a couple on the street. They ask me if I am married, since I am pregnant, and I answer 'yes'. Then they ask who my husband is, and I give his name. Then they look at each other and say: 'He is already married, and has children'. Oh, no, I was so shocked. I

go home, cry, and get great pains in my stomach. I fall, and an ambulance takes me to hospital ... I have been duped. ... I lie to my mother [who comes for a visit to Denmark], saying he works in Germany. ... She asks why he never calls, so I make a woman I know from kindergarten call me, and I say 'hi', and talk with her, and trick my mother into believing he called me.

The interview makes apparent that Saida's 'marriage', while certainly not valid according to Danish law, may not even have been a *nikah* with an imam but rather a show with no legal or other validity, made to dupe her into having a sexual relationship with the 'husband'. Also, the husband did not disclose to her that he was already married to another woman. Afterwards, the 'husband' gave Saida little of his time and support, materially or otherwise. Despite his infrequent visits, Saida ended up becoming pregnant again, further entrenching her in a life as a *de facto* single mother.

An extreme example of male exploitation of a vulnerable woman, Saida's case must be understood within the context of migration, which had first made her easy prey for her Turkish 'husband', and left her unable to forge a better life for herself after realizing that she had been deceived. While the case may have initially occurred due to the man's desire for intimate relations with more than one woman, the outcome was considerable ill-being for Saida and her two children.

The case of the Danish Helle, a convert to Islam, presents another example where spousal abuse, polygamy, and the husband's disregard for state family laws converge, leading to women's vulnerability and inability to opt out of a marriage. Helle had both a civil and a religious marriage to a refugee from a Middle Eastern country. The couple had three children. The relationship was troubled, as the husband had both psychological problems and a criminal record. He was rarely at home, and then Helle discovered that he had married another woman in a religious ceremony and fathered a child with the second wife. When the husband went to jail, Helle divorced him according to Danish law. The husband, however, did not agree to dissolving their *nikah* and fully ending their relationship. Although Helle knew that she could have her *nikah* dissolved without his consent, as they were not living together, she did not dare take such an action. She feared both that the children might be abducted to the husband's country of origin and that her husband would physically harm her, if she unilaterally had the *nikah* dissolved:

If you are aware of how one's man's temperament can be, and what he can do, just if he feels like it. How much he disregards the Danish system – because he is already a convicted criminal, and has been in a Danish jail, which is not nearly as bad as in his own country. I know he won't accept a divorce, because then you are kind of 'free on the market'. ... It's like I still belong to him.

Helle's case also involves an initially secret polygamous marriage. Her story, however, has less to do with the dynamics of migration and transnational social space *per se*, and more with male domination and gendered violence that render the wife vulnerable and lacking agency to end the marriage for fear of the consequences. Indeed, both friends and Danish case workers had offered Helle help with going underground and starting a new life elsewhere in Denmark – the perceived prerequisite if she was to succeed in leaving her husband for good. However, she had refrained from this drastic solution, choosing to live instead with a 'husband' who still had a key to her flat and regularly showed up at her home without warning.

In short, while some women fared better than others in the above-mentioned polygamous marriages, on the whole, women tended to be negatively impacted by these unions compared to men. In exceptional cases polygamous marriages (at least in name) contributed to increasing female wellbeing. In the case of a Turkish woman, Su, a polygamous marriage existed for a while because she wanted to have a *nikah* with her new husband before the civil divorce from her first husband was clear. Under conditions of transnationalism, legal, social, and religious systems co-exist in complex ways. In Su's case, this co-existence enabled her to start married life with a man earlier than otherwise, because she married him in a religious *nikah* even though her official civil divorce had not yet come through.

Su's story parallels that of a Pakistani couple in Bristol: in the British case, the groom's divorce from his first wife was not yet finalized. The couple nevertheless had a *nikah*. Even though they were not yet living together, the *nikah* gave them the freedom to go unchaperoned on shopping trips for jew-ellery, overcoming the traditional prohibition against contact between engaged couples (Charsley, 2006).

Conclusion

Returning to the question of how polygamous practices among Muslim ethnic minorities in Europe are associated with individual aspirations towards well-being in transnational social spaces, the analysis shows that the practices are complex and may evolve over time as the initial migration stream develops into settled ethnic minority communities. The analysis also shows that while influenced by historical, geographical, and social processes (and in some cases driven by complex family needs), polygamous marriages predominantly remain gender-unequal constructs, with the playing field advantaging men. Hence, in most of the empirical material, these marriages generally appeared motivated by male aspirations that the initial monogamous marriage had left wanting, e.g., male desire for care, 'better wife', heirs, or migration.

Moreover, the analysis shows that the marriages were strongly shaped by the transnational social spaces in which they took place: the distances of such spaces could allow men to keep wives from knowing of one another, at least for a time, or could contribute to some women being vulnerable and socially isolated enough to be tricked into entering polygamous marriages that they could later have difficulties leaving. In such spaces, different religious and legal systems could also co-exist, enabling individuals to enter into different kinds of polygamous 'marriages'. While male aspirations underlie most of these polygamous marriages, the greatest hardships were suffered by the women involved. These gendered experiences, as well as the link between polygamous marriages and family conflict, align with more general research on polygamous marriages and wellbeing (Al-Krenawi, Graham and Slonim-Nevo, 2002; Ozkan, 2006; Slonim-Nevo and Al-Krenawi, 2006).

The analysis also testifies to the changing gender relations in the context of migration. In the countries of origin, women's dependence on men for material and relational wellbeing could make them agree to become a second wife (rather than remaining unmarried). Such gendered dependence most likely contributed to the relative stability of polygamous marriages, with all wives firmly anchored in the country-of-origin context. In comparison, immigrant women in Europe can often command a relatively high degree of self-determination, especially when they are descendants of immigrants (rather than migrants themselves) with European linguistic and educational skills. Such resourceful women may have relatively good options for leaving unsatisfying marriages. Thus, especially in a welfare state such as the Danish one, such women can survive on their own, even as mothers of young children, because they have money that they either earn or receive through social welfare. The associated changes in the gendered balance of power may indeed underlie some men's aspirations for finding 'better' (possibly less independent) second wives than their European-raised first wives, in an attempt to recoup masculine authority.

Some women may see advantages in or desire a husband, and polygamy offers opportunities for women who might not be able to marry otherwise. Similarly, other studies document that polygamous marriages may also contribute to the wellbeing of women (Majeed, 2016; Anderson, 2000). Such positive examples, however, were hardly present in the empirical material upon which this chapter is built, likely because this material was partly drawn from studies focusing on marital discord and divorce. In line with existing research on polygamy and wellbeing, this chapter thus also points to such marital arrangements often being associated not with happy and harmonious family arrangements but with marital problems.

Note

1   This chapter has received financial support from The Danish Victims Fund.

Bibliography

Abbott, F., 1962. Pakistan's new marriage law: A reflection of Qur'anic interpretation. *Asian Survey*, 1(11), pp.26–32.
Akpinar, A., 2003. The honour/shame complex revisited: Violence against women in the migration context. *Women's Studies International Forum*, 26(5), pp.425–442.

Al-Krenawi, A. and Graham, J.R., 1999. The story of Bedouin-Arab women in a polygamous marriage. *Women's Studies International Forum*, 22(5), pp.497–509.

Al-Krenawi, A., Graham, J.R. and Slonim-Nevo, V., 2002. Mental health aspects of Arab-Israeli adolescents from polygamous versus monogamous families. *The Journal of Social Psychology*, 142(4), pp.446–460.

Altman, I. and Ginat, J., 1996. *Polygamous Families in Contemporary Society*. Cambridge, UK: Cambridge University Press.

Anderson, C.M., 2000. The persistence of polygyny as an adaptive response to poverty and oppression in apartheid South Africa. *Cross-Cultural Research*, 34(2), pp.99–112.

Asad, M., 1980. *The Message of the Qur'an*. Sharjah, UAE: Dar al Andalu Limited.

Ataca, B., Kagitcibasi, C. and Diri, A., 2005. The Turkish family and the value of children: Trends over time. In: G. Trommsdorff and B. Nauck, eds. 2005. *The Value of Children in Cross-cultural Perspective*. Berlin, Germany: Pabst, pp.91–119.

Bao, J., 2008. Denaturalizing polygyny in Bangkok, Thailand. *Ethnology*, 47(2/3), pp.145–161.

Bourdieu, P., 1977. *Outline of a Theory of Practice*. Cambridge: Cambridge University Press.

Brouwer, L. and Priester, M., 1983. Living in between – Turkish women in their homeland and in the Netherlands. In: A. Phizacklea, ed. 1983. *One Way Ticket: Migration and Female Labour*. London: Routledge and Kegan Paul, pp.113–130.

Castels, M., 1997. *The Power of Identity*. Oxford: Blackwell Publishing.

Chamie, J., 1986. Polygamy among Arabs. *Population Studies*, 40(1), pp.55–65.

Charsley, K., 2006. Risk and ritual: The protection of British Pakistani women in transnational marriage. *Journal of Ethnic and Migration Studies*, 32(7), pp.1169–1187.

Charsley, K., 2013. *Transnational Pakistani Connections: Marrying 'Back Home'*. London: Routledge.

Charsley, K. and Liversage, A., 2013. Transforming polygamy: Migration, transnationalism and multiple marriages among Muslim minorities. *Global Networks*, 13 (1), pp.60–78.

Charsley, K. and Liversage, A., 2015. Silenced husbands: Muslim marriage migration and masculinity. *Men and Masculinities*, 18(4), pp.489–508.

Elbedour, S., Onwuegbuzie, A.J., Caridine, C. and Abu-Saad, H., 2002. The effect of polygamous marital structure on behavioral, emotional, and academic adjustment in children: A comprehensive review of the literature. *Clinical Child and Family Psychology Review*, 5(4), pp.255–271.

Hassouneh-Phillips, D., 2001. Polygamy and wife abuse: A qualitative study of Muslim women in America. *Health Care for Woman International*, 22(8), pp.735–748.

Lang, G. and Smart, J., 2002. Migration and the "second wife" in South China: Toward cross-border polygyny. *International Migration Review*, 36(2), pp.546–569.

Liversage, A., 2009. Vital conjunctures, shifting horizons: High-skilled female immigrants looking for work. *Work, Employment and Society*, 23(1), pp.120–141.

Liversage, A., 2012a. Gender, conflict and subordination within the household – Turkish migrant marriage and divorce in Denmark. *Journal of Ethnic and Migration Studies*, 38(7), pp.1119–1136.

Liversage, A., 2012b. Muslim divorces in Denmark – findings from an empirical investigation. In: W. Menski and R. Mehdi, eds. 2012. *Interpreting Divorce Law in Islam*. Copenhagen: DJØF Publishers, pp.179–201.

Liversage, A., 2012c. Transnational families breaking up: Divorce among Turkish immigrants in Denmark. In: K. Charsley, ed. 2012. *Transnational Marriage: New Perspectives from Europe and Beyond*. London: Routledge, pp.146–160.

Liversage, A., 2014. Minority ethnic men and fatherhood in a Nordic context. In: G.B. Eydal and T. Rostgaard, eds. 2014. *Caring Fathers in the Nordic Welfare States – Policies and Practices of Contemporary Fatherhoods*. Bristol: Policy Press, pp.209–230.

Liversage, A. and Ottosen, M.H., 2014. Changing times – Family formation processes among Turkish immigrant women and their Danish majority peers. *Journal of Comparative Family Studies*, 45(4), pp.459–474.

Liversage, A. and Ottosen, M.H., 2015. When family life is risky business, immigrant divorce in the women-friendly welfare state. In: T.T. Bengtsson, M. Frederiksen and J.E. Larsen, eds. 2015. *Risk and the Modern Welfare State – Sociological Investigations of the Danish Case*. New York: Palgrave Macmillan, pp.109–123.

Liversage, A. and Rytter, M., 2015. A cousin marriage equals a forced marriage: Transnational marriages between closely related spouses in Denmark. In: A. Shaw and R. Aviad, eds. 2015. *Cousin Marriages: Between Tradition, Genetic Risk and Cultural Change*. Oxford: Berghahn, pp.130–153.

Majeed, D., 2016. Ethics of sisterhood: African American Muslim women and polygyny. In: J. Bennion and L.F. Joffe, eds. 2016. *The Polygamy Question*. Logan: Utah State University Press, pp.85–102.

Mallett, S., 2004. Understanding home: A critical review of the literature. *The Sociological Review*, 52(1), pp.62–89.

Mashhour, A., 2005. Islamic law and gender equality: Could there be a common ground? A study of divorce and polygamy in Sharia law and contemporary legislation in Tunisia and Egypt, *Human Rights Quarterly*, 27(2), pp.562–596.

Ozkan, M., 2006. Mental health aspects of Turkish women from polygamous versus monogamous families. *International Journal of Social Psychiatry*, 52(3), pp.214–220.

Qureshi, K., 2013. Sabar: Body politics among middle-aged migrant Pakistani women. *Journal of the Royal Anthropological Institute*, 19, pp.120–137.

Rooij, F.B.van, Balen, F.van and Hermanns, J.M.A., 2009. The experiences of involuntarily childless Turkish immigrants in the Netherlands. *Qualitative Health Research*, 19(5), pp.621–632.

Schrock, D. and Schwalbe, M., 2009. Men, masculinity and manhood acts. *Annual Review of Sociology*, 35, pp.277–295.

Shaw, A., 2000. *Kinship and Continuity: Pakistani Families in Britain*. Amsterdam: Harwood.

Shepard, L.D., 2013. The impact of polygamy on women's mental health: a systematic review, *Epidemiology and Psychiatric Sciences*, 22(1), pp.47–62.

Slonim-Nevo, V. and Al-Krenawi, A., 2006. Success and failure among polygamous families: The experience of wives, husbands, and children. *Family Process*, 45(3), pp.311–330.

Welchman, L., 2007. *Women and Muslim Family Laws in Arab States: A Comparative Overview of Textual Development and Advocacy*. Amsterdam: Amsterdam University Press.

White, D.R., 1988. Rethinking polygyny: Co-wives, codes, and cultural systems, *Current Anthropology*, 29(4), pp.529–572.

White, S.C., 2008. *But What is Wellbeing? A Framework for Analysis in Social and Development Policy and Practice*. Paper for Regeneration and Wellbeing: Research into Practice, University of Bradford, 24–25 April 2008. University of Bath, Centre for Development Studies. Available at: http://staff.bath.ac.uk/ecsscw/But_what_is_Wellbeing.pdf [Accessed September 25, 2018].

White, S.C., 2010. Analysing wellbeing: A framework for development practice. *Development in Practice*, 20(20), pp.158–172.

Zeitzen, M.K., 2008. *Polygamy: A Cross-cultural Analysis*. Oxford: Berg.

6 Transnational families navigating the law

Marriage, divorce, and wellbeing

Iris Sportel, Betty de Hart and Friso Kulk

Introduction

In the rich and varied literature on transnational families, the role of the law in their everyday lives generally escapes attention. Although transnational families are, in their everyday activities and relationships, at least potentially influenced by multiple sets of laws and institutions (Levitt and Glick Schiller, 2004) which may involve plural and fundamentally different legal systems and normative orderings, we know relatively little about how transnational families are confronted with the law, how they use the law, and how it impacts their everyday lives. This is remarkable, as many life events, such as marriage, divorce, or the birth of children, are not just intimate family matters, but also legal matters. For members of transnational families, this often means dealing with legal systems from multiple countries. In this chapter, we aim to contribute to the literature on transnational families by drawing attention to the role of law. We do this by shedding light on how transnational Dutch-Moroccan and Dutch-Egyptian families relate to multiple family law systems in cases of marriage and divorce. How do family members experience the legal regulation of intimate relationships? How do they navigate between two family law systems and with what results? We specifically examine how the process of navigating the law is related to their wellbeing.

We start with a brief theoretical note on the relationship between law and wellbeing, followed by some background information on Dutch-Moroccan and Dutch-Egyptian transnational families, our research methods, and the interlocutors. Subsequently, we will go into more detail on three dimensions of wellbeing and the law for transnational families. Lastly, we will look at differences between the interlocutors in how they dealt with the law, particularly the resources needed for dealing with bureaucracy and inequalities in access.

Law and wellbeing

Although it is often assumed that law is related to wellbeing, there is very little work on what this relationship looks like. Furthermore, the existing literature has mostly perceived this relationship from the narrow angle of how the law best serves the interests of transnational family members. Accordingly, the focus has been mainly on tangible outcomes such as accessibility of legal systems and access to justice (in terms of available information about the law and obstacles related to a lack of financial resources); the need to make family members' legal position similar in the two countries to avoid so-called 'limping' legal situations (being married or divorced in one country and not in the other) (Van Den Eeckhout, 2000; Kruiniger, 2015; Rutten, 2004); and finally, accommodation of cultural and religious claims in law (Foblets, 1997; Hoekema and van Rossum, 2010).

Instead, we seek a more complex and layered understanding of the relationship between law and the wellbeing of transnational families. Drawing on the approach proposed in the introduction of this volume, we examine the wellbeing of transnational families and its interplay with law as a multidimensional process, comprising material, relational, and ethical aspects. With regard to the material aspects of wellbeing, we shift the direction of our gaze from formal laws that can be found in law books and courts to the more mundane work of documents and bureaucracy with which transnational family members have to deal. Law comes to them often in the form of documents that have to be acquired or submitted (e.g. marriage or birth certificates) in order to make actual family relationships into legal facts (a valid marriage or a registered birth).

We approach the relational aspect of wellbeing through the notion of 'kin work'. For members of transnational families managing kin ties in two countries often requires legal work, such as arranging passports or visas for family visits or ensuring the legal validity of a marriage or divorce. The extent to which family members engage in such legal work may also depend on the closeness of their transnational ties. In this respect it is relevant to keep in mind that transnational families are not always cooperative units and kin ties are not stable. Like all families, transnational families are full of tensions, conflict, power relationships, and inequalities (Dreby and Adkins, 2010). Events such as death, marriage, or divorce transform kin ties, and may not only strengthen, but also sever them. In this context, law may also be purposely used to sever kin ties, especially, but not only, in cases of family break-up (Morano-Foadi, 2007). Using the term *managing* kin ties encompasses both the maintenance and obstruction or severance of family ties through law.

Third, in the ethical dimension, law is just one of the systems of meaning pertinent to the lives of transnational families. Transnational couples live in a complex normative context, made up from their own and their partners' wishes and desires, those of two extended families, public discourses on religion and migration, the legal regulations of two (or even more) states, as well as culture and religion. The complexity of the diverse normative contexts implies that there is no clear-cut relationship between the norms and values that people cherish and their expectations of the law. Rather, we found that transnational family members navigate this complex normative context, often trying to avoid conflict and friction with the multiple actors in this environment and choosing pragmatic solutions.

For all these three dimensions of wellbeing, the processes through which family relationships and rights are negotiated between individual members of the families on the one hand, and vis-à-vis state laws and institutions of two (or more) countries on the other hand, vary. Dealing with the law requires financial, social, and language resources. Hence, it is related to inequalities based on gender, ethnicity, nationality, and/or social class.

Dutch-Moroccan and Dutch-Egyptian transnational families

We understand transnational families to include not only spouses, parents, and children, but also the extended family (in-laws, grandparents) living across borders. Labelling them transnational families means only that members of these families have crossed borders and potentially encountered two family law systems; we cannot reach any conclusions about the extent to which they actually lead transnational lives or identify transnationally; this differs significantly for individual cases.

Moreover, we move beyond a singular understanding of transnational Muslim families by researching diverse categories of families. Our research sample includes families where one of the partners migrated from Morocco or Egypt to the Netherlands or vice versa. We include persons who in the Netherlands are labelled 'second-generation migrants': in our case they are persons of migrant origin, born in the Netherlands, with or without Dutch citizenship, who marry a partner from the country of origin of the parents.[1] We also include so-called 'mixed families', where a Dutch-born man or woman concludes a marriage with a partner from Morocco or Egypt.[2] Generally, these two groups are perceived very differently and are thought to be incomparable. In our view, however, the two research groups are similarly situated in several respects: as families where one partner migrated, who have family ties in at least two countries, and who potentially come into contact with two different legal systems and institutional arrangements. For the non-migrant partner transnationality may not be central in their lives, and they may never visit the other country. However, following Levitt and Jaworsky (2007, p.132) we claim that they live in households where people, values, goods, and claims from somewhere else – including family law – are likely to be present on a daily basis. Comparing these two different research groups enhances our insights into the role of law in the lives of transnational families.

Furthermore, we put forward a dynamic understanding of the category of 'Muslim', based on the diverse experiences of our interlocutors concerning Islam and its normative significance in their lives. In some of the families in our research, both partners considered themselves Muslim. Some were religiously mixed (Christian-Muslim or non-religious-Muslim), while in other families the non-Muslim partner converted to Islam.

Moroccan migrants and their children are one of the largest immigrant groups in the Netherlands, and they are predominantly of Muslim background. They mostly marry spouses from the same ethnic group, although the number of migration marriages (i.e., marriages with a partner from Morocco not already living in the Netherlands) has dropped significantly in the last 15 years due to changing patterns of family formation and immigration restrictions.[3] People of Egyptian descent form a much smaller migrant group in the Netherlands, with a significant Christian minority and a larger percentage of mixed marriages, evidenced by the fact that over half of the 'second-generation children' are from a mixed relationship.[4] Little is known about Dutch migrants living in Egypt and Morocco. Estimates are that around 600 Dutch nationals live in Morocco, and around 1,500 Dutch nationals in Egypt.[5]

Methodology

We interviewed couples and divorcees living in Morocco, Egypt, or the Netherlands on their experiences with the different family law systems. Our multi-sited research enabled us to study the reciprocal connections between the Netherlands and Morocco, and between the Netherlands and Egypt. Interviews took place in two sub-projects: one dealing with marriage and the legal relationships between parents and children (33 interviews with parents), the other with divorce (26 interviews with spouses).[6] In addition, around 40 professionals involved in legal matters relevant to transnational families, such as lawyers, embassy personnel, translators, and NGO representatives were interviewed. The interviews were conducted in the period from 2008 to 2012.

We approached the interlocutors in a variety of ways: through our own networks and through (online and offline) networks of NGOs, migrant communities, and lawyers. For the project on divorce, we also approached the interlocutors through the Dutch courts and by contacting lawyers of published court cases. Lastly, we spent time at locations and events relevant to transnational couples, especially for the Dutch communities in Morocco and Egypt. Most interviews were held in Dutch, others in (mixtures of) Arabic, French, or English. They lasted from 45 minutes to four hours. Most interviews took place at the homes of the interlocutors, others at the homes of family members or friends, at the workplace, or in cafés.

It is not easy to provide a profile of our research group due to the interlocutors' diversity and mobility. The country of residence serves as an example. While 16 interviews were conducted in Morocco, 13 in Egypt, and 29 in the Netherlands, not everyone lived in the country in which they were interviewed. A considerable proportion of the interlocutors had moved from one country to the other, or even to a third country, during their marriage or after divorce.[7] There were also important differences between the interlocutors for the two sub-projects, especially in terms of education, employment, and income.

Table 6.1 Overview interlocutors

Background	Parenthood		Divorce		Total
	Dutch-Moroccan	Dutch-Egyptian	Dutch-Moroccan	Dutch-Egyptian	
Number of interviews	20	13	15	11	**59**
Mixed marriages	14	13	6	11	**44**[8]
Migration marriages	6	0	9	0	**15**
Number of interlocutors[9]	29 (18 women/ 11 men)	17 (12 women/ 5 men)	15 (12 women/ 3 men)	11 (9 women/ 2 men)	**72 (50 women/ 22 men)**

Although the majority of the interviewees had completed some form of higher education, the interlocutors in the research group on parenthood were, generally speaking, more highly educated than the divorcees. In the case of most of these couples, both partners had paid employment, and in half of the cases, both spouses earned enough to be financially independent. In the divorcee group, however, only a small minority of the families (4) had two partners with a substantial income, and in most of these families (18) one of the spouses was the main or sole provider: both men (10) and women (8).[10] Despite considerable efforts, we did not manage to find enough male participants to attain a gender balance, especially for the interviews on divorce. The interlocutors were also a very diverse group with regard to age, ranging from early twenties to late seventies.

The material dimension of wellbeing

Family law is not just about court procedures and conflicts, but also, and perhaps more so, about everyday legal paperwork such as arranging the documents for a marriage or registering the birth of a child or the death of a relative. Many authors assume that, in dealing with bureaucracy and law, transnational families want 'the best of both worlds', acting strategically to maximize their position in dealing with multiple legal systems in which rights and obligations differ (Ackers and Dwyer, 2004; Foblets, 1998; Jansen Frederiksen, 2011). However, in our research we found little evidence of such strategic behaviour: most people had no (long-term) strategic plan, but rather obtained information and took legal steps as they went along.

For example, when a Dutch-Moroccan husband wanted to register the birth of his first child in the Netherlands, the Dutch civil registry warned him that the spelling of the child's name would not be accepted in Morocco. This would mean that the Moroccan authorities would refuse to register the child and it would consequently not acquire Moroccan citizenship.

> [Husband:] At first I wrote it differently. In French. They took the book [of names accepted by Morocco], looked it up, and said: "you'd better spell this differently". And I reacted a bit and said: "I'll decide myself how I name my son". And the lady said: "I only want to warn you. If you go to the consulate, they will refuse" (Mimoun, October 2011).[11]

Having learned from this experience, the couple took a different approach with the next two children and went to the Dutch civil registry during the wife's pregnancy to choose a name from the Moroccan 'name book'.

As this example illustrates, transnational families tend to come into contact with bureaucracies of two (or more) countries, and are confronted with requirements in both bureaucracies that at times contradict each other. Steps taken in one country are not automatically known or valid in the other country; legal status such as marriage or even the name of a child can be different in the two countries involved. Furthermore, documents such as marriage or birth certificates often need to be officially translated and legalized by embassies or a Ministry of Justice before they can be used in the other country. Dealing with bureaucracy in two countries thus not only involves 'double work', but also complicates the work that needs to be done.

Consequently, documents have an independent meaning both in legal practice and social life, constituting family relationships both in a legal and a social sense (Kulk, 2013; Yngvesson, 2006; Hegel-Cantarella, 2011; Mulla, 2011). Moreover, because of the interconnectedness of family law and migration law, family law status may have consequences for residence and nationality: without a valid marriage there may be no possibility of family reunification or a child may not acquire the citizenship of the father. It is therefore not surprising that an important part of the stories of our interlocutors was about their dealings with bureaucracy. For example, a Dutch-Egyptian couple explained the process they went through to marry in the Netherlands:

> H: I think all that I needed from here was my birth certificate. And what did I need, you remember? [to wife]
> W: You needed a document that you were not married before.
> H: I mean besides this?
> W: You needed the documents that you didn't have a criminal record ... and you needed to come to Holland to have a meeting with the immigration police.
> H: That wasn't very smart from them. Because in Holland, they assumed that because I'm a foreigner, we're going to live in Holland. This was not the case ... And it was actually annoying at the time. It was in the middle of the semester here. So it was really in the middle of my work. And

[wife] insisted that I have to come because it was one of the procedures to get married. And I have to meet the police for it. And when I went there, well, she asked me for my passport. I give her my passport and she gave me a stamp and she said: "Mister, you can stay now for six months". I said: "I'm sorry; I have to leave in two days, back to Egypt. I can't stay for six months. Why?" Then she [immigration officer] finally understands that we were not going to live actually in Holland. ... And that was the only reason for me to get a plane ticket to Holland, and one week to get out from my work, from my annual leave, just to go there to discover that it was a misunderstanding (Farouq and Brigitte, October 2010).

This interview excerpt illustrates three important points. First, it shows the complexity of the procedures and the difficulties in acquiring the correct legal information. As the couple was inquiring about the necessary steps, the Dutch authorities assumed that they would want to establish life in the Netherlands, and thus started the migration procedure to make that possible. It was only after spending significant amounts of time, energy, and money, that it became clear that it had not been necessary. Second, it shows how an important part of the legal and bureaucratic work by the interlocutors is aimed at managing kin relationships. Even though marrying in Egypt, where the couple was going to live, would have been more practical, the couple wanted to marry in the Netherlands to enable the wife's mother, who was ill and could not travel, to attend the wedding. In other words, this legal process was a form of 'kin work'. We will elaborate on this concept in the next section.

Legal work as kin work: the relational dimension

The literature on transnational families discusses the means needed to maintain family across borders: family visits, telephone calls (Horst, 2006) and the Internet (Vertovec, 2004), sending remittances or gifts (Tilly, 2007), sharing productive and caring work (Wilding, 2006), rituals and material culture (Zontini, 2004), and emotional and moral support (Gardner and Grillo, 2002). All these activities to maintain family ties have been labelled 'kin work': the conception, maintenance, and ritual celebration of cross-border household ties (Baldassar, 2007).

The law is one of the factors shaping transnational ties between those migrating and those staying in the country of origin (di Leonardo, 1987). However, we know little about how law shapes transnational family relationships and family dynamics, as this issue is rarely studied systematically (de Hart, van Rossum and Sportel, 2013; Dreby and Adkins, 2010; Mazzucato and Schans, 2011). Nevertheless, dealing with law is necessary for the conception, maintenance, and ritual celebration of kin ties across borders. A lot of the activities to maintain family ties, such as family visits, care, or marriage celebrations in the home country are not possible without some form of dealing with the law. Consequently, the law can be a tool to maintain kin ties, but also a hindrance to doing so.

For instance, the family visit. While migration law and citizenship are well known in enabling or, rather, frustrating people in maintaining family relationships by family visits, family law status is equally important. When parenthood (e.g., paternity or parental authority) is not legally established or not recognized in a country, parents may not be able to enter or leave with their children. Moreover, unmarried sexual relationships are illegal in Egypt and Morocco, and remarriage after a divorce that is not legally recognized may lead to prosecution for bigamy.

These were some of the issues Dutch-Moroccan Naima faced when she wanted to visit her family in Morocco with her new partner and their child. Years earlier, she had been pressured by her family into marrying a Moroccan spouse during the summer holidays, while still underage. After conducting a legal marriage in Morocco, Naima returned to the Netherlands, where she was supposed to start the migration procedure for her husband to join her. However, she managed to postpone the wedding event – that would make them socially married – and registering the marriage in the Netherlands until she had graduated from high school. After spending another summer in Morocco, she decided that she did not want to start married life. This meant a significant breach with the life she had had before:

> And then I left home. I wandered. I saw all the dark sides of life …. For me, nobody existed. They [family and husband] were just in Morocco, it did not bother me. And I did not register in the Netherlands that I was married or anything. Just did not register it. Because I did not plan to continue with him anyway. … And then I met my [new] partner. … And I got pregnant. And *that's* when it came back. Because then I had a big problem. Now I was not only married, but I was married in Morocco *and* I was in the Netherlands *and* I was pregnant from another man. … When the child was a few months old, I thought: now I have to go to Morocco and start the court case [for divorce], or I'll never get rid of it (Naima, November 2009).

In the period before the Moroccan family law reform of 2004, divorce was not easy. The process took several years, during which Naima was afraid to take her child to Morocco:

> N: All that time I was afraid that he [husband] would find out that I had a child.
> I: You never took the child to Morocco?
> N: No, and I hated that. Because I felt like: it's my child. You want to show your child to your family, show your country. I love Morocco as well. It was dreadful. And his father is a Turk, by the way. And we went there [to Turkey] on holiday in the summer. But I could not take them to Morocco.

Naima's complex story demonstrates that although she initially avoided Morocco and Moroccan family law, this no longer worked when she had a new partner and a child because she wanted to maintain her transnational ties with Morocco and her family there.

Hence, relationships with family and friends are a major motivator to do legal work across borders. While most divorced interlocutors arranged for divorce in their country of residence, only some of them also arranged the divorce in the other country to which they had transnational ties or intended to do so in the future. In the absence of such transnational links to the other country, the interlocutors simply saw no need to go through the trouble of arranging the divorce there. However, it is important to stress that the presence or absence of such ongoing transnational ties cannot be presupposed based on ethnic background. Some migrant spouses in our study had lost all ties to their country of origin, whereas some non-migrant informants greatly valued the connections they had built in the country of origin of their former spouse.

The ethical dimension

In the academic literature on migrants in Europe, it is often assumed that dealing with family law is strongly shaped by religious or cultural ethical considerations in which migrants want the law of their 'own culture' or religion applied to their family (see for example: Foblets and Verhellen, 2000; Menski, 2001; Yilmaz, 2002). In the Dutch context, issues like 'sharia wills', the possible presence of 'sharia courts' (Bakker, et al., 2010), and the application of 'Islamic' foreign family law by Dutch judges have caused intense public and political debate (Van Den Eeckhout, 2003; Sportel, 2017). However, this focus on the 'accommodation' of culture and religion in law was far less prominent in our interviews than one would have expected based on this literature. While for some interlocutors religion was an important part of their everyday life, with some impact on how they dealt with the legal aspects of their family relationships, religious accommodation was hardly raised as an issue by respondents. Rather than expecting the law to accommodate their religious wishes, the informants tried to solve normative issues in pragmatic ways, navigating multiple legal systems, social networks, and practical concerns (Kulk, 2013; Storms and Bartels, 2017; Vigh, 2009). Just like transnational ties, religiosity cannot be presupposed based on the ethnic background of the partners. One Moroccan non-religious woman complained that her Dutch ex-husband took his new faith far too seriously after he converted to Islam for the sake of their marriage. Conversely, some Dutch informants had already converted before meeting their spouse, and were explicitly looking for a Muslim partner.

This does not mean that religious and ethical concerns were entirely absent. Most importantly, religion played a role in the decision to get married rather than choosing cohabitation, which in recent years has become a popular family form in the Netherlands.[12] Some informants valued getting married before living together as part of their religious obligations. For other couples it was their families or social environment that encouraged an early marriage. As a Dutch woman living in Egypt explained:

> When we started a relationship together, we got married *'urfi* straight away. Because here, in [city], well, they keep an eye on you. And [husband] is someone from, not a good family, but a middle-class family. Where reputation is very [important]. He did not want to be addressed by a police officer: "Can I see your papers?" He wanted to be able to show [the papers]. So we conducted the *'urfi* right away. ... For me it did not feel like a marriage at all. More like, well, we have the right papers and, and now we can just be on the streets together, rent an apartment together. It felt more like living together (Petra, October 2010).

In this case, getting married was necessary to be able to be together in public spaces without damaging the family's reputation or being harassed by local authorities. An informal *'urfi* marriage, which this informant believed had no legal value, meant that they could fulfil the community's demands. It also served her own interests, as she did not want to enter into a 'real', formal marriage so soon and without living together first.

Furthermore, as this quotation also shows, in Morocco and Egypt, state prohibitions of sexual relations outside marriage are key in couples' decisions to get married. Especially in Egypt, unmarried sexual relationships are actively policed, particularly in tourist areas, when showing affection in public, or checking into a hotel together (Behbehanian, 2000). This is why many couples conducted informal *'urfi* marriages, sometimes only a few days or weeks after meeting. Later, when the relationship proves to be stable, and especially when children are born, they formally register the *'urfi* marriage with the Egyptian authorities.

Another potential topic of ethical and religious considerations is religious conversion. While many of the native Dutch partners at some point converted to Islam, most of them described this primarily as a pragmatic step. For example, in Morocco or Egypt religion is relevant in inheritance law (Muslims and non-Muslims cannot inherit from one another), and many Dutch women believed it to be relevant when Moroccan or Egyptian courts decided on child custody after divorce or death of a spouse. Many Dutch women shared stories of formally converting to Islam as a safety measure for child custody or safeguarding their inheritance if their spouse should die. However, it must be noted that while most conversions we came across could be described as instrumental, people often had multiple aims, such as acceptance by their family-in-law, wanting to share their spouse's faith, or an interest in spirituality. For example, a Dutch man who married in Egypt spoke about his conversion as part of an entertaining anecdote rather than a life-changing religious event:

It was so easy. I sat next to a couple from the US. The wife married an Egyptian and wanted to become Muslim because he wanted her to. She did not know anything of [the religion] either. She wore a little silk scarf over her hair which kept falling off, and she put it back on, giggling all the time. ... And at some point he [religious official] asked: "Do you know what Islam is about?" And I said something like: "Well, more or less." And she [the American woman] as well. And he [religious official] said: "The most important thing is that you do not believe Jesus is God." And we said: "We don't believe that." "OK, that's all right then. Please repeat." And then he started saying some sentences in Arabic and we had to repeat them in Arabic, more or less phonetically, and then we got our certificate (René, August 2009).

For him, the conversion was a necessary step in the legal work required to get married in Egypt, including spending several days arranging all the paperwork, finding the right offices, and getting the right stamps. It was also a compromise at the relational level. His religious wife accepted that he was not religious, as long as he did not remain Christian. Before getting married she insisted that their children would be raised as Muslims, to which the husband agreed. Thus, conversion to Islam could be a practical solution for material reasons as well as for relational and ethical concerns. This is where the three forms of wellbeing come together.

While some interlocutors or their social environment put religious value on marriage, religious considerations seemed to be of limited importance in dealing with divorce. Almost all the interlocutors divorced in their country of residence, regardless of their views on its legal system or the fairness of its divorce procedures. While some interlocutors referred to religious or cultural norms on divorce, these norms did not seem to translate into specific choices during the legal process of divorce, such as divorcing in Morocco or Egypt rather than in the Netherlands, or asking Dutch judges for accommodation of religious norms. For example, a mixed couple of a Moroccan man and a Dutch woman living in the Netherlands had taken great care in writing a marriage contract which would be legally valid in both countries.[13] Fitting with the Moroccan family code at the time, they chose complete separation of spousal property. However, after the divorce, they ignored this contract and amicably arranged to equally split their property, as is customary in the Netherlands, and divided assets such as furniture according to their needs. In the interview, the Dutch wife recalled how surprised she was by her husband's insistence that she should keep her dower (*mahr*):

In the [marriage] contract there had to be a dower, at least according to the Moroccan norms of [marriage year, 1970s]. In the end we decided that [husband] had bought a 15-volume encyclopaedia. It was very expensive back then .... It was his, but he thought it would be a nice, symbolic dower for me, not just because of the monetary value, but because of the symbolic value .... So when we separated I suddenly got the encyclopaedia. I thought, "you need it more than I do", but no, he insisted: "This is yours" (Eva, January 2010).

For this husband, making sure his former wife kept her dower was an ethical issue, separate from the material issue of division of other property. Similarly, while some interlocutors felt that their former spouse did not handle the divorce in accordance with their religious norms, none took action by involving religious authorities in their divorce or having religious or cultural norms addressed in their court cases.

As these examples illustrate, one of the most important findings of our study is that family members navigated a complex web of demands from their social environment, legal requirements, family relationships, and religious and cultural norms, dealing with the law and bureaucracy as they went along. As we also saw, dealing with multiple bureaucracies across borders is not easy. It requires different kinds of resources: financial resources, the ability to travel, knowledge of dealing with bureaucracy, and transnational networks. Furthermore, access to and use of these resources was often connected to inequalities based on nationality and gender. In the next section, we will look further into how these factors and inequalities have impacted the ways in which transnational families dealt with bureaucracy and law.

Inequalities in transnational families

The interactions of transnational families with multiple legal systems and the possibilities of reaching their goals are strongly influenced by the resources accessible to them. These resources can effectively be divided into three kinds of capital as distinguished by Bourdieu (1986): economic capital, social capital, and cultural capital. Whether and how people had access to these forms of capital was influenced by their social position, which could be different in the countries of settlement and origin. In particular, nationality was a major source of inequality, as not all nationalities provide equal access to other resources. Aptly termed 'hierarchical citizenship' by Castles (2005), differences shape the legal work necessary for maintaining transnational family ties, as visas for Europe can be difficult for Moroccan and Egyptian nationals to obtain, while Dutch nationals can easily travel within and outside Europe.

Next, we discuss the three forms of capital, economic, cultural, and social, in relation to transnational families dealing with the law.

First, economic capital was important for the legal work entailed in managing 'kin work'. For example, obtaining documents in two countries and having them translated and legalized for use in the other country can be a costly affair. Securing documents also often involves travelling across borders. Travelling costs were a major obstacle, especially in the past, before the introduction of cheap flights. Hence, for some of the older interlocutors, travelling to their country of origin was a rare event. Even within Morocco or

Egypt travelling long distances can be costly and complicated. For example, while local Egyptian couples can marry in any city, marriage with a foreigner can only be concluded at a specific office in Cairo. The distances between the capital and the homes of people interviewed often meant that doing such legal work required multiple days away from a job or care responsibilities, as well as costs for travel and hotels. Such costs prevented some family members from arranging legal issues.

Second, dealing with bureaucracy requires cultural capital in the form of specific knowledge and experience. What is important here is not so much legal knowledge, but rather the awareness that something needs to be done and how it needs to be done. This requires not only language capability and knowledge of how and where to find information, but also embodied knowledge on how to behave and interact with 'the people of the law' such as civil registrars, lawyers, or judges. For transnational families in this study, such cultural capital was unequally distributed within the family as members had grown up in different countries. Those who had grown up in the country where things needed to be arranged were in a privileged position. We found that many of the interviewed family members took this into account by assigning the legal work to the spouse with the most experience of that particular system. Gender also played a role here, especially in Morocco and Egypt, where bureaucracy is generally dealt with by husbands and fathers, and women tend to have less experience in this field.

Third, we found that social capital played an important role in dealing with complex bureaucracies. Family members and friends living in countries of origin and settlement could provide important support in acquiring legal information and documents. However, the use of these family relations was not unconditional, and at times there was a lack of support, for example, when family members opposed a marriage or divorce.

Dutch-Moroccan families, in particular, made use of professional actors, such as NGOs and translators, for whom dealing with transnational families is an important part of their job. When migration law issues came up, professional support was particularly indispensable.

For example, Dutch-Moroccan Samira had migrated to Morocco with her parents when she was 17. Once in Morocco, she could not continue her education because she lacked the required Arabic language skills. After a while, she gave in to her parents' pressure to marry a Moroccan family member. After an unhappy marriage, her husband divorced her and she wanted to return to the Netherlands, where she had been born, had friends, and felt at home. However, her return was complicated as she had never acquired Dutch citizenship, and in her absence she had lost her residence rights. Dutch friends helped her contact a specialized office in Morocco that provided legal services and translations for Moroccan migrants from the Netherlands. The office guided her through the many steps needed to start the procedure for renewal of her residence permit in the Netherlands. The first step was to convince her ex-husband to hand over her passport. After the passport turned out to be valid for only a few more months, it needed to be renewed, for which a birth certificate was required. As Samira had been born in the Netherlands, she needed to travel to Rabat for the document. For Samira, who had never visited the capital before, and had been kept mostly indoors by her husband, this was a big step:

> Well, [director of specialized office] arranged it all for me, because I was so scared. ... It's as if you're on the street on your own for the first time. I was alone and I was afraid. ... Well, and then I went to Rabat. ... and it turned out there was a problem with my birth certificate. Because my name, our last name, here in Morocco was not the same name as was written in [her Dutch birth certificate] (Samira, November 2009).[14]

Samira had to start a Moroccan court procedure to have the spelling mistake in her Dutch birth certificate corrected. She could then finally apply for a new passport, and apply for renewal of her residence permit in the Netherlands.

This example demonstrates that, at times, specialist expertise of multiple legal systems and family law as well as migration law is called for. Regular Moroccan or Dutch lawyers often lack the necessary knowledge of two legal systems, even if Samira had had the financial means to hire one. Moreover, the availability of the necessary expert knowledge is, depending on the specific transnational context, not obvious. Whereas there is a strong network of NGOs, specialized lawyers, and private offices active between Morocco and the Netherlands (Sportel, 2011), the Dutch-Egyptian context lacks such a strong field of specialized legal aid. This difference can be explained by variation in size, visibility, and level of organization of the migrant communities involved. Hence, established larger migrant communities have easier access to specialized help for legal needs in complex situations than smaller or newer communities.

Conclusion

In this chapter, we aimed to contribute to the literature on transnational families by drawing attention to the role of law. As we have shown, law is of great importance for the wellbeing of transnational families. Living a family life across borders requires dealing with multiple laws and bureaucracies. Our most important finding is that people navigate the law, taking legal steps and finding legal information as they go along. Mistakes are made and confusion arises along the way. Moreover, rather than acting from a single interest or aim, there were several interconnected factors contributing to their wellbeing in multidimensional ways. Our findings indicate that the transnational families in our study did not interact strategically with the law to maximize material gain. Rather, their interests were relational, taking on complicated and often expensive legal work and finding compromises on normative issues in order to manage kin ties across borders. Travelling, visits, and enabling family and friends to attend important life events such as marriage ceremonies may all require extensive legal work. As such, legal work was often kin work.

Dealing with law requires several kinds of resources. Family members need economic, social, and cultural capital to deal with multiple bureaucracies. Existing inequalities in terms of nationality and gender thus impact the possibilities of transnational family members achieving their aims. Furthermore, the opportunity structures present in the different transnational contexts are also of importance in understanding differences in transnational family members' abilities to navigate the law.

We have also demonstrated the importance of a law-in-everyday-life approach in investigating the relationship between the law and the well-being of transnational families. Looking at law in everyday life shifts attention to the importance (and cost) of legal work, of forms, translations, and bureaucracy. Approaching the law from the everyday life of transnational families also requires transcending boundaries between different fields of law. People's experiences with the law are shaped by all their interactions with a legal system. For transnational families, especially family law and migration law interact in shaping people's experiences. Furthermore, a law-in-everyday-life approach allows for a more nuanced picture of transnational families and their needs and wishes. Studies on transnational families and the law often make assumptions on how transnational families seek accommodation of their religious or cultural values by legal systems. However, as we have shown, transnational families navigate multiple aims, demands, and aspirations, and their religiosity or transnational ties cannot be presupposed based on ethnicity. Future studies on the wellbeing of transnational families should take these complexities into account to get a fuller grasp of their lived reality.

Notes

1 While we consider the term 'second-generation migrants' quite problematic, it is commonly used in Dutch official and policy documents and statistics. We put the term between inverted commas to indicate its problematic character.

2 We use the terms 'mixed marriages' and 'mixed couples' in spite of their problematic character. As all marriages contain aspects of sameness and difference, it is only those differences that are marked as significant, especially by the social environment, that make a marriage mixed (Waldis, 2006). The marker of difference for mixed couples in this article is 'ethnicity' and/or 'race'.

3 In 2015, there were 380,755 persons of Moroccan descent living in the Netherlands. Of this group, 212,304 are so-called second-generation, the majority of whom have two parents who were born abroad (CBS Statline, 2017). Statistically, 70% of the second generation marry a partner of Moroccan descent already living in the Netherlands. For women, 12% marry a partner from Morocco and 7% a native Dutch partner. For men, 7% of spouses are from Morocco and 12% native Dutch.

4 In 2015, 22,700 people of Egyptian origin were living in the Netherlands, of whom 12,776 were born in Egypt (first-generation migrants); 4,783 have two parents who were born abroad; and 5,141 are children of one Egyptian parent and one Dutch parent (CBS Statline, 2017).

5 Estimations made by representatives of the Dutch embassies in interviews in Rabat in October 2009 and Cairo in December 2010. As there is no obligatory registration, the Dutch authorities cannot provide exact information on how many Dutch emigrants live in Morocco and Egypt.

6 Interviews for the sub-project on parents and children were done by Friso Kulk while interviews for the sub-project on divorce were done by Iris Sportel. About half of the interviews with professional actors were done by Friso Kulk and Iris Sportel together, the others by one of these two researchers. A third sub-project concerned cross-border custody disputes; interviews in this project are not included in this contribution. The entire project was led by Betty de Hart and financed by a VIDI grant she received from the Netherlands Organisation for Scientific Research.

7 Two interlocutors had moved to another country after divorce. One of these interviews was conducted by phone, the other in person.

8 A large majority of mixed families consisted of a Dutch woman and a Moroccan or Egyptian man, five out of 44 consisted of Dutch men and Egyptian (2) or Moroccan (3) women.

9 Many of the interviews on parents and children were held with both parents.

10 Interlocutors were asked about the situation during the marriage. When there was no communal household this was mostly due to complications in migration procedures.

11 All names in this chapter are pseudonyms.

12 In 2015, 44% of babies born in the Netherlands had unmarried parents, with 52% of first children born out of wedlock (CBS Statline, 2017).

13 Technically, what this couple wrote was a pre-nuptial agreement with a notary, as the Netherlands does not have marriage contracts.

14 Part of this quotation is also used in Sportel, 2016, p.224.

Bibliography

Ackers, L. and Dwyer, P., 2004. Fixed laws, fluid lives: The citizenship status of post-retirement migrants in the European Union. *Ageing and Society*, 24(3), pp.451–475.

Bakker, L.G.H., Gehring, A.J., Mourik, K.van, Claessen, M.M., Harmsen, C. and Harmsen, E., 2010. *Sharia in Nederland. Een studie naar islamitische advisering en geschilbeslechting bij moslims in Nederland* [Sharia in the Netherlands. A study on Islamic consultation and conflict resolution among Muslims in the Netherlands]. Nijmegen: Radboud Universiteit Nijmegen, Instituut voor Culturele Antropologie en Ontwikkelingsstudies / Radboud Universiteit Nijmegen, Instituut voor Rechtssociologie/WODC.

Baldassar, L., 2007. Transnational families and aged care: The mobility of care and the migrancy of ageing. *Journal of Ethnic and Migration Studies*, 33(2), pp.275–297.

Behbehanian, L., 2000. Policing the illicit peripheries of Egypt's tourism industry. *Middle East Report*, 30(3), pp.32–34.

Bourdieu, P., 1986. The forms of capital. In: J. Richardson, ed. *Handbook of Theory of Research for the Sociology of Education*. New York: Greenwood, pp.241–258.

Castles, S., 2005. Hierarchical citizenship in a world of unequal nation-states. *PS: Political Science and Politics*, 38(4), pp.689–692.

CBS Statline database, 2017. Available at: http://statline.cbs.nl/Statweb/ [Accessed February 17, 2017].

Dreby, J., and Adkins, T., 2010. Inequalities in transnational families. *Sociology Compass*, 4(8), pp.673–689.

Eeckhout, V. van den, 2000. De wisselwerking tussen materieel en internationaal privaatrecht: eenrichtings- of tweerichtingsverkeer? [The interplay between substantive law and private international law: One-way traffic or two-way traffic?]. *Rechtskundig Weekblad*, 63(37), pp.1249–1265.

Eeckhout, V. van den, 2003. Gelijkheid in het internationaal privaatrecht. Een kritiek op de gangbare structurering van het debat [Equality in private international law. A critique on the common structures of the debate]. *Nemesis*, 19(5/6), pp.177–189.

Foblets, M.-C.S.F.G., 1997. Conflicts of law in cross-cultural family disputes in Europe today: Who will reorient conflicts of law? *The Comparative and International Law Journal of Southern Africa*, 30(1), pp.22–36.

Foblets, M.-C., 1998. *Marokkaanse migrantenvrouwen in gezinsgeschillen: wat zijn passende juridische oplossingen?* [Moroccan migrant women in family conflicts: What are fitting legal solutions?]. Antwerpen: Maklu.

Foblets, M.-C. and Verhellen, J., 2000. Marokkaanse migrantenvrouwen in gezinsgeschillen. Wat zijn passende juridische oplossingen? [Moroccan migrant women in family conflicts: What are fitting legal solutions?] *Recht van de Islam*, 17, pp.90–115.

Gardner, K. and Grillo, R., 2002. Transnational households and ritual: An overview. *Global Networks*, 2(3), pp.179–190.

Hart, B. de, Rossum, W. van and Sportel, I., 2013. Law in the everyday lives of transnational families: An introduction. *Oñati Socio-Legal Series*, 3(6), pp.991–1003.

Hegel-Cantarella, C. 2011. Kin-to-be: Betrothal, legal documents, and reconfiguring relational obligations in Egypt. *Law, Culture and the Humanities* 7(3), pp.377–393.

Hoekema, A.J. and Rossum, W.M.van, 2010. Empirical conflict rules in Dutch legal cases of cultural diversity. In: M.-C. Foblets, J.-F. Gaudreault-Desbiens and A. Dundes Renteln, eds. 2010. *Cultural Diversity and the Law: State Responses from Around the World: Proceedings of the Colloquium "The Response of State Law to the Expression of Cultural Diversity", Brussels, September 2006*. Bruxelles: Bruylant, pp.851–888.

Horst, H.A., 2006. The blessings and burdens of communication: Cell phones in Jamaican transnational social fields. *Global Networks*, 6(2), pp.143–159.

Jansen Frederiksen, K., 2011. Mahr (dower) as a bargaining tool in a European context: A comparison of Dutch and Norwegian judicial decisions. In: R. Mehdi and J. S. Nielsen, eds. 2011. *Embedding Mahr in the European Legal System*. Copenhagen: DJØF Publishing, pp.147–190.

Kruiniger, P., 2015. *Islamic Divorces in Europe: Bridging the Gap between European and Islamic Legal Orders*. Den Haag: Eleven International Publishing.

Kulk, F., 2013. *Laverend langs grenzen. Transnationale gezinnen en Nederlands en islamitisch familie – en nationaliteitsrecht* [Navigating across borders. Transnational families and Dutch and Islamic family and nationality law]. Nijmegen: Wolf Legal Publishers.

Leonardo, M.di, 1987. The female world of cards and holidays: Women, families, and the work of kinship. *Signs: Journal of Women in Culture and Society*, 12(3), pp.440–453.

Levitt, P. and Jaworsky, B.N., 2007. Transnational migration studies: Past developments and future trends. *Annual Review of Sociology*, 33, pp.129–156.

Levitt, P., and Glick Schiller, N. 2004. Conceptualizing simultaneity: A transnational social field perspective on society. *International Migration Review*, 38(3), pp.1002–1039.

Mazzucato, V. and Schans, D., 2011. Transnational families and the well-being of children: Conceptual and methodological challenges. *Journal of Marriage and Family*, 73(4), pp.704–712.

Menski, W., 2001. Muslim law in Britain. *Journal of Asian and African Studies*, 62, pp.127–163.

Morano-Foadi, S., 2007. Problems and challenges in researching bi-national migrant families within the European Union. *International Journal of Law, Policy and the Family*, 21(1), pp.1–20.

Mulla, S. 2011. Introduction to forging family: Legal documents as new kinship technologies. *Law, Culture and the Humanities*, 7(3), pp.352–358.

Rutten, S., 2004. Recognition of divorce by repudiation (talaq) in France, Germany and the Netherlands. *Maastricht Journal of European and Comparative Law*, 11, pp.263–285.

Sportel, I., 2011. Transnational divorce in Dutch-Moroccan families: The semi-autonomous social field of legal aid. *Recht der Werkelijkheid*, 32(3), pp.37–51.

Sportel, I., 2016. *Divorce in Transnational Families: Marriage, Migration and Family Law*. London: Palgrave MacMillan.

Sportel, I., 2017. Who's afraid of Islamic family law? Dealing with sharia-based family law systems in the Netherlands. *Religion & Gender*, 7(1), pp.53–69.

Storms, O. and Bartels, E., 2017. The reform of the Moroccan family law and women's daily lives: Navigating between structural constraints and personal agency. In: L. Touaf, S. Boutkhil and C. Nasri, eds. 2017. *North African Women after the Arab Spring: In the Eye of the Storm*. London: Palgrave MacMillan, pp.191–209.

Tilly, C., 2007. Trust networks in transnational migration. *Sociological Forum* 22(1), pp.3–24.

Vertovec, S., 2004. Migrant transnationalism and modes of transformation. *International Migration Review*, 38(3), pp.970–1001.

Vigh, H., 2009. Motion squared: A second look at the concept of social navigation. *Anthropological Theory*, 9(4), pp.419–438.

Waldis, B., 2006. Introduction: Marriage in an era of globalisation. In: B. Waldis and R. Byron, eds. *Migration and Marriage. Heterogamy and Homogamy in a Changing World*. Berlin: Lit Verlag, pp.1–20.

Wilding, R., 2006. 'Virtual' intimacies? Families communicating across transnational contexts. *Global Networks*, 6(2), pp.125–142.

Yilmaz, I., 2002. The challenge of post-modern legality and Muslim legal pluralism in England. *Journal of Ethnic and Migration Studies*, 28(2), pp.343–354.

Yngvesson, B., 2006. Backed by papers: Undoing persons, histories, and return. *American Ethnologist*, 33(2), pp.177–190.

Zontini, E., 2004. Immigrant women in Barcelona: Coping with the consequences of transnational lives. *Journal of Ethnic and Migration Studies*, 30(6), pp.1113–1144.

7 Somali parents in Sweden

Navigating parenting and child wellbeing

Rannveig Haga

Introduction

This chapter examines how Somali parents[1] in Sweden understand and pursue the wellbeing of their children. Parents' aspirations for their children and the challenges they encounter in raising them are situated in the former's everyday experiences of racism, and in particular in relation to parents' experiences of marginalization in their encounters with institutions working with their children. In these encounters, parents experience, I argue, 'epistemic injustice', that is, they are marginalized and silenced as knowing and capable parents (Haga, 2015; 2016).

Sweden has a very heterogeneous Muslim population, resulting from half a century of immigration from all parts of the world. Somalis, with an approximate total number of 100,000, are the fourth largest group of Muslims after Iraqis, those from the Balkans, and Iranians as well as being the largest African group (Statistics Sweden, 2017). The mass migration of Somalis to Sweden began with the Somali civil war of the late 1980s.

Studies on Islamophobia in Sweden are few; however, the existing research indicates that overall there is a negative view of Islam among the native populations (Gardell and Muftee, 2017; Abrashi, Sander and Larsson, 2015; Equality ombudsman, 2013). A study reported that 47% of Swedes have, on the whole, a negative attitude towards religious diversity (Abrashi, Sander and Larsson, 2015). This was particularly evident in relation to Islam. For example, the study reported that 64.4% of the surveyed population held the view that Muslim women with scarves were oppressed (Abrashi, Sander and Larsson, 2015, pp.497–498). Discourses in which Islam is presented as a threat to the rights of women and children tend to affect Muslim parents' encounters with institutions working with their children. While this particular issue is currently understudied, an earlier study indicated a bias on the part of social workers against Muslims. The researched social workers held the view that parents from cultures that were assumed to be most distant from the Swedish culture were lacking in parenting capabilities (Eliassi, 2006, p.262). Somalis, being of African descent, and also commonly visibly Muslim, experience the above-mentioned racial, economic, and religious marginalization.

Sweden is also highly segregated and, in areas with many immigrants, schools have few, and in some cases no, 'ethnic' Swedish pupils. Thus, meeting places between the majority and Muslim minorities are few. It is mainly through the media that various groups learn about each other. And since media reports often focus on that which is different and problematic as opposed to that which is familiar and recognizable, the 'we' versus 'them' narrative – i.e., the Swedish majority versus Muslim minorities – tends to be pronounced (Roald, 2013).

In this chapter, I use the concept of wellbeing as a central analytical lens (see the introduction in this volume and the editors' iteration of the concept). Sarah White (2008) writes of wellbeing and its multidimensionality, which encompasses: material, relational, and subjective aspects, all of which are intrinsically intertwined. By using a similarly layered understanding of wellbeing, I examine the multidimensionality of the good life that Somali parents in Sweden aspire to for their children, and which goes beyond fulfilling needs and encompasses securing ethical resources and capabilities as well. I focus here on White's conceptualization of the subjective dimension of wellbeing, which concerns what people value and hold to be good, the desires they identify, and how they feel about their lives. Paying close attention to this dimension of wellbeing enables us to understand that perceptions of a good life are always grounded in cultural frameworks. These frameworks vary, as does the degree to which they are contested. However, in no case are they 'just there': they are situated in and are the means of significant exercise of power (White, 2008, p.9). Within European popular discourse, the focus is usually on the culture of minorities, a discourse that does not take into account that cultures are not static, but an ongoing process (Haga, 2009). The underlying assumption is that it is minorities that have culture. But what is not acknowledged is that the policies and practices of social institutions are also located in cultures and agendas that are part of broader normative frameworks and ideologies (see Kamali, 2002).

The chapter is structured into three sections. First, I present the research informing this analysis. Second, I examine Somali parents' aspirations for their children and their understanding of their children's wellbeing/good life. I identify, in particular, two issues that are pertinent to parents' understandings and pursuit of their children's wellbeing, namely: navigating Islamic teachings, Somali culture, and Swedish norms and creating family practices and relationships that foster strong family ties and support. Third, I situate parents' aspirations for their children in the context of the former's daily experiences of racism and in particular their experiences of marginalization (or epistemic injustice) in their encounters with different institutions working with their children, such as schools. I show, for example, how parents experience mistrust from these institutions and how they in turn also (mis)trust them. I shed light on the impact of these challenges on parents' relationship with their children. I also highlight how parents' aspirations for their children's wellbeing are shaped by their context and daily experiences of marginalization. I end with concluding reflections.

Research context and methodology

The data presented in this chapter is part of an ethnographic research project sponsored by the Swedish Research Council. In 2008, during a field trip to Dubai for my doctoral research, I noticed that a number of Somali-born women were moving to Dubai from Europe and North America because of the challenges they were facing raising their children in their countries of resettlement. These mothers were finding it difficult to raise their children as Muslims, and also felt that their parental capabilities were continually questioned by the institutions that were relevant to the children's lives. This gave me the idea to undertake the much-needed research on the parenting norms, practices, and experiences of Somali mothers and fathers in Sweden and Finland, which I did in the period from 2011 to 2015. This chapter is based on this research, focusing on the findings from the Swedish context.

I conducted in-depth interviews and follow-up interviews with nine mothers in three cities, some of them with the help of my assistants Amina Kasem Noor and Sahra Shukri Mohamoud. I also draw on data collected from six focus group discussions with mothers, fathers, and religious leaders. The focus group discussions with the fathers and religious leaders were conducted by the Public Health researcher Dr Barni Nor, who was hired to work with me on the project. Dr Nor and I also conducted together two focus group discussions with mothers, while I carried out two additional focus group discussions, and numerous informal conversations, with mothers and fathers. Furthermore, Dr Nor and I conducted participant observation of a highly popular educational programme "Better Parenting and Parenting Coach" for Somali parents in Stockholm.[2]

Altogether, 30 mothers took part in this research. They were from Uppsala, Stockholm, and Sundsvall. At the time of the research about half of the mothers had been living in Sweden for more than 20 years, while the other half had been living in the country for less than ten years. Most of the mothers were full-time care providers for their children. About one third worked in the healthcare sector or as interpreters and as teachers. 15 mothers had only elementary school education, two had no schooling, ten had a high school diploma and three had higher education. The age range was between 22 and 60. The mothers had from one to nine children, most of them had between two and six children, and the children were of all ages from seven months to 30 years old. Most of the women (24) were married; four were divorced, and two were widows.

The thirteen fathers who took part in the research were living in Stockholm and had participated in the above-mentioned parental education programme. Four fathers were also imams. All the fathers were married, except for one. They had from one to eleven children and their age range was 32–59. Most of the fathers were employed as interpreters, bus drivers, or had their own business. Only one of them was unemployed. Eight fathers had higher education, four had a high school diploma and one had only elementary school education. About half of them had been over 20 years in Sweden, while the other half had been in the country for less than ten years. In this chapter I focus mainly on the mothers, but in some cases I also refer to the fathers.

Parents' aspirations and child wellbeing

The interviewed parents had multidimensional understanding of the good life that they wanted for their children. This good life was not confined to material accomplishments such as securing a good education and jobs, but also encompassed ethical wellbeing that was primarily grounded in Islamic teachings. In line with White's (2008) findings, the moral dimension of wellbeing, in this case bearing a religious expression, was central for the parents in this study, who often emphasized that no matter how much they cherished their children and struggled for them to have a good education, their children being Muslims was their first priority. Furthermore, being a Muslim was described primarily in moral terms about being kind, respectful, and helping those in need. However, the ethical wellbeing that parents sought for their children also meant learning how to navigate Islam, Somali culture, and Swedish norms in relation to one another, as the three normative systems were relevant to the daily work of raising children.

Children's wellbeing also required, in the parents' views, creating healthy and close parent–children relationships and cooperative spousal relations, both of which entailed changes in family practices. In what follows I will elaborate on parents' understandings of the wellbeing that they sought for their children.

Navigating Islam, Somali culture, and Swedish norms

The interviewed parents spoke of the importance but also of the complexity of navigating the three normative systems that were relevant to the daily work of raising their children: Islamic teachings, Somali culture, and Swedish norms. Parents also differed in the ways they tried to navigate these three systems. For some, Islam and Somali culture were compatible with one another, and raising their children according to their religious norms was of paramount importance, even if this made them visibly different from the larger society. One mother put it as follows:

> We (Somalis) are a people who hold tightly to our religion and culture and we will not abandon them. Many of the people from other Muslim countries do not have as strong a culture as Somalis and they adapt more easily, but for us, Sweden has their culture and it is for them and we will not leave our religion for this. We cannot say to our children to party, drink alcohol, have sex and other things that are counter to our religion and our culture. ... We can go into the society, but we cannot leave our

religion because we follow it strongly. We will leave this earth one day, no one lives forever.

Other parents spoke of how it is necessary to adapt to the society and to let their children be part of the Swedish society, without abandoning their religion. These parents emphasized the importance of learning about the Swedish society and encouraging their children to embrace an identity and a lifeworld that were not confined to being Somalis. As one father said:

> An important thing to have in mind is that our children are no longer only Somali. They are Somali in addition to something. Is this something Swedish? Is it another nationality? One must define this. What I have noticed is that Somali children in Sweden are not only Somalis, of this I am convinced.

In particular, parents who had lived a longer time in Sweden emphasized that it was not possible to live in the country without adapting, as one mother phrased it:

> We live here, and we raise our children here, but we already had our values when we came, and hopefully we will keep them throughout our lives. What will happen is that we will adapt. During the time of the Prophet there was a man who travelled far in order to ask advice from a man. The man answered that he could not answer his question as he did not know the circumstances and the living conditions at the place where the man lived. It is true. I am only referring to the adaptation. It is true that we do not live in our country, we live in another country where different problems can arise, and there are a lot of problems.

Some of the interlocutors, for example, spoke about the problems that arose in situations where some parents were ignorant of the language and culture of the Swedish society and thus their children had to take the lead in navigating the daily encounter of the family with the outer world (see also Phoenix in this volume). In the words of one mother:

> In Sweden it is very important to be open, you must look at how the Swedes are raising their children, you must understand how the rules are. You must know how the school works, if not, it is difficult, then the children ... Sometimes ... a thirteen-year-old child is taking care of everything. When someone calls she is the one who is translating, when a letter comes she is reading it for her mother and father, and that could turn out wrong ... Sometimes there is a cultural clash between the parents and the child and that is not easy. But for me, I have made a great effort to understand the society that we live in. I must understand what my children are a part of, where they are and what they are doing. So, I

gave the freedom to go out and have friends, to socialize with friends with boundaries.

Another mother pointed to the problems encountered by such parents who did not learn the Swedish language: "Imagine, the child has done something, and the parents want to know what happened, and the child gets to be the interpreter. What will the child say?" Therefore, learning the Swedish language and culture were seen as very important strategies for raising children and being better able to work towards the children's wellbeing and stronger ties with them. As one mother said: "You cannot keep the children close if you do not know the language that the children know. So, it would be good for the parents to learn the language, it would make them come closer."

The compatibility between Islamic teachings and Somali cultural norms in raising children was also a point of disagreement among parents. An older woman, a mother and grandmother, argued that the religious tenets on how to raise children were the same as those advocated by Somali culture. The problem, she noted, was that people lacked good knowledge of both their religion and their culture:

> Our religion says that one should not be hard on the children and hit them, it says be soft towards the children. We have a (Somali) saying: Never pass the line for those who are weak. A child cannot ... she is in your hands. Do not be hard on them. A Somali proverb says so. *Inta aamusan lagaa raac.* If you do something towards those that are quiet, you will get back. If they are afraid of telling you off. The culture says that one should protect the weak and be soft and tender. That is originally from the culture.

Other parents differentiated culture from religion. They associated the former with negative parenting practices such as physically disciplining the children. Parents' views on both the cultural and religious norms regarding raising children depended on their own childhood experiences. Parents also differentiated between ideals and actual practices on the ground, whether in relation to Somali culture or Islamic tradition. One woman explained it as follows:

> They (i.e., Somalis in the country of origin in the past) hit their children when they, when a child makes a mistake, then the fathers or the mothers or the cousins ... yes, they hit the children. And it is a system of raising the children in my country, it is not that they hate children, but it is a system that has won ground. But I do not raise my children like that even though I was hit by my parents. I love them and I think, they did it for my sake and not because they hated me or didn't like me, but because they were raised that way themselves, so they raised me the same way. But me, and my generation, I think it is wrong. And to hit the children

does not help the upbringing to become better ... They hit really hard and it is allowed. It was allowed, even that the teachers in the school and the parents, like everyone, it was common that the children were beaten there. But now, even in my home country, even here, we learn that this is not good.

She explained how this way of thinking now has changed "because my religion (Islam) does not allow hitting children, but it is our culture, it won ground and it just continued that way."

Interestingly, learning more about Islam was seen to be a way to help families integrate into Sweden (see Al-Sharmani in this volume). For example, the teacher of the educational parenting programme saw many parallels between new research on child development and Islamic teachings on child-rearing practices. The teacher pointed out, for example, that both Islamic teachings on parenting and modern child development theories emphasized the importance of speaking softly to children, creating a positive atmosphere within the home, and abandoning physical disciplining of children. He quoted a *hadīth* [3] from the Prophet Muhammad on how to raise children, and which reflected the prevalent notion in child psychology which advocates parental communication skills that are dynamic and appropriate to the different stages of their children's development. The *hadīth* says that parents should play with the children and teach them to behave until they are seven; when they are seven they are ready to know the difference between right and wrong, and one should educate them until they are age 14. After 14 one should befriend them, and then let them be after age 21. Moreover, in class he encouraged the parents to change their culturally influenced ways of raising their children by quoting from the Qur'an that God does not change the circumstances if they do not change themselves, and a *hadīth* where the Prophet Muhammad says that God loves it when you attempt to improve.

The parents who took part in this programme were very satisfied as they trusted that it was in line with Islamic teachings and at the same time it equipped them with better parenting skills. The parents reported, for example, that their communication with their children improved. In the ceremony marking the end of the programme, the parents showed their great appreciation, and one mother even said now that she had participated in the programme, she changed her mind about moving with her family to Egypt.

Developing good relationships within the family

Parents put great emphasis on the relational aspects of children's wellbeing, which was also tightly connected to the ethical dimensions. Many saw that their children's relational wellbeing required two important goals to be attained: close and cooperative relations between the two parents as well as healthy and close parent–children relationships. These goals were seen to require changes in family practices both with regard to spousal relationships and parenting.

In the absence of the extended family, the role of both parents as caregivers and guides for their children became even more important. Hence, close and cooperative relationships between fathers and mothers were crucial so that children would learn these values from the parents' example. Also, lacking the support of their extended family, mothers in Sweden needed help from fathers with housework and childcare. This meant that parents taking on more flexible and egalitarian gender roles became crucial for the efforts to raise children and enhance their wellbeing. Some of the parents even argued that cooperative and flexible gender roles were reflective of Somali cultural values as well as Islamic norms, both of which emphasized the importance of family members helping and supporting one another.

Another important strategy to realize children and parents' wellbeing was to foster close ties and relationships among family members and develop a sense of belonging and solidarity within the family, which the parents saw as a central value in both Somali culture and Islam. With the absence of the extended family, it was within the nuclear family that children needed to learn interdependence. Although children also learned interdependence through how their parents connected with relatives across the world, their first-hand experience was mainly with parents and the relatives who happened to live nearby.

Thus, parents sought to teach the children interdependence because they viewed it as important for the wellbeing of children. Traditionally, the Somali extended family functions as a welfare system, and, as one parent put it, "even if you are a grown-up you need your family." They would teach their children that life was a circle and that just as parents nurtured the children, they would need their support when they became old, and then the children would have children who again would support them in old age. Parents would remind their children of how much they went through to raise them in order to teach the children the importance of reciprocity, and for them to remain committed to the family and take care of each other. A good relationship between the parents and the children was seen as crucial in order to teach the children the values that sometimes were referred to as part of a we-culture as opposed to an I-culture, which is how they described the Swedish culture, and particularly the fact that many Swedes let their parents stay in a retirement home was, according to them, symptomatic of this.

Although some parents noted that the circumstances were different in Sweden, and that it might not be possible for their children to take care of them at home, they emphasized the importance of remaining close, and were heartbroken if they saw older people in retirement homes who were rarely visited by their children. The moral dimension of the children's wellbeing was tightly connected to the relational aspects as it was through these family relationships and ties that children were taught about reciprocity, and about the importance of sharing and helping those in need. As one mother expressed it:

I will try to raise my children to tell the truth, respect and love each other like brothers and sisters, that they should have a relationship as siblings, to share everything, and that they share with others as well. And all this is the basis of my religion, Islam. It says in Islam that one should respect the parents, respect others and that one should share. One should not just think: "but this is mine!", one should help those in need. Hence, I bring them up so that my children when they are older also will try to help those who are in need and those who need help.

According to the parents, the understanding of sibling relationships which they wished to inculcate in their children was wider than what was commonly the case in Sweden: "The family belongs together, and the cousins from the father's and mother's side and everyone, they keep together." The concept of parents was also wider and included aunts and uncles and even teachers, who also should be given the same respect as parents. But many of the interviewed parents also agreed that good parent–children relationships required that they depart from some of the common parenting practices in Somali culture. As one mother said:

If you want to say something you can talk with the children instead of saying "no, you can't do that." You have to speak with the children. I think it is better that way. One should not scream, one should take the time and talk with them. In Somalia the mother would say, you must do this or that and we listened. But here this doesn't work. We come from the same country my husband and I and so we raised the children the same way. In Somalia the children listened to their parents, one learned the Qur'an and one could not talk back. Here it is different. We must adapt. Here you cannot say, "you must do as I say." One must talk and come to an agreement.

Parents also noted the changes in their parenting practices as a result of adopting some new norms from the Swedish culture. For example, some parents pointed out that they learned from the Swedish culture the importance of viewing small children as individuals who could have valuable opinions worth listening to. Some of the mothers said they had learned this valuable lesson in Sweden, and they wanted to combine the respect for the elderly that was part of Somali culture with the respect for their children's opinions, which they saw as part of Swedish culture. I talked to a mother and grandmother in Uppsala, who said she tried to convince other Somali mothers in Sweden that children had many thoughts worth listening to, and that it was only because of the way they were raised themselves that they thought otherwise. She remembered how she as a child had many thoughts when growing up in Somalia, but that she was afraid of the grown-ups who would not let her and other children "talk back" as they insisted that it was adults who knew everything as they had more experience. She joked that it felt like she and the other children had a "cap on their mouth". She thought the way the children were taught to relate to those who are older in Somalia was good and bad. When I asked her to explain, she said:

> To respect each other and listen to each other and listen to the grown-ups, they have experience and they know more than you, it is good to listen; that is positive. But sometimes you can see, the child cannot say anything, he cannot question anything, and that is negative. Children have many thoughts and a lot of questions and they can say many good things. And if they cannot say anything, and you always say "no," that is very negative, that is not good.

Another mother, who grew up in Sweden, thought that while maintaining strong family ties was very important, the family could also have too much power over the children, to the detriment of the latter. She said, "In Somalia the family ties are very strong and sometimes it can be very negative also. It can be a power that the family has if it goes overboard. It is about finding the balance."

This mother also described the school and the parents as being two powers and emphasized the importance of communicating well with the teachers instead of only asking the child about the school, which she said was often the case. This way, she explained, children would not get caught up between these two powers.

> In Somalia the parents have the power. They have the power to control their children. They decide which school the children should go to, and the child cannot say: "No, I am not comfortable in this class." "No, I know what is best for you, I am your mother or father." But here in Sweden you cannot say this. The child does not accept it. I also think the combination between the parents and the teachers is the biggest problem. Because the teachers have a lot of influence on the children's lives. If they become two powers, and the teachers think ... the children end up in the middle. But imagine if they could understand each other. It is good to have contact with the children's teacher, that one contacts about how they are doing in school, do you understand what I mean?

She added that she would always first ask the teachers how her child was doing in school so that she first understood the teachers' point of view as this would lead her, in her opinion, to better understand her child's views – her motivation being to have a more informed picture of the issue or the encounter reported by her child. According to her, many parents would get their knowledge of the teachers from the children, and then they would feel accused, as, for instance, the child would tell them that the teachers asked about how they are doing at home. She was slightly critical of other parents who, according to her, would put the child in the middle, but she also thought that the distrust of parents in institutions working with their children was caused by the real threat of the social services taking away the children. She described how she was first met by these institutions with prejudice, but it became easier once she was able to communicate with them well in Swedish, while parents who did not know Swedish and did not have an interpreter were forced to ask the children to help with communication. She wanted the parents and the teachers to cooperate and communicate as adults instead of both asking the children and giving small children responsibilities they could not shoulder.

Suspect parenting: epistemic injustice

Somali parents' aspirations for their children are to be understood in relation to parents' experiences of marginalization in their encounters with institutions working with their children. My interlocutors frequently spoke about being questioned and undermined as parents and communicated a feeling of distrust between them and actors in these institutions. Parents were repeatedly met with suspicion and judgement rather than affirmation. A mother, for example, articulated this problem as follows:

> My kids, when they are in school, if I am an immigrant woman, if something happens, a small thing, it is already a big deal. Because I am a parent who is an immigrant, [I am seen to be someone] who does not know how to educate my child in a good way. That is a great [challenge], it still is, and I do not know when this will change (quoted in Haga, 2015, p.51).

The parents also felt they were not heard by school officials when they tried to report their children's experiences of racism in the school. Parents pointed out that their children would be called 'nigger' in school, usually by other children, and in some cases even by teachers, as reported by some parents. If the children reacted to this by becoming angry, the parents attempted to explain to the teachers the children's reactions. Yet, the teachers would ignore the parents' interpretation of the situation and instead characterize their children as being problematic. Thus, the parents felt that they were perceived by school officials as incapable of interpreting the experiences of the children. As the parents were not viewed as a resource for their children or for the school, their interpretations and meanings were not considered or listened to.

This negative view of their parenting also made them lose legitimacy in the eyes of the children and impacted their relationship, especially when this discourse was highlighted by social services (see also Osman, 2017, p.46). Many parents felt they had completely lost the ability to influence their children and to guide them. Ayaan, one of the women I interviewed, explained this problem:

I have seen it myself. They (parents) cannot speak to the children or, we cannot do anything for the children. Children threaten their parents, "if you do not do this for me, I will tell the social services." They threaten, they use it as a weapon against their parents. It is good if the children listen to their parents. A mother and a father only want what is best for their children.

Ideally, both the parents and institutions want what is best for the children. They have a common interest. If they do not work together, the children's wellbeing suffers. But what can explain the parents' experiences? These experiences are located in the interlocutors' daily realities of racism.

Afro-Swedes, including Somalis, are marginalized in all sectors of Swedish society, such as education, health, housing, and employment (Hübinette, Kawesa and Samson, 2014; see also Salat, 2010). For example, the risk of being unemployed is significantly higher among the higher-educated Afro-Swedes compared to other groups in Sweden with the same education. In addition, Afro-Swedes born in Africa are also overrepresented among the low-income groups (Hübinette, Kawesa and Samson, 2014). Somalis, in particular, have the largest rate of unemployment among the immigrants, a problem which is often linked to their lack of education (Mohme, 2017; Open Society Foundations' At Home in Europe Project, 2014). Moreover, stereotypes of Africa and Africans that date back to the era of colonialization still prevail and affect the everyday lives of people of African origin. However, because the dominating discourse in Sweden denies the existence of racism as an institutional problem, it is difficult for Afro-Swedes to articulate and make sense of their everyday experiences of racism (Hübinette, Kawesa and Samson, 2014; see also Motsieloa, 2003).

Somali parents' encounters with school, social services, and other 'childhood experts' happen in and are part of these racialized relations. I suggest that this everyday racism functions, in particular, through a mechanism in which 'the racialized other' is constructed as a lesser knowing agent; culturalist explanations are given for all the challenges the parents face in the upbringing of their children. But what is at stake when parents' ability to take care of their children's wellbeing is frequently questioned? The parents felt that they were marginalized as inadequate and incapable of good parenting. I argue that, crucially, it was their capacity as knowers that was questioned directly and indirectly in these encounters. In order to analyse this process in which parents were or felt they were questioned by institutions that work with their children, I borrow the term 'epistemic injustice' from the work of the philosopher Miranda Fricker (2007).

Fricker argues that there are two kinds of injustice that can be done to people in their capacity as knowers: testimonial and hermeneutical injustice. Testimonial injustice occurs when prejudices cause a hearer to give less credibility to a speaker's word than he/she rationally deserves. Hermeneutical injustice occurs in a prior stage and is about how some types of injustices are not recognized within the society, as those who experience them do not participate equally in generating social meanings. In such a case it becomes difficult to articulate and understand the experience, and when it is expressed, acknowledgement might be resisted.[4]

Parents in this study experienced epistemic injustice, whether testimonial or hermeneutical, in four distinct ways: they were not perceived as a resource for their children; parents' accounts of their children's experiences of racism in school were not heard and validated by school officials; the children were surrounded with an institutional discourse that promoted a notion of freedom which excluded parents' guidance of their children; and there was distrust between the parents and the school officials. In what follows, I will elaborate on these experiences of epistemic injustice.

Parents felt that teachers did not view them as a resource for their children, but rather as a liability: they experienced epistemic injustice as they were judged to lack knowledge, both of the Swedish language and of how to raise their children well, simply because of their religious and racial background. One mother explained this challenge as follows:

> Poor you with the hijab and everything. In the Swedish society, they assume you can do nothing if you are a Muslim. "Of course I can", you have to constantly say: of course I can. I am a resource. You must change this way. Life is more than this. We will be here; our kids will be here. We need to change this idea (quoted in Haga, 2015, p.52).

Another aspect of the epistemic injustice that parents encountered was related to the schools' discourse on children's freedom, which assumed that Muslim parents did not want their children to be independent. Children were often told by teachers that they were free, and that their parents could not mistreat them. For example, a mother told me that her son was given the phone number of the police by the school in case his parents mistreated him, and she asked me, "why do they assume we abuse our children?"

The parents emphasized that they wanted the same things that most parents would aspire to for their children. This institutional discourse that depicted Somali parents as controlling, interestingly, did not take into account that personal independence is an important value in Somali culture (see Haga, 2015). Furthermore, it did not pay attention to its possible detrimental effect on Somali parents' relationships with their children. As one mother noted,

> We have asked young people what the meaning of 'free' is. "Free?! Well, I can come home any time I want, I can go from home at any time, I'm an adult." What happens with the education? Be free, but I say, being free does not mean you're free. It's about free with responsibility. That means a lot, education is a part. You have all your life in front of you. If you destroy your future today, who will push your development forward later?

You are small now and have to listen to me, I usually say. So, what you can say now is that the way the word 'free' is used in Sweden is wrong, we do not agree with this. If you want to use freedom (free) in this context, the word 'liability' must be linked to it. To explain that education and knowledge are in focus. And from our side, it is also important with the Muslim doctrine and religion, to worship God and pray the five daily prayers, make it mandatory, do not worry people and much more. However, when using the word 'free' in the context of young people, which leads to the fact that they do not get good results in school and do not enter university is one thing. That is what people have problems with.

As the parents were not viewed as a resource for their children or for the school, their interpretations and meanings were not considered or listened to. This negative view of their parenting impacted their relationship with their children. Many parents felt they had completely lost the ability to influence their children and to guide them as I have shown above.

When teachers highlight children's right to freedom, their underlying assumption is the children's right to be free from the power of parents' cultural values. But what is left unacknowledged by the teachers is that their own views and perceptions of what constitutes a good life for the children are also shaped by a broader normative framework that also has its power on the children's lives. Thus, the communication between the teachers and parents is hampered although both parents and teachers seem to want the children to be independent and responsible and have a good life. But the concerns of the parents are: how can their children make informed decisions about how to balance different normative frameworks within their own lives? How can they be free with responsibility, and understand the consequences for their own lives and their future?

As a result of the above-mentioned challenges, parents felt distrusted by school officials. The parents themselves also experienced great fear of their children being taken away from them. This fear influenced all their encounters and communication with institutions and as one mother said: "When persons feel threatened, they will defend themselves. ... It does not matter what you say to the person, she will only think that you are accusing."

It is in light of these experiences of marginalization that parents' aspirations for their children and their changing parenting practices become more understandable. Thus, navigating dynamically the role of Islamic teachings, Somali cultural norms, and Swedish societal values on child rearing becomes an important strategy in parents' daily efforts to care for and raise their children. Many parents, accordingly, seek to inculcate the importance of close family bonds – a key Somali cultural value – in their children while at the same time learning from the experience of living in Sweden the importance of nurturing the autonomy of their children and valuing their opinions. Additionally, flexible and cooperative gender roles for both parents become part of the parental strategy to overcome the marginalization resulting from their racial and cultural othering, particularly in the absence of an extended family and the support it normally provided in the home country. Parents, however, as shown previously, were differentiated in their perspectives and strategies.

Conclusion

In this chapter I have shown how the interviewed Somali parents had a multi-dimensional understanding of the good life they aspired to for their children. This good life was not confined to material accomplishments such as securing a good education and jobs but also encompassed ethical wellbeing that was primarily grounded in Islamic teachings. The ethical wellbeing that parents sought for their children also meant learning how to navigate Islam, Somali culture, and Swedish norms in relation to one another. Parents, for example, wanted their children to become successful members of Swedish society while holding on to Islamic and Somali values. They emphasized the importance of teaching children respect for the elderly in the family as well as in the larger community. They aspired for their children to find a balance between freedom and responsibility and to be autonomous while valuing family relationships based on reciprocity and interdependent rights and responsibilities. Actualizing children's wellbeing required, in the parents' views, their creating healthy and close parent–children relationships and cooperative spousal relations, both of which entailed changes in family practices. For example, learning how to communicate with their children and supporting their autonomy was highlighted as a new parenting practice that became necessary in the new context.

Somali parents' aspirations for their children and their changing parenting practices were situated in the larger Swedish context where these parents were experiencing everyday racism and marginalization in their encounters with institutions working with their children. Parents experienced being othered by a racist discourse adopted by these institutions that defined them as incapable parents without knowledge of how to raise their children. They experienced what I call 'epistemic injustice'.

I employed the concept of wellbeing to take my analysis a step further from focusing only on the marginalization of racialized groups, in this case Somali parents, to examining their aspirations for their children and the experiences, values, and perspectives that underlie these aspirations. A shift towards wellbeing can, therefore, be a way to work for epistemic justice as it highlights and validates how parents understand the wellbeing of their children. What is needed in future research is to focus on how the children understand wellbeing themselves (see Ismail in this volume on the Finnish context).

There may be notable differences between Somali and Swedish cultures. However, the problem is not the existence of these differences, but rather how differences are commonly misnamed, misunderstood, and unnecessarily emphasized in the encounters with Swedish institutions. A focus on Somali parents' aspirations for their children's wellbeing enables us to understand these differences in a more nuanced and dynamic fashion. It will also help us resist reductionist explanations attributing challenges that immigrant parents may confront with their children, often as a result of marginalization and discrimination, to their culture. If the aspirations of immigrant parents are in focus, it may facilitate better communication between these parents and the institutions that are in charge of their children's education and welfare; it may help parents and these different institutional actors find common ground and, ideally, learn from each other.

I will end with a quote by Audre Lorde and with the aspiration that we can create a more epistemically just society and overcome divisions with greater understanding and communication, as "It is not our differences that divide us. It is our inability to recognize, accept, and celebrate those differences" (Lorde, 2001, p.315). Or, perhaps, it is most of all our inability to listen. My aspiration is that my research is seen as an attempt to listen and an encouragement to listen, more than an attempt to explain. What I have heard when speaking to these mothers is that they have many experiences and much valuable knowledge of the specific challenges of raising their children in Sweden.

Notes

1 I refer to the interviewed mothers and fathers as "Somali parents" because they identify themselves as Somali, and this is what they have in common and what is in focus in this chapter. This does not exclude the possibility that some also identify as Swedish-Somali, Swedish, or Muslim parents in different contexts.
2 The programme is led by Ismail Miad, who has a master's degree in human resource development and a practitioner qualification in neuro-linguistic programming (NLP). The programme took place in a mosque in Stockholm and was given in the Somali language. The parenting course started with a small group of mothers seeking knowledge, but grew quickly, and soon it also included a growing number of fathers.
3 A *hadīth* is a saying attributed to the Prophet Muhammad.
4 An example of this is the concept of sexual harassment and how the participation of the victims in generating social meaning through the #MeToo Movement has made sexual harassment more visible and easier to express.

Bibliography

Abrashi, A., Sander, Å. and Larsson, G., 2015. Islamophobia in Sweden. National Report 2015. In: E. Bayrakli and F. Hafez, eds. 2015. *European Islamophobia Report 2015*. Istanbul: Seta, pp.492–526. Available at: https://www.islamophobia europe.com/reports/2015/en/EIR_2015_SWEDEN.pdf [Accessed August 13, 2018].

Eliassi, B., 2006. Diskriminerande föreställningar inom socialtjänsten [Discriminatory perceptions in social services]. In: M. Kamali, ed. 2006. *Den segregerande integrationen. Om social sammanhållning och dess hinder*. Stockholm: Fritzes, pp.251–294.

Equality ombudsman, 2013. *Forskning om diskriminering av muslimer i Sverige: En översikt över forskning publicerad vid universitet och högskolor i Sverige sedan år 2003* [Research on discrimination of Muslims in Sweden: An overview of research published at universities and colleges in Sweden since 2003]. Stockholm: Oxford Research. Available at: https://www.do.se/globalassets/publikationer/rapport-fors kning-diskriminering-muslimer-sverige.pdf [Accessed July 10, 2018].

Fricker, M., 2007. *Epistemic Injustice: Power and the Ethics of Knowing.* Oxford: Oxford University Press.

Gardell, M. and Muftee, M., 2017. Islamophobia in Sweden. National Report 2017. In: E. Bayrakli and F. Hafez, eds. 2017. *European Islamophobia Report 2017.* Istanbul: Seta, pp.618–646. Available at: http://www.islamophobiaeurope.com/wp-content/uploads/2018/04/Sweden.pdf [Accessed August 13, 2018].

Haga, R., 2009. *Tradition as Resource: Somali Women Traders Facing the Realities of Civil War.* PhD. Uppsala University.

Haga, R., 2015. 'Freedom has destroyed the Somali family.' Somali parents' experiences of epistemic injustice, and its influence on their raising of Swedish Muslims. In: M. Sedgwick, ed. 2015. *Making European Muslims: Religious Socialization Among Young Muslims in Scandinavia and Western Europe.* New York: Routledge, pp.39–56.

Haga, R., 2016. Storytelling as a way to reconnect and co-create spiritual contexts: Conversations with five Swedish-Somali mothers. In: V. Reimer, ed. 2016. *Angels on Earth: Mothering in Religious and Spiritual Contexts.* Canada: Demeter Press, pp.209–229.

Hübinette, T., Kawesa, V. and Samson, B., 2014. *Afrofobi: En kunskapsöversikt över afrosvenskars situation i dagens Sverige* [Afrophobia: A knowledge review about the situation of Afro-Swedes in today's Sweden]. Stockholm: Multicultural Centre. Available at: http://mkcentrum.se/wp-content/uploads/2014/12/Afrofobi-20140203-f%C3%B6r-webben.pdf [Accessed August 13, 2018].

Kamali, M., 2002. *Kulturkompetens i socialt arbete: Om socialarbetarens och klientens kulturella bakgrund.* Stockholm: Carlsson bokförlag.

Lorde, A., 2001. Our difference is our strength. In: B. Ryan, ed. 2001. *Identity Politics in the Women's Movement.* New York: New York University Press, pp.315–319.

Mohme, G., 2017. Somali Swedes' reasons for choosing a Muslim-profiled school – Recognition and educational ambitions as important influencing factors. *Journal of School Choice*, 11(2), pp.239–257.

Motsieloa, V., 2003. *"Det måste vara någonting annat": En studie om barns upplevelser av rasism i vardagen* ["It must have been something else": A study of children's experiences of everyday racism]. Stockholm: Save the Children Sweden. Available at: https://resourcecentre.savethechildren.net/sites/default/files/documents/2605.pdf [Accessed August 27, 2018].

Open Society Foundations' At Home in Europe Project, 2014. *Somalis in Malmö.* Somalis in European cities. New York: Open Society Foundations. Available at: https://www.opensocietyfoundations.org/reports/somalis-malmo [Accessed July 13, 2018].

Osman, F., 2017. *Ladnaan – Evaluation of a Culturally Tailored Parenting Support Program to Somali-born Parents.* PhD. Karolinska Institutet.

Roald, A.-S., 2013. Majority versus minority: Governmentality and Muslims in Sweden. *Religions*, 4(1), pp.116–131.

Salat, O.A., 2010. *Settling in? A Case Study of Somalian Refugees Living in Stockholm, Sweden.* PhD. University of Birmingham.

Statistics Sweden, 2017. Population Statistics. 31 December 2017. Available at: http://www.scb.se/en/finding-statistics/statistics-by-subject-area/population/population-composition/population-statistics/ [Accessed July 13, 2018].

White, S.C., 2008. *But What is Wellbeing? A Framework for Analysis in Social and Development Policy and Practice.* Paper for Regeneration and Wellbeing: Research into Practice, University of Bradford, 24–25 April 2008. University of Bath, Centre for Development Studies. Available at: http://staff.bath.ac.uk/ecsscw/But_what_is_Wellbeing.pdf [Accessed July 13, 2018].

8 Transnational Finnish–Somali families and children's wellbeing

Abdirashid A. Ismail

Introduction

The goal of this chapter is to study the impacts of the transnational engagements of the Somali parents in the diaspora on the wellbeing of their children living with them. The chapter will do so mainly by examining the perspectives of Finnish-Somali youth and relating their views to perceptions and experiences of Finnish-Somali parents. The central emphasis is on how transnational engagements of the parents affect both the stability of the family (conflict/divorce) and family resources (time and money). The basic assumption of the study is that family stability and resources, which are central to child wellbeing (Thomson, Hanson and McLanahan, 1994), are affected by the family's transnational life.

During the past two decades, a growing number of studies have researched the daily practices and experiences of transnational families (Baldassar and Merla, 2014; Baldassar, et al., 2014; Goulbourne, et al., 2010). Bryceson and Vuorela (2002, p.3) defined transnational families as "families that live some or most of the time separated from each other, yet hold together and create something that can be seen as a feeling of collective welfare and unity, namely 'familyhood', even across national borders". Research on the transnational family has also investigated the consequences of living apart on parental and spousal relationships (Dreby, 2006; 2010; Schmalzbauer, 2004; Pribilsky, 2004). Specifically, some authors have looked at transnational motherhood (Parreñas, 2001; Hondagneu-Sotelo and Avila, 1997) and others have emphasized transnational fatherhood (Fresnoza-Flot, 2014; Kilkey, 2014; Pribilsky, 2004). Literature on transnational fatherhood is relatively scarce and new (Dreby, 2006). Existing research findings show that migrant fathers put their focus on providing economically for their families. Migrant mothers, on the other hand, were found not only to communicate more with their children but they also were more generous in remitting to their children (Mazzucato, 2014; Fresnoza-Flot, 2014). Research findings also indicate that in general the negative impact of the father's migration on children's wellbeing (i.e., educational challenges, emotional difficulties, and health problems) is less harsh compared to the mother's migration (Mazzucato, 2014).

This literature has also studied the influence of living in a transnational family on children (Dreby, 2010; Parreñas, 2005; Suárez-Orozco and Suárez-Orozco, 2001). A common goal of these studies was to understand the impacts of living apart on family lives when one or both parents migrate and leave their children behind; children, in particular, have been found to face serious challenges (Zontini, 2010; Suárez-Orozco and Suárez-Orozco, 2001). Valentina Mazzucato (2014) provides a thorough review of these studies (see also Mazzucato and Schans, 2011; Zontini, 2010). However, children may be impacted directly or indirectly by the transnational engagement of their parents even when they live together with them. This aspect of transnationalism, which has not been at the centre of most previous studies, will be explored in this chapter.

Most previous studies have focused on the impact of Latin American parents who migrated to the United States and left their children behind, while the increasing trends in transnational families in other migrant-sending areas, such as Sub-Saharan Africa, are largely ignored (Mazzucato and Schans, 2011). By studying Somalis in Finland, this chapter intends to fill this gap. In addition, the chapter builds on and contributes to the growing body of literature on transnational Somali families (Al-Sharmani and Ismail, 2017; Tiilikainen, 2017; Hautaniemi, 2011; Mohme, 2014; Al-Sharmani, 2010; Horst, 2006).

In this chapter, transnationalism is understood as a process in which immigrants generate and maintain multidimensional social relations with their families and kin residing outside their country of settlement. In this definition, the intensity and diversity of their relationship with relatives is in the focus (Basch, Glick Schiller and Szanton Blanc, 1994, pp.7–8). In addition, as Alejandro Portes, Luis Guarnizo and Patricia Landolt (1999) have stressed, transnational involvement of immigrants can primarily be understood as socio-cultural, economic, and political activities of individual actors. However, although the perceptions and experiences of individual actors are central to my analysis, I locate these activities within the context of the family because this individual "is embedded within the family. Such an individual originates, continues along the road of life, and sees their social being within the context of family of birth and family of creation scattered across physical spaces and memorial times" (Goulbourne, et al., 2010, p.10). Furthermore, transnational engagements by immigrant family members are more than just physical movements by individuals or exchange of goods. As noted above, family transnationalism also comprises a range of other border-transcending social relations that link family members despite the cross-border separation (Goulbourne, et al., 2010; Basch, Glick Schiller and Szanton Blanc, 1994).

Parental involvement has a positive impact on various dimensions of child wellbeing. For instance, educational success is positively associated with parental involvement (Jeynes, 2005; Hoover-Dempsey and Sandler, 1995). Particularly, money and time are two key resources in parental involvement that enhance children's wellbeing (Thomson, Hanson and McLanahan, 1994, p.222). Studies have also linked children's wellbeing to family stability

(Amato, 1993). In the literature, there are various definitions of family stability, but in this chapter the family is considered a stable one in a situation where both profound and prolonged marital conflict and critical change in family structure (divorce) are absent (Baldridge, 2011, pp.1–2). I am not suggesting that divorce is always detrimental to child wellbeing, but I have chosen to analyse particular cases of divorce and marital conflict and how participants perceived them to be connected to the wellbeing or ill-being of children and youth.

In this chapter wellbeing of children and youth is understood as a dynamic and multidimensional concept which describes their quality of life and which takes into consideration children's status both now and in future life. By studying child wellbeing, the chapter brings forward youth's perspectives, but also considers parents' views and experiences (OECD, 2009).

Specifically, this chapter will utilize the conceptual framework on wellbeing developed by Sarah C. White (2008; 2010. See the introductory chapter of this volume.) In the logic of that framework, child wellbeing has material, relational, and ethical dimensions. Regarding the material dimension, this chapter will give particular attention to how children's wellbeing, such as their educational performance and their leisure time, is affected by their parents' transnational practices as the latter cut into family resources, time, and income. Concerning the relational dimension, the focus will be the parent–child relationship as well as the relationship parent and children have with their transnational family members and how these relationships impact the children's wellbeing. Finally, regarding the ethical dimension, the chapter will consider how Islamic values and societal norms inform the interlocutors' perceptions of how parents' transnational behaviour, i.e., spending their income and time, is related to the children's wellbeing. I will focus, in particular, on the negative implications of certain practices. I do so because these practices may have serious but less well understood implications for the wellbeing of children in the countries of resettlement.

The chapter is organized as follows. First I present the research background. This is followed by an overview of the transnational practices of Finnish-Somali parents. I then proceed with a section on the influences of the parental transnational practices on child wellbeing. This is followed by a section on the impact of the father's absence from the family life on child wellbeing. Then I end with a conclusion.

Research background

Somalis in Finland

In 2015, the number of foreign language speakers in Finland was 329,562 out of a total population of 5,487,308. Since the early 1990s, a large group of Somali asylum seekers have been arriving in Finland. In 2015, Somalis were the third largest foreign language speaking group in the country, after

Russians and Estonians. More than 60% of the 17,871 Somalis were 24 years old or younger. Gender-wise, close to 48% (8,521) were female and over 52% (9,350) male. A remarkably large number of the Finnish-Somalis, around three quarters, live in the Uusimaa region, particularly in Greater Helsinki (Statistics Finland, 2016).

Somalis in Finland face a great number of challenges. Adults face a harsh situation in the labour market. Their children have the highest school dropout rate and least educational achievements compared to other migrant communities (Kilpi, 2010). Identity crises and lack of a sense of belonging are also major problems among the Somali youth and children (Open Society Foundations, 2013). Notable difficulties within families, most of which also tend to have a large number of children, are also reported. A significant number of the children (38% in 2012) are raised by single mothers (Helminen and Pietiläinen, 2014).

Data and method

For this chapter,[1] I will principally draw on data from four focus groups for youth, but also on data from 22 individual interviews with parents and four focus group discussions with adults.[2] As only a few of the participants in the adult focus groups were not parents, I therefore use the term parents instead of adults.

Of the youth focus groups, with a total of 33 participants, two were organized for girls and two for boys. 17 of the participants were female and 16 were male. 28 participants were between the ages of 15 and 18 and five were in their early and mid-twenties. 32 were single and one had already formed his family. Out of the 33, 19 were high school students, six were lower secondary school students, one was studying a combination of vocational training and high school, one was studying at an adult high school, another was studying at a higher education institution, two were employed, and another three were neither students nor employed. 29 were born in Finland and four in places other than Finland. The married one lived with his wife and the rest with their parents/siblings.

Among the 22 individual interviewees, nine were mothers and 13 fathers. Among the nine mothers, six were married and three divorcees. Among the fathers, there were eight married and five divorcees. The average age of mothers and fathers was about 32 and 43 years respectively. 14 parents were relatively well educated with a minimum of vocational training and maximum of an MA degree. At the time of the interview, two mothers and two fathers were unemployed. Two fathers and one mother were part-time employees, one was a stay-at-home mother and another mother was a student. The rest were in fulltime work.

Four focus groups (two for women and two for men), with a total of 29 participants, 13 women and 16 men, were organized for adults. Overall, participants were between 26 and 68 years old. Most of them were married, while there were more women than men in the divorced group. Regarding their educational status, there were a few with a postgraduate degree and some with little formal schooling, but most of them had some tertiary education. 15 were employed, five were students and the rest were unemployed, stay-at-home mothers, pensioners, or did not provide information on their employment status.

Data collections were conducted from September 2013 to July 2016 and the interlocutors were recruited through personal networks and organizations. I interviewed the two adult male focus groups, four youth focus groups, and the adult male individuals, while interviews with the adult women (focus groups and individuals) were conducted by Mulki Al-Sharmani.

Various mechanisms for recruiting participants, such as use of social networks, snowball sampling, and approaching people in public spaces, were employed to ensure the participants were diverse. All interviews were conducted in Somali and lasted between about one and three hours. All interviews, except one individual interview, were recorded and all recorded interviews, except one focus group, were transcribed.

Transnational practices of Finnish-Somali parents

Finnish-Somalis are involved in extensive kin-based transnational practices (Al-Sharmani and Ismail, 2017; Tiilikainen, 2017; Hautaniemi, 2011). This is a common feature for other Somali diasporic groups as well (Mohme, 2014; Al-Sharmani, 2010; Horst, 2006).

The transnational practices of Finnish-Somali parents could be divided into two broad categories. The first is kin-based transnational practices. These practices (i.e., communication, holidays and other visits, and remittances) are primarily motivated by the interest of immediate family in Finland or the needs of their kin residing outside Finland. The second type is non-kin-based transnational practices. Here some parents engage in transnational activities that are not primarily motivated by the interest of family in Finland or relatives elsewhere. However, the boundaries between these two practices are not clear cut.

Although all our interlocutors were engaged in these practices, there were gendered and generational differences. For instance, children, compared to their parents, were less involved in sending remittances and communicating with family members in Africa. In addition, both male and female interviewees highlighted that Somali women were more responsive to the financial needs of their relatives in Africa.

In some situations, a mother and children might move to a third country to seek a presumably religiously and culturally appropriate environment and better educational opportunities, such as Islamic education and education where the medium of instruction is either English or Arabic, for their children. It is predominantly mothers who engage in this practice (Ismail, 2016).

Finnish-Somalis also seek employment and establish businesses in Somalia or elsewhere. Some of them are also directly involved in Somali politics (Ismail, 2011). Some of these practices can be considered kin-based activities, as the main motive for the father's absence could be to provide for his family. These practices are usually male dominated and require a father's long-term travel and generate his absence from the family life. For convenience, I call this 'fathers' long-term travels'.

Finnish-Somalis also engage in other transnational practices where the interests and needs of the family in Finland or relatives are not the main incentives. Our interlocutors pointed out three non-kin-based transnational activities – investing in property or business, *fadhi-ku-dirir*, and *khat* chewing. The last two activities are undertaken by fathers while they physically remain in Finland. Investing in property or business is a practice by some parents, both fathers and mothers, where they buy properties or business shares mainly in the Horn of Africa. In this case, contrary to previously discussed fathers' long-term travels, they may pay a short visit to Africa for conducting business transactions, or others may represent them, but long-term absence from the family is not needed. Although in general, family goals can possibly be the main drivers of investing in property or business elsewhere, our interlocutors considered it detrimental to the wellbeing of the Finnish-Somali children. *Fadhi-ku-dirir* (meaning literally, "fighting one-another while seated") is a custom for some Somali men, who meet in cafés and heatedly debate Somali politics and clan-related issues. According to Doug McGill, who has observed *fadhi-ku-dirir* in Minneapolis, "instead of fighting to the death, they '*fadhi-ku-dirir*'. They order shots of espresso, sit across coffee tables from one another, and hurl rhetorical ordnance for hours at a time" (McGill, 2006). One reason for *fadhi-ku-dirir* could be that some of these men are unemployed and just want to kill time for what they see as a good cause – i.e., defending clan dignity and interest. Others are employed and partially for that reason *fadhi-ku-dirir* is typically conducted in the evenings.

I consider *fadhi-ku-dirir* as a transnational activity because participants primarily discuss Somalia-related issues and, in addition, before they meet, participants collect relevant information from social media, the Somali websites, and informed relatives and friends in Somalia or elsewhere. Here I follow scholars who consider reading newspapers from and keeping in touch with politics in the country of origin as a transnational political activity (Snel, Engbersen and Leerkes, 2006).[3]

Khat chewing is another transnational practice for some Finnish-Somali men. *Khat* is a plant (*Catha edulis*) native to East Africa and Yemen that releases a stimulant when its narcotic leaves are chewed. Some Somalis even in the diaspora, particularly men, chew it and spend a considerable amount of money and time on the consumption. Previous research found that in the UK Somali migrants chewed *khat* three days a week on average, six hours and 2.5 bundles per session. In 2005, before *khat* was banned, a bundle in the UK used to cost between £4 and £6 (Patel, Wright and Gammampila, 2005). The price is much higher in the context where *khat* is illegal (Osman and Söderbäck, 2011, p.215). Furthermore, traditional social rules that regulated *khat* use and minimized its socioeconomic consequence in pre-civil war Somalia

(Patel, Wright and Gammampila, 2005, p.1) are not observed in the diaspora, which may increase the socioeconomic impact of *khat* chewing on the family.

Although *khat* use has probably been less prevalent among Finnish-Somalis compared to those in the UK and other Nordic countries, there was growing concern about *khat* use within the community before 2014 when the UK banned it. Presumably the ban has reduced the inflow of *khat* into Finland.

Khat is mostly consumed in a group in specific cafés and venues devoted to chewing *khat,* often called *mafrish,* as well as private homes. I consider *khat* chewing as a transnational activity. Here I follow scholars who considered consuming nostalgic goods imported from countries of origin such as traditional food and clothing as transnational because it is a "way of maintaining cultural traditions from the home country" (Orozco, et al., 2005, p.12). I do so because some chewers believe that their practice supports sustaining the Somali culture (Patel, Wright and Gammampila, 2005, p.45).[4] In addition, like the participants in *fadhi-ku-dirir, khat* chewers at consumption meetings often discuss Somalia-related issues.

Somali parents' transnational engagement and child wellbeing

Almost all participants believed that in general transnational engagements are positive and have certain advantages for the family wellbeing. From the youth's perspective, parental transnational engagement positively influences child wellbeing by, for instance: enhancing their social network (e.g., they cultivate close relationship with relatives); improving their personal character (e.g., it improves their empathy towards others and thus enhances one's self-esteem); enhancing their awareness and information (e.g., they gain updates about their parents' home country and other Somali-populated regions of the world); and providing them with opportunities to travel and spend holidays elsewhere when they visit relatives with their parents. This section, however, examines the perceived negative effects of transnational practices, in particular, how remittances and investments, fathers' long-term travels, and *fadhi-ku-dirir* and *khat* chewing would divert meagre parental resources from children's use and how these engagements would generate family instability.

Remittances and investments

For almost all young respondents, the small amount remitted to a family member did not directly impact their wellbeing. For example, a high school student voiced this point of view as follows:

> My mom used to pay this one and two hundred euros, even when I was born, it is almost the same, and I lose nothing from that. But if something big happens and a large amount of money is needed, really in that case they (children) will feel it. (18-year-old female, focus group, May 2015)

Most of the young interviewees believed that large remittances to relatives and the practice of making investments such as building houses or establishing businesses elsewhere would significantly reduce the amount of money available for the children's needs. In addition, many young interlocutors believed that in some situations remittances might generate marital conflicts and thus would indirectly affect child wellbeing. This mainly happened in situations where families were facing financial challenges and one of the parents was still committed to remitting to relatives. As a 17-year-old high school female student put it: "It is possible … that one parent, or the father, is considering about his mom (to send money to), the wife would say 'no, we have to consider our family first'! That can possibly generate conflict."

So, although the youth had a positive attitude towards remittances to relatives, they thought that remittance is problematic when it creates a burden on family and generates marital conflict.

There is a relational dimension to remittance sending because by generating marital conflict, which sometimes results in divorce, it reduces fathers' physical and emotional availability for their children. It also has an ethical dimension. For instance, young respondents' views on remittances (e.g., whether sending remittances was justified on the basis of the needs of the recipient or parents needed to consult one another) were mainly informed by religious values and cultural norms. In addition, the main reason that investments were perceived as predominantly negative relates to the ethical dimension because the caregiving obligation towards extended family attached to the remittance is not present in the case of investment. Therefore, investment is perceived as neither useful for a Finnish-Somali family nor necessarily helpful for needy family members elsewhere. For instance, according to a young interviewee, this care dimension was present even if the amount remitted was large. She highlighted several contexts in which a large amount of money was needed to support a relative, including a situation where a sick person in Somalia needed help for medical treatment in a foreign country and concluded: "You (the child) might feel bad because you cannot get new shoes, but you need to understand you don't need these new shoes as much as the (sick) person in the hard situation needs (medical treatment)" (18-year-old female, focus group, May 2015). Again, these perceptions are apparently informed by the Islamic teachings that encourage helping the needy, particularly relatives, as well as traditional kinship rules that make kin-relations a base for social welfare.

Like the youth, most parents perceived that small remittances and other financial contributions to needy relatives were not detrimental to children's wellbeing. They also agreed, however, that in some situations remittances may become problematic. For instance, a father in a focus group discussion observed how Somali parents, both fathers and mothers, were willing to support their relatives, even at the expense of their children. He referred to Somali parents, who unlike the mainstream parents were not engaged in the practice of giving weekly pocket money to their children and concluded that "our people don't have this kind of things for the kids, they only think about Somalia and the relatives".

The experiences of the parents support the youth's view on the impact of large remittances on family stability. For example, the second marriage of 41-year-old Beelwade, a father of four, broke up because of conflicts with his wife over his obligations towards his relatives. At one point, after five years of his marriage, he had to send 1,000 dollars to a female cousin to escape to Sweden from the conflict in Somalia. However, his wife was not happy with it. His cousin migrated to Sweden and at one time wanted to visit Finland for a few days and asked him to host her, as he was the only relative she had in Finland. His wife refused and this led to an open conflict between the two. This coincided with the death of his older brother who left a large family – a wife and six children in a Horn of Africa country – who turned to rely on him for their survival, along with other relatives in need of help. Beelwade started sending a considerable amount of money every month to his relatives. These factors created marital conflict that eventually resulted in their divorce.

Both mothers and fathers also noted that lack of prior consultation between the spouses about when, how much, and to whom money was to be sent was another reason why remittances created marital conflicts. In fact, one of the mothers in a focus group discussion claimed that 80% of the Somali women made decisions about remitting to relatives without prior consultation with their husbands. As she put it, "Someone (who is in need of her help) is talking to me on the telephone, so I have to say yes or no (make a decision)".

Marital conflicts over remittances also arose when one spouse felt injustice about how they were distributed between the families of both spouses. As one of the male participants in a focus group discussion noted, "when one of the spouses says I will send 700 dollars to my family and 200 to your family". This is an example of those situations where kin-based transnational activities, though contributing to the wellbeing of the family, conflict with an important ethical value, fairness. On the other hand, couples who succeeded in managing family time and finance enjoyed strong marriages and family stability, even at times of serious challenges (Al-Sharmani and Ismail, 2017, p.46).

Some parents pointed out that remittances became a serious problem when parents failed to observe and prioritize the needs that they were facing in a given context. A father pointed out that some parents did not give proper consideration to their children's needs. He stressed the immorality and unfairness of sending money to a young and healthy family member, who can survive without it, at the expense of the children. Emphasizing the ethical dimensions of remittance, he quoted the religious instruction that says "*ibda' bi-man ta'uul* – begin with your dependants" and explained that grandparents and children are to be given first priority.

Long-term travel

Youth participants highlighted that certain transnational practices by fathers (Somali politics, conducting business or working abroad) required long-term travel that was regarded harmful to the wellbeing of the family in general, and that of children in particular, because these transnational commitments considerably decreased the parental time available for the family. A high school student, talking about the impact of the absences of her father, who had business abroad and travelled extensively, described how hard it was not only for her mum who "had to do everything alone" but also for the siblings:

> Yeah, it affects the wellbeing because I feel like my dad is not home … clearly things are not right, so it is either my sister is not home, like my brothers are like late outside … It does affect our family, especially my (younger) sister, when my dad is not home she does not do her homework or like she doesn't really care about school. When he is home she does care about her homework, I feel like she wants her dad to be part of her … (17-year-old female, focus group, May 2015).

Here she emphasizes how her father's absence was a source of many ills in their family. Her mother suffers due to lack of support in household tasks and chores. The children are suffering due to lack of supervision and support. In the discussions she conveyed that all members of the family needed her father's presence.

Youth participants also mentioned that, due to their long-term absence, some fathers may take a second wife. They noted that this practice would further result in more absence by the fathers as they took on other responsibilities because of the second marriage, especially if new children were born from this marriage. In addition to diverting the father's time, this also fuelled family instability.

The youth believed their relationship with their absent fathers would not be negatively impacted if they were informed about the reason for his absence and it was justified. For instance, a high school male student noted how it was all right with children if their father went abroad for work to help the family, and not for his own interests. This is one of the situations where the boundary between transnational kin- and non-kin-based practices is somewhat fuzzy. Depending on its influence on the family wellbeing, father's long-term travel is perceived as kin- or non-kin-based transnational practice. It is the ethical dimension attached to it that makes the difference. Here, as the cases above illustrate, the father's absence was acceptable as long as his absence was perceived as the best way to meet his religiously and culturally informed father/husband role in the overall family wellbeing.

Conversely, if his absence was perceived as not useful for the family, the case was different. An 18-year-old high school female student in one of the youth focus groups reported that her own father, although employed in Finland, tried to establish his own business in Somalia, which necessitated his travelling frequently to Somalia. She was not happy with this situation because she believed that her father's absence was unnecessary as he already had an opportunity to work in Finland. Furthermore, for her, her father's unnecessary absence from the family would potentially threaten the family's stability.

Parents' experiences also show these practices generate family instability. For instance, Bile, a 47-year-old father of four, was married twice and both marriages ended in divorce. His first marriage was a happy one before he became heavily engaged in Somali politics. His first wife, mother of his four children, was not pleased with that because it required him to travel frequently. This became a source of tension between the two. One day he informed his wife about his intension to travel to Africa, but this time his wife made up her mind and warned him that it would be the end of their family. However, Bile, believing that he would be able to change her mind upon his return, departed. He was wrong, and that was the end of his first marriage. From the family perspective, this kind of transnational practice is not justifiable and it is considered negative as it generates the father's absence without contributing to family wellbeing.

The case of Saruuro, a 34-year-old divorced mother of eight, substantiates how an absent father's marriage to another wife would impact family resources and stability. Her husband, who was working in another European country, got married to another wife in that country. Although her main issue was that he took another wife without even letting her know, she was also annoyed that his role in the family, particularly regarding child rearing, had dramatically decreased. They finally divorced.

Fadhi-ku-dirir *and* khat

In addition to travel, young participants highlighted a number of other activities that leave fathers absent from family life even while they are present in Finland. For instance, working long hours and/or working evening and night shifts were main factors that made many Somali fathers less available to their children's life. *Fadhi-ku-dirir* and *khat* chewing were perceived negatively, affecting children by diverting badly needed time and financial resources from the children's needs. Although *fadhi-ku-dirir* and *khat* were not included in our interview questions, the youth raised them when discussing factors that made some fathers absent from their family life. Their claim corroborates community discourses that these practices are impacting the wellbeing of the Somali family. Parents also brought up these issues when discussing how time was one of the two main sources of family conflict, money being the other.

The youth noted that *fadhi-ku-dirir* and *khat* make some fathers absent from their children's lives and emphasized that these practices increase the likelihood of marital conflict. For instance, an 18-year-old high school male student believed that fathers who spend long hours sitting in cafés or chewing *khat* have no time for their children. For him, this also fuels marital conflict as mothers would expect fathers to contribute to child rearing.

Here the father is perceived as spending his time and money on worthless practices at the expense of the children's and family's wellbeing. Thus, there is an ethical dimension to *khat* chewing and *fadhi-ku-dirir*. Our interlocutors perceived these practices as incompatible with the image of a good husband and father. A high school male student, for example, associated *fadhi-ku-dirir* and *khat* chewing with bad Somali fatherhood. This participant, talking about why some fathers were not sufficiently engaged with their family noted, "It is possible that the father in question is not a good father!" He went on to describe a bad father, "A father who is a *khat* chewer or who for 24 hours of the day is sitting in cafés, who is careless about his children's interests."

In addition to the impact of *fadhi-ku-dirir* and *khat* on family time, parents' views and experiences also show the impact of these practices on family finances. Saluugla's case illustrates the matter.

Soon after Saluugla and her baby were reunified with her husband and father of the child, after a year of marriage in Africa, Saluugla (currently a single mother of eight) realized her husband was not the kind of husband and father she and her children would want to live with. He was neither supporting her in household activities nor letting her seek formal education. However, the imminent challenge was that he was addicted to *khat* and gambling and used to spend the family income on these habits. Mainly due to authorities who helped her solve the financial issue, her marriage survived ten more years. In addition, probably because of his preoccupation with *khat* chewing and gambling, he had no time for the family. Finally, they divorced.

Like the youth, the parents also emphasized the role of *khat* chewing and *fadhi-ku-dirir* in marital conflicts and divorces. According to Subkan, a 32-year-old married woman:

> Factors that usually contribute to family conflicts are the men who chew *khat,* they create a number of problems. Another source of this problem are the people who are here but are engaged in Somali politics, and for that they are busy, mainly men are very busy in activities of that sort, such as an extensive *fadhi-ku-dirir*. These are sources of serious issues in the family. (Individual interview, December 16, 2013)

Parents also shared a similar perception on the ethical dimensions of *fadhi-ku-dirir* and *khat* chewing. According to them, a man who chewed *khat* and took part in *fadhi-ku-dirir* could not be a suitable husband.

Child wellbeing and the father's absence from family life

As noted, transnational practices that led fathers to be absent from family life (fathers' long-term travels, *fadhi-ku-dirir*, and *khat* chewing) reduced the amount of time and money available for the children and generated family instability. Youth participants also observed that these practices had other negative implications for children's wellbeing. For instance, they emphasized that the father's absence from children's life affected the child's self-esteem (a father's absence would make his child feel shame in front of other children) and mental health (the child may feel abandoned and become depressed), and generated sadness and lack of parental care and support. Lack of a role model was another negative effect of the father's absence. Some of the youth believed that the lack of a role model had strong implications in particular for boys. Some of them also noted that the father's absence from family life would generate conflict between the father and his children.

The views and experiences of the parents also matched those of the youth. For instance, parents observed that, in the case of divorce, parental resources, particularly time, available for the children severely shrank, as Somali husbands tended to become less involved in childcare. In the words of one mother, "The main problem is that they (husbands) will never look back to their families." Parents mentioned that this was a serious issue in the Somali family because the Somali family is typically large and because many Somali mothers are not well prepared to support their children outside the home, for example, with school and leisure time activities.

Parents also noted that the father's absence has negative emotional implications for the children. Saluugla, for instance, noted that after her divorce her children were, due to their father's absence, "feeling that a window is open out there", meaning that there was emptiness in their lives. Some fathers narrated, based on their personal experiences, that, due to the divorce, open competition between the two parents over their children's loyalty had negatively impacted the children's love and feelings towards their parents.

In addition, parents mentioned that the father's absence from their children's life contributed to sons becoming delinquent and getting involved in fights and shoplifting. Furthermore, parents also talked about some indirect impacts of divorce on the wellbeing of their children. One was that the pressure generated by demanding household tasks and chores (due to large family size) on the mother's health, resulting in stress and depression, also adversely affecting children's wellbeing. Another adverse effect from divorce was what many interlocutors perceived to be excessive monitoring and possible interventions by child protection authorities who, according to the interlocutors, held the view that the mother alone might not be able to take care of so many children in one family. A commonly held fear was that such intervention would lead to children being taken away from the mother. A father, school teacher, and activist who participated in a focus group noted:

> Divorce engenders family destruction. It also causes stress on the wife. Many are mentally sick and in hospitals with *buufis* [mental distress]. That is the result of the excessive workload in the household and that (unlike in Somalia) there is no one helping her to have some rest. In case

the social worker provides home services, they are not confident in accepting it.

Affirming the above-mentioned concerns and fears, he added:

> They (service providers) watchfully observe the living conditions of the family, especially if there are five or more children, with the perception that the family is too large and that she (the mother) alone could not take care of it. That would generate the assumption that she cannot take care of all these and the kids need to be saved.

Conclusion

The goal of this chapter was to study the impact of the transnational engagements of Somali parents in diaspora on the wellbeing of their children living with them in Finland. The chapter examined youth's views, complemented by parents' perspectives and experiences, on how transnational engagement of Finnish-Somali parents would impact the wellbeing of their children. The central emphasis was on how these parental engagements affected both the stability of the family (conflict/divorce) and family resources (time and money).

Interviewed youth stressed how their family, particularly their parents, was vital for their wellbeing. They highlighted that their happiness was intertwined with their parents' roles in their lives and pointed out that, in general, their parents strived to enhance their wellbeing. However, they also highlighted several transnational parental practices that negatively impact their wellbeing.

From the youth's perspective, large remittances and investments, fathers' long-term travels, and *fadhi-ku-dirir* and *khat* chewing negatively impact child wellbeing. These practices deplete family resources, time, and money, resulting in family instability and the father's absence from family life. They also stressed that long-term travel and *fadhi-ku-dirir* and *khat* chewing are male dominated activities.

Interestingly, our interlocutors gave particular attention to the role of fathers and transnational practices that lead fathers to be absent from their children's lives. The youth emphasized that the father's absence generates emotional difficulties, lack of a role model, and marital conflict as well as child–father conflict, particularly with boys.

The perspectives and experiences of the interviewed parents also corroborate the youth's perspectives. This is also in line with the overall community discussions that put fathers (e.g., uninvolved fathers and absent fathers) at the centre of the many challenges confronted by Finnish-Somali families, such as children's educational underperformance. A relevant concern is that the proportion of Finnish-Somali families with children headed by a single mother is the highest among all ethnic groups and the number of single-mother families among Finnish-Somalis is probably increasing (Ismail, 2016). Thus, transnational practices that generate fathers' absences from their families' life could perhaps be a determining factor behind the high proportion of single motherhood among the Somalis.

Perhaps this conclusion supports the findings of the literature on transnational parenting highlighting that migrant fathers are less effective, compared to mothers, in their adjustment to the parental needs of the integration context (Parreñas, 2008). This may partially be negligence by some fathers, as the cases of *khat* chewing and *fadhi-ku-dirir* illustrate, but also partially a response to the fact that the lack of socioeconomic opportunities to fulfil traditional fatherhood roles (Carling, Menjívar and Schmalzbauer, 2012) drives some fathers to seek better opportunities elsewhere.

Furthermore, the three dimensions of wellbeing elaborated in the introductory chapter are relevant in both children's views and parents' experiences and perceptions. Regarding the material dimension, these parental practices may divert resources away from the children. For the relational dimension, for instance, the father's absence from family life impacts his physical and emotional availability for his children. Concerning the ethical dimension, for instance, the youth's perceptions of parental attitudes were to a large extent shaped by religious and cultural norms.

These dimensions are also relevant in the division of transnational practices into kin- and non-kin-based activities. For instance, parental transnational practices are perceived as justified and even beneficial to the wellbeing of the larger family when they fulfil the needs of the family in Finland or contribute to the interest of relatives elsewhere. In addition to the kinship ties, which traditionally are at the centre of the welfare system in Somali society, these understandings and perceptions are primarily informed by Islamic teachings and values.

Although non-kin-based transnational practices are the main source of family conflict, kin-based practices may also generate marital conflicts. This is mainly when they lose their ethical values, as the case of unfair distribution of remittance to the two relatives of the spouses above illustrates.

To conclude, this chapter has elaborated on transnational activities of Somali parents that may adversely influence the wellbeing of their children who are living with them in the resettlement country. However, this does not substantiate the notion that parental transnational practices are principally negative.

Finally, this chapter examined the perspectives of the youth as well as parental perspectives and experiences. But further in-depth research on the youth's experiences of the influence of their parents' transnational practices on their wellbeing is needed.

Notes

1 The chapter is part of a larger project, 'Transnational Muslim Marriages in Finland: Wellbeing, Law, and Gender' (2013–2017), funded by the Academy of Finland and directed by Dr Marja Tiilikainen at the Department of Social Research,

University of Helsinki. The main sub-study, 'Transnational Somali Families in Finland: Discourses and Lived Realities of Marriage', is designed and led by Dr Mulki Al-Sharmani at the Faculty of Theology, University of Helsinki. The overall research project investigates how Muslims in Finland organize and experience marriage in transnational space, and how the Finnish legal system and state institutions meet their needs and enhance their wellbeing. A large set of data from different sources, including individual interviews, focus groups, participatory observations, and life-stories, was collected for this project.

2 I excluded the fifth focus group, which was also mixed, because most of the participants were young people who were not parents.

3 This author is not aware of any research on *fadhi-ku-dirir*.

4 However, as Klein (2007, p.59) rightly asserted, there is no evidence that *khat* chewing was originally part of Somali culture and the historical origin of this consumption pattern shows the opposite.

Bibliography

Al-Sharmani, M., 2010. Transnational family networks in the Somali diaspora in Egypt: Women's roles and differentiated experiences. *Gender, Place and Culture*, 17(14), pp.499–518.

Al-Sharmani, M. and Ismail, A.A., 2017. Marriage and transnational family life among Somali migrants in Finland. *Migration Letters*, 14(1), pp.38–49.

Amato, P.R., 1993. Children's adjustment to divorce: Theories, hypotheses, and empirical support. *Journal of Marriage and Family*, 55(1), pp.23–38.

Baldassar, L., Kilkey, M., Merla, L. and WildingR., 2014. Transnational families. In: J. Treas, J. Scott and M. Richards, eds. 2014. *The Wiley Blackwell Companion to the Sociology of Families*. Sussex: John Wiley & Sons, Ltd, pp.155–175.

Baldassar, L. and Merla, L. eds. 2014. *Transnational Families, Migration and the Circulation of Care. Understanding Mobility and Absence in Family Life* New York: Routledge.

Baldridge, S., 2011. Family stability and childhood behavioral outcomes: A critical review of the literature. *Journal of Family Strengths*, 11(1), Article 8, pp.1–24.

Basch, L., Glick Schiller, N. and Szanton Blanc, C. eds. 1994. *Nations Unbound: Transnational Projects, Postcolonial Predicaments and Deterritorialized Nation-states*. New York: Routledge.

Bryceson, D. and Vuorela, U. eds. 2002. *The Transnational Family: New European Frontiers and Global Networks*. Oxford and New York: Berg.

Carling, J., Menjívar, C. and Schmalzbauer, L., 2012. Central themes in the study of transnational parenthood. *Journal of Ethnic and Migration Studies*, 38(2), pp.191–217.

Dreby, J., 2006. Honor and virtue: Mexican parenting in the transnational context. *Gender and Society*, 20(1), pp.32–59.

Dreby, J., 2010. *Divided by Borders: Mexican Migrants and Their Children*. Berkeley, Los Angeles and London: University of California Press.

Fresnoza-Flot, A., 2014. Men's caregiving practices in Filipino transnational families. In: L. Baldassar and L. Merla, eds. 2014. *Transnational Families, Migration and the Circulation of Care: Understanding Mobility and Absence in Family Life*. New York: Routledge, pp.170–184.

Goulbourne, H., Reynolds, T., Solomos, J. and Zontini, E., 2010. *Transnational Families: Ethnicities, Identities and Social Capital*. Abingdon: Routledge.

Hautaniemi, P., 2011. Transnational life course, human development and diverse landscapes of opportunities among young Somali men. *Nordic Journal of African Studies*, 20(1), pp.11–27.

Helminen, M-L. and Pietiläinen, M., 2014. Maahanmuutto moninaistaa lasten perheitä [Immigration diversifies families of children]. *Hyvinvointikatsaus*, 1, Statistics Finland. Online Report 47/05. Available at: http://www.stat.fi/artikkelit/2014/art_2014-02-26_002.html?s=0 [Accessed April 12, 2017].

Hondagneu-Sotelo, P. and Avila, E., 1997. 'I'm here, but I'm there': The meanings of Latina transnational motherhood. *Gender and Society*, 11(5), pp.548–571.

Hoover-Dempsey, K. and Sandler, H., 1995. Parental involvement in children's education: Why does it make a difference? *Teachers College Record*, 97, pp.310–332.

Horst, C., 2006. Connected lives: Somalis in Minneapolis, family responsibilities and the migration dreams of relatives. *New Issues in Refugee Research*. Research Paper No. 124. Geneva: UNHCR.

Ismail, A.A., 2011. Diaspora and post-war political leadership in Somalia. *Nordic Journal of African Studies*, 20(1), pp.28–47.

Ismail, A.A., 2016. Somali children in Finland are raised by their mothers. *Afrikan Sarvi*, 2. Available at: http://afrikansarvi.fi/issue12/128-artikkeli/328-somali-children-in-finland-are-raised-by-their-mothers [Accessed April 13, 2017].

Jeynes, W.H., 2005. A meta-analysis of the relation of parental involvement to urban elementary school student academic achievement. *Urban Education*, 40(3), pp.237–269.

Kilkey, M., 2014. Polish male migrants in London. In: L. Baldassar and L. Merla, eds. 2014. *Transnational Families, Migration and the Circulation of Care: Understanding Mobility and Absence in Family Life*. New York: Routledge, pp.185–199.

Kilpi, E., 2010. *The Education of Children of Immigrants in Finland*. PhD. University of Oxford.

Klein, A., 2007. Khat and the creation of tradition in the Somali diaspora. In: J. Fountain and D.J. Korf, eds. 2007. *Drugs in Society: European Perspectives*. Oxford: Radcliffe Publishing Ltd, pp.51–61.

Mazzucato, V., 2014. Child well-being and transnational families. In: A.C. Michalos, ed. 2014. *Encyclopedia of Quality of Life and Well-Being Research*. Dordrecht: Springer, pp.749–755.

Mazzucato, V. and Schans, D., 2011. Transnational families and the well-being of children: Conceptual and methodological challenges. *Journal of Marriage and Family*, 73(4), pp.704–712.

McGill, D., 2006. The coffee shop warriors of Minnesota-Somalia. The McGill Report. Available at: http://www.mcgillreport.org/fadhikudirir2006.htm [Accessed April 13, 2017].

Mohme, G., 2014. "Samira doesn't live here any more": Somali-Swedes' mobility as transnational practice. *Nordic Journal of Migration Research*, 4(3), pp.118–125.

OECD, 2009. *Doing Better for Children*. Paris: OECD. Available at: http://www.oecd-ilibrary.org/social-issues-migration-health/doing-better-for-children_9789264059344-en [Accessed July 24, 2017].

Open Society Foundations, 2013. *Somalis in Helsinki*. New York and London: Open Society Foundations.

Orozco, M., Lowell, B.L., Bump, M. and Fedewa, R., 2005. *Transnational Engagement, Remittances and their Relationship to Development in Latin America and the Caribbean*. Washington, DC: Institute for the Study of International Migration. Available at: http s://monroecollege.edu/uploadedFiles/_Site_Assets/PDF/Remittances-and-Developm ent-in-Latin-A-and-CA.pdf [Accessed April 13, 2017].

Osman, F.A. and Söderbäck, M., 2011. Perceptions of the use of khat among Somali immigrants living in Swedish society. *Scandinavian Journal of Public Health*, 39, pp.212–219.

Parreñas, R.S., 2001. *Servants of Globalization: Women, Migration, and Domestic Work*. Stanford, CA: Stanford University Press.

Parreñas, R.S., 2005. *Children of Global Migration: Transnational Families and Gendered Woes*. Stanford, CA: Stanford University Press.

Parreñas, R.S., 2008. Transnational fathering: Gendered conflicts, distant disciplining and emotional gaps. *Journal of Ethnic and Migration Studies*, 34(7), pp.1057–1072.

Patel, S., Wright, S. and Gammampila, A., 2005. Khat use among Somalis in four English cities. London: Home Office. Online Report 47/05. Available at: https:// webarchive.nationalarchives.gov.uk/20110218135832/http:/rds…uk/…/r266.pdf [Accessed April 12, 2017].

Portes, A., Guarnizo, L.E. and Landolt, P., 1999. The study of transnationalism: Pitfalls and promise of an emergent research field. *Ethnic and Racial Studies*, 22(2), pp.217–233.

Pribilsky, J., 2004. 'Aprendemos a convivir': Conjugal relations, co-parenting, and family life among Ecuadorian transnational migrants in New York City and the Ecuadorian Andes. *Global Networks*, 4(3), pp.313–334.

Schmalzbauer, L., 2004. Searching for wages and mothering from afar: The case of Honduran transnational families. *Journal of Marriage and Family*, 66(5), pp.1317–1331.

Snel, E., Engbersen, G. and Leerkes, A., 2006. Transnational involvement and social integration. *Global Networks*, 6(3), pp.285–308.

Statistics Finland, 2016. Population structure. Helsinki. Helsinki: Statistics Finland. Available at: http://pxnet2.stat.fi/PXWeb/pxweb/en/StatFin/StatFin__vrm__vaerak/? tablelist=true#_ga=2.148432823.1645356295.1501155723-837017718.1497456011 [Accessed July 27, 2017].

Suárez-Orozco, C. and Suárez-Orozco, M.M., 2001. *Children of Immigration*. Cambridge, MA: Harvard University Press.

Thomson, E., Hanson, T.L. and McLanahan, S.S., 1994. Family structure and child wellbeing: Economic resources vs. parental behaviors. *Social Forces*, 73(1), pp.221–242.

Tiilikainen, M., 2017. 'Whenever mom hands over the phone, then we talk': Transnational ties to the country of descent among Canadian Somali youth. *Migration Letters*, 14(1), pp.63–74.

White, S.C., 2008. *But What is Wellbeing? A Framework for Analysis in Social and Development Policy and Practice*. Paper for Regeneration and Wellbeing: Research into Practice, University of Bradford, 24–25 April 2008. University of Bath, Centre for Development Studies. Available at: http://staff.bath.ac.uk/ecsscw/But_what_is_ Wellbeing.pdf [Accessed July 26, 2017].

White, S.C., 2010. Analysing wellbeing: A framework for development practice. *Development in Practice*, 20(20), pp.158–172.

Zontini, E., 2010. *Transnational Families, Migration and Gender: Moroccan and Filipino Women in Bologna and Barcelona*. New York and Oxford: Berghahn Books.

9 Raising children of Somali descent in Toronto

Challenges and struggles for everyday security and wellbeing

Marja Tiilikainen

Introduction

In the spring of 2013 I was sitting in a townhouse in the West End of Toronto interviewing a Somali mother whom I call Ayaan. It was already dark, and suddenly we heard people running outside the house and saw torch lights. "They are here, the police," she said quietly as the interview was interrupted. The neighbourhood and its surrounding areas are predominantly government-housing neighbourhoods that some young people in my interviews called 'hoods', i.e., ghettos. For Ayaan, the presence of the police did not invoke a sense of relief or trust, but rather painful memories and feelings of insecurity. In general, the Canadian-Somali community members expressed mistrust towards the police and their willingness to solve issues that concerned the community, and in the case of Ayaan the issues were of enormous scale: one of her sons had been violently killed in Canada in dubious circumstances.

The tragedy of Ayaan and other parents whose children had experienced gun violence, but also discrimination and stigmatization because of their race, ethnicity, or religion, were widely discussed in the community and impacted the wellbeing of the community and families. Yet despite their sense of injustice and powerlessness in the face of the legal and societal structures and practices in Canada, parents were not passive, but tried, and acted in many ways, to support and protect their children from the dangers that they identified both inside and outside Somali and/or Muslim communities.

In this chapter I will explore, on one hand, some of the vulnerabilities and challenges that Somali parents face when raising children in Toronto, and on the other hand, parents' resources and agency to safeguard and support them. The focus is on their experiences and organization of everyday security, which is further seen as a central component of individual and family wellbeing. The focus on human security redirects attention from the security of nation-states to the security of individuals, groups, and communities (Williams, 2008; Kubo, 2010; Inglehart and Norris, 2011). One of the basic principles in the human security approach is people-centredness. Hence, the aim of the analysis is to understand what makes people feel safe or unsafe, what the processes of vulnerability are, and what are resources people draw on to create security in their daily lives. In this chapter I use the term *everyday security* (Crawford and Hutchinson, 2016) to refer to the study participants' lived experiences related to (in)security as well as the mundane, often family-centred practices that they engage in to live with insecurity and foster security.

The concepts of everyday security and wellbeing, as presented in the introductory chapter of this book, are linked to each other. Based on Sarah C. White's three-dimensional model (2008; 2010), wellbeing is seen to be comprised of material, relational, and ethical dimensions. First, both wellbeing and security have material and physical dimensions that in the case of Canadian Somali families and parents refer to, for example, the neighbourhoods they live in, available housing and services, income of the family, educational and religious institutions they are attached to, and public spaces. Many Somali families who came to the country as refugees have ended up living in social housing projects in poor neighbourhoods where inhabitants often struggle with marginalization and also crime (Tiilikainen, 2015). This condition increases the vulnerability of the Canadian Somali families. Neighbourhood (in)security is a significant factor in the overall perceptions and experiences of everyday (in)security (Inglehart and Norris, 2011, pp.82–83).

Second, both wellbeing and security have a relational dimension that refers to family members locally and transnationally, local networks (for example, with neighbours or other women), and religious communities. In addition, wellbeing and the sense of security among the Canadian Somali parents is impacted by their relationships and interactions with institutions and structures of power – for example school, police and the justice system, mosques, and organizations – that parents trust, or mistrust, in varying degrees. Lack of trust in these institutions (that are designed to enhance the wellbeing of families, citizens, and residents) resulting from, for example, experiences of being racialized and, therefore, having limited opportunities for education or work, or experiences of not receiving justice from police and the legal system, add to the vulnerability of parents and their children.

Third, the concepts of wellbeing and security refer to systems of meanings and norms, values, and religious beliefs. The ethical dimension includes, for example, religious and other norms and values that guide and empower Canadian Somalis, but also racism, pathologization of black immigrants, public discourse on Muslims as extremists, and securitization measures that impact the everyday life of Muslim parents and their children in Canada (e.g. Nagra, 2017). Furthermore, the emergence of violent radicalized groups that claim to act in the name of Islam have shaken the sense of security of Somali Muslim parents.

The experiences related to everyday security are gendered, as, on one hand, in North America young black men, in particular, have been marginalized and criminalized, and face great challenges in trying to improve their social mobility (Davis, 2017; Berns-McGown, 2013). In addition, young black males are often targets of violence in general and force by the police in particular (Brunson and Miller, 2006; Staggers-Hakim, 2016). On the other hand,

Somali mothers often carry the biggest responsibility for taking care of children and daily matters inside families. In addition, over one third of the Somali families in Canada (37.9%) are single-parent families and in most cases (82%) these families are led by single mothers. Consequently, almost 52% of all Canadian Somali children are raised by single parents, mostly their mothers (Mata, 2011, pp.19–25). The situation has consequences for the wellbeing and everyday security of families, as lone-parent families in Canada are likely to live in poverty (ibid., p.27).

According to White (2008; 2010), wellbeing should not be seen as mere outcome, but rather as a multidimensional process which also entails aspirations as well as strategies to overcome challenges and create wellbeing. Similarly, senses of security and insecurity are not static, but change spatially and temporally. For Somali parents who left Somalia primarily due to civil war and conflict, finding a secure place for themselves and their children was of utmost importance (Tiilikainen, 2015). They escaped civil war in Somalia to find physical security, but also a better life and opportunities for their families. Hence, in this chapter I will link the concepts of wellbeing and everyday security as this helps, on one hand, to highlight the different dimensions of vulnerabilities that Somali parents face as they pursue a good life (i.e., wellbeing) for their children and families and, on the other hand, to capture aspirations and agency of parents that are enabled or constrained by the material, relational, or ethical dimensions of their everyday lives.

Research background

The chapter is based on ethnographic data and qualitative interviews that I conducted as part of my larger research project on transnational Somali families.[1] I collected the data in Canada, Finland, and Somalia, but for this chapter I use only the data collected in Toronto, Canada, in particular interviews with parents. In Canada, eight families participated in the study.[2] Among these eight families, I interviewed eight mothers (five of them were either divorced or widowed) and three fathers, in addition to some of their (mostly adult) children. In the selection of the families I wanted to include families of different socioeconomic status, from different neighbourhoods in Toronto and regional backgrounds in Somalia. Furthermore, I tried to find both families who had done well socioeconomically, as well as families who were struggling economically and/or families where parents were confronting challenges in raising their children. In one of the studied families, a child had been killed in Canada.

At the time of my approximately nine-month-long fieldwork in Toronto, starting in November 2012, violent deaths of young Somali men in Toronto and other big cities in Canada were a grave concern for the community, and therefore, in order to better understand the experiences of those families who had lost their children to gun violence, I purposely searched out and interviewed another mother whose child had been shot and another whose child had been injured in gun violence. Furthermore, I conducted some other individual and focus group interviews with other parents (and young people) who do not belong to actual research families, but who enrich the data through various experiences. For this chapter, in addition to the previously mentioned individual interviews, I also draw from three focus group discussions (two with mothers, one with fathers), as well as some other interviews and discussions with imams, representatives of Somali community organizations, and the police. In addition, during the fieldwork I regularly participated in meetings and activities of the Task Force on the Success of Students of Somali Descent, set up by the Toronto District School Board, which aimed at creating recommendations (TDSB, 2014) to improve the achievement of students of Somali descent in schools. I conducted the interviews in English, apart from a couple of interviews that were partly conducted in Somali with the help of a female assistant. Most interviews were done in homes. The names are pseudonyms and some details may have been changed to conceal the identities of the interlocutors.

In the eight studied families, the age of the parents ranged from 41 to 68, and they had been living in Canada for between 13 and 32 years. They were all born or grew up in either Somalia or neighbouring Ethiopia, and hence they can be called first-generation migrants. The socioeconomic backgrounds of the studied families varied: On one hand, in six of the interviewed families either both parents or a single mother were working, and they managed financially well enough so that they did not need to worry about their daily maintenance. Some of these families had even been able to pay for their children's university fees or had bought property. On the other hand, in two of the families the monthly income hardly covered living expenses and the parents struggled to survive. Also, the two additional mothers whom I interviewed and whose sons had been affected by gun violence were low-income single mothers.

According to unofficial estimates, over 100,000 people of Somali descent live in the greater Toronto area, the biggest concentration of Somalis in the country and one of the largest outside Somalia. In general, the community has faced socioeconomic challenges, and the majority live in poor neighbourhoods where school dropout and crime rates are high (MacDonnell, et al., 2004; Charron, 2009; Tiilikainen, 2015). At the same time, there are adults and youths who have done extremely well in education and employment. Hence, even though my data is not representative, I have tried to capture the diversity of the community in the selection of participants solicited for this study.

The parents and families in my study are transnational in the sense that parents, in particular, maintain connections to family members in the Horn of Africa as well as in the diaspora and, when necessary, utilize transnational family relationships to raise their children. For many parents who migrated to Canada due to the civil war, Somalia and the Horn of Africa, including their cultural and religious values, still represent 'home'.

In addition, 'transnational' in this chapter refers to parents raising their children in a global world where new, violent ideologies also cross borders and may impact children. In this changed world, familiar religious values and norms may also be questioned.

In this chapter, I will discuss the experiences of wellbeing and everyday security through two narratives from the data. The examples capture some of the common concerns, vulnerabilities, and insecurities of the participating parents, also reflecting the material, relational, and ethical dimensions of wellbeing. In addition, the selected two examples show different kinds of vulnerabilities that parents confront as well as differences among the interlocutors in terms of class, their access to resources to create everyday security and enhance wellbeing, and ability to cope and act in situations where children need protection. Finally, these examples demonstrate how wellbeing can be seen as a process (White, 2010), as people are striving for it without knowing the end result.

The first story takes us back to Ayaan, who was introduced in the opening of the chapter.

Struggles of a single mother

I needed someone to help me, but did not get any help: I lost my child

Ayaan escaped Somalia with her two children after the civil war in Southern Somalia had broken out. She undertook a dangerous trip by small boat, packed with other refugees, to Yemen, and further to a Middle Eastern country where she worked to maintain the family. The husband joined her later, but divorced Ayaan after a few years. Finally, she managed to enter Canada with her three children, at which time the oldest son was nine years old. Ayaan herself was 33. She wanted to continue her studies but realized that finalizing high school studies was too difficult as she did not master English well enough. Instead, she started working in a factory to maintain the family. She was worried for her teenage boys and mentioned the names of three different low-income neighbourhoods where she had lived in government housing while in Toronto, all having bad reputations as places with high rates of criminality and violent incidents. She related how she always changed the neighbourhood once she had noticed that her sons had got bad friends: "that's why I ran".

When the oldest son was 14 years of age, Ayaan decided to take him over to Kenya to live with his uncle, to get him away from his friends and their bad influence. She had never met the brother of her ex-husband, but as she saw the situation with her son, she called his uncle and asked for help. She told him, "this is my son, you are his uncle, please I need help; I will send the money, please take care of my son. He said, 'okay'." Ayaan took the son to Kenya and stayed with him one month. Then Ayaan left the boy saying, "You have to learn. We don't have a choice. You have to learn how the people here live and survive." She had a plan to bring the boy back once he was mature, but after two years he got seriously ill, and the mother brought him back to Toronto. According to the mother, the boy had changed (for the better) when he returned to Toronto, but soon he was again spending time with his old friends who were involved in robberies and drugs. He went back to school. Ayaan was very concerned about how the son would do there, and she went to school every day to check that everything was okay. She also went to see the principal, who convinced her that the boy was behaving well. But after three months he already was in trouble and explained to his mother that he had to follow his old friends. Ayaan narrated how she once even took the boy to a police station and complained that the boy did not listen to her, but always wanted to go out with his peers. She asked the police to help her, but the policeman laughed and said that they could not help as the boy had not done anything criminal. According to Ayaan, "they told me, kick him out of your house; he is 16; it is not your responsibility anymore."

Two years later Ayaan got a telephone call at night, and she was told that the boy had been shot and seriously injured. Ayaan quit her factory job to take care of the son whose recovery took a year. When he recovered, he decided to travel to Alberta in West Canada to search for a job. Ayaan was against the move, but the son left. After three weeks he was dead. Ayaan travelled to Alberta to bury her son. The stories of the Somali community, on one hand, and the police on the other were different: according to the information circulating in the local community, the son's death had been a targeted killing. According to the police, the incident was basically robbery, not manslaughter, regardless of Ayaan's reassurance and information from the Somali community. Ayaan moaned, "I told the police, I talked to the judge. I say, I don't have money to get a lawyer – I'm not working, I'm on welfare that time because I quit [my job] because of my son …. And I said, everybody has time to die, he never comes back; thank you God, that's it. I left, I never went back."

Insecure neighbourhoods

Ayaan's story, along with my other data, emphasizes the role of neighbourhoods as sites that powerfully determine the flow of daily life and sense of security among Canadian Somalis as well as their future opportunities. Like Ayaan, many Canadian Somali families have no other choice but to live in social housing in low-income neighbourhoods, as their income is not high enough to rent from the private market, and hence the choices regarding the place where they want to live are limited (e.g. Murdie, 2003). Living in a 'ghetto' often means insecurity, poor housing conditions, under-resourced schools and limited opportunities for getting a job. For example, my young interlocutors have given several examples of how employers do not even invite them for an interview when they see their postcode in an electronic application. In addition, parents have complained that the schools in low-income neighbourhoods are less resourced than in affluent neighbourhoods, and this impacts the future opportunities of the children.

In Toronto, some of the low-income neighbourhoods, such as Dixon, Jane and Finch, Rexdale, or Jamestown, where many Somali families lived, have a bad reputation as many shootings and drug-related fights take place there. In some of these neighbourhoods, inhabitants needed to consider how and when they went outside, in particular after dark. Some interviewees explained, for example, how they would carefully watch if strange cars drove in the area. A young woman also related that she would always speak to her mother on her mobile phone when she got off the bus as she walked home for five minutes so that her mother would know in case something happened to her. This does not mean, however, that only families that lived in low-income neighbourhoods were potential victims of violence, as violence and random shootings also happened elsewhere.

When Somalis arrived in Canada, they were not aware of the risks that their children might be exposed to outside the home, as they were used to letting children play freely in the neighbourhood. In Somalia, it was a collective duty of all adults to watch and take care of the children, whereas in Canada this collective responsibility was absent: in Canadian society, family issues were perceived as a private matter, and strangers would not interfere if they saw unknown children misbehaving. In addition, the neighbourhoods where Canadian Somalis lived were multicultural and migrants originating from different countries were not seen to share the same cultural values and habits. Furthermore, not even all Somali families in the area were automatically trusted if families did not know each other. Families soon realized that they were not able to leave their children unattended outside, but had to take them, usually by car, to a playground preferably outside the neighbourhoods where they lived. It was, however, difficult to keep teenagers inside the house as the apartments were usually crowded. Furthermore, Ayaan and other single mothers with several children often did not have enough time and resources to follow what their teenage children were doing outside the home, and they felt that a man at home would have been important in raising boys in particular.

Ayaan explained how she moved from one neighbourhood to another once she noticed that her sons spent time in bad company. The same strategy also came up in other interviews: those interlocutors who were able to move from areas where they felt insecure or where the school was not considered good enough, did so. One of the families in the study explained how their life had greatly changed after they had moved away from their low-income area to an area where most people were employed and owned their property: it was a relief not to have to worry about walking home late in the evening. Families who lived in an affluent neighbourhood often described how their child was the only black child in the school, or there were very few children of Somali descent or Muslims in general. Sometimes the situation was experienced as positive, sometimes negative.

As a low-income single mother, Ayaan did not have material resources to move to a more affluent neighbourhood, and, moreover, she might not even have known of all the available opportunities to get affordable housing in better neighbourhoods due to her poor English language skills. Therefore, she was powerless in the face of structural constraints.

(Mis)trusted relationships and the search for support and justice

Ayaan's example shows how she tried to approach authorities and institutions of power and seek help for her son at different stages of her son's struggle: she visited the school and had discussions with the principal and teachers, and she even took her son to the police station, hoping that they could force him to listen to his mother. The police, however, did not have any advice to offer other than to kick him out of the house. Finally, once the son had died, Ayaan felt that even the justice system was failing her: she felt that the police did not do a proper investigation and, because of her poverty, she could not get a good lawyer who could have helped find justice for her deceased son.

Not just Ayaan, but most interviewed parents complained that they did not trust that the police would seriously try to investigate the violent deaths of Canadian Somali youths, as most of the cases remained unsolved after several years. Hence, they experienced that the security system designed to protect people and ensure their wellbeing did not provide those services for them: they felt that they did not get justice as a community because they were people of colour and had a refugee background. Mistrust of the police was reinforced by the experiences of both parents and the youths. Young black men, in particular, were profiled by the police: the interlocutors told me about police who frequently patrolled the neighbourhoods, harassing and stopping and asking for identification papers from young black men (also Berns-McGown, 2013; Brown, 2006). Some young men mentioned how they had been stopped by the police and questioned about why they were driving such an expensive car.

The police on their part complained that the Somali community did not cooperate and report what they knew about assaults and other violence. From the point of view of the parents and families, silence might be a way to protect their own families: even if they had seen things happening in the backyards and side alleys, they might not want to reveal their information as they wanted to protect their own families and sons. Hence, violence and fear affected the neighbourhood relations, even though at the same time other women or trusted neighbours were mentioned by a few female participants as an important aspect of living in certain insecure neighbourhoods.

Migration from Somalia and dispersal of families impacted the roles inside the families. Some parents, often those who had been successful in raising their children, described how they had worked as a team and supported each other in the absence of other relatives. Some families had been lucky to sponsor other family members to Canada, and, for example, the presence of a grandmother in the family had been of great help with taking care of the children. Single mothers had often struggled the most, in particular those with low education. However, even if there were two parents in the family, mothers commonly complained that they were the ones who had the main responsibility of raising the children while fathers stayed most of the time outside the home, often at Tim Horton's (popular franchised coffee shops) which some mothers described as 'a playground' of fathers.

In addition to immediate family, extended family and clan relationships could also be mobilized during a crisis. For example, money was collected through clan and community networks to pay for lawyers when someone's child had been in court – some parents explained that they contributed gladly because one day they might need the same support themselves. As in Ayaan's case, transnational family ties were utilized when a child was taken to Africa or the Middle East to learn more about religion and culture, or to be protected from gun violence and bad influences. The role of transnational family in organizing care and treatment in different contexts has been well documented (Al-Sharmani, 2006; 2010; Bledsoe and Sow, 2011; Tiilikainen, 2011; Tiilikainen and Koehn, 2011; Baldassar and Merla, 2014). For Ayaan, reliance on the patrilineal family relationships in trying to save her son indicates trust in the traditional family institutions in Somali culture.

Ayaan's example, in short, shows how the insecurity and ill-being experienced by the parents are interlinked with the material and relational dimensions of their daily lives. Poor, racialized families often inhabit rough neigbourhoods where male youths in particular are more likely to be dragged into drugs and robberies and become victims of violence than their age-mates living in neighbourhoods that are usually safe. Single mothers, such as Ayaan, who struggle with financial insecurity and who try to raise their boys in the absence of a father figure or other supportive family ties in Canada are in an especially vulnerable position. In addition, parents feel powerless in the face of institutional structures, available service systems, and law enforcement that seem to ignore or fail to recognize and respond to the needs of Somali parents. Mistrust in authorities and the institutions of power increases the feelings of vulnerability and insecurity among the parents as they lack resources to protect their children from threats and violence that they encounter daily in their residential areas and other public spaces.

Next, I present another ethnographic example that demonstrates how not just the physical environment and access and relationship to supportive structures changed due to migration, but how the meanings of religious tradition and the mosque as a safe space also changed as part of temporal and contextual processes.

Contested religion

You want your child to be connected to religion, but you worry who may meet him in a mosque

Farhia and Abdulkadir are educated parents of a well-off family. Both parents have been working since the time they moved to Canada, and they have never qualified to live in government housing. Instead, they have rented from the private market and live in a spacious house in a nice neighbourhood. All the children have already completed or are in the process of completing their university degrees. Farhia relates how one of the challenges of raising children in the neighbourhood where the majority are Christians was to make small children understand that they had another religion, religious practices, and celebrations, yet not to deprive them of the experiences that their friends were experiencing. For example, at school their children also participated in exchanging Christmas gifts or Christmas concerts. At the same time, parents educated them about Islam. Abdulkadir used to teach them the Qur'an and how to pray. By the time the children became teenagers they knew well what being Muslim entailed and nowadays two of the three sons are more serious about religion than the parents are.

The two sons engaged with religion in a new way when they started university. They met practising Muslims and they started to search for information about Islam by attending religious lectures and reading books about Islam. Moreover, they started to pray all the prayers at the mosque and also spend more time there otherwise. At the start of the third year of university, one of the brothers told the parents that he wanted to stop studying at the university and concentrate instead on the practice of religion alone, which caused a family crisis.

At the time of the religious awakening of the two boys, some Somali young people had left Toronto and joined Al-Shabaab in Somalia, which made Farhia and Abdulkadir fear that their sons had been brainwashed and that they might be planning something similar. They related:

> We were always talking to them, to understand what they are thinking and how they are thinking, and to tell them stories about what's happening, like what's happening is against the religion, and how it's not right to kill a human being that hasn't done anything to you. You kill somebody when you are defending yourself … That's the only time you can kill somebody. But you cannot kill somebody just because his government is doing something somewhere. And we keep on talking to them all the time.

Farhia also used to take her sons for a long ride so that she could talk to them. When she was going for groceries, she complained that it was hard for her to push the cart and therefore, she wanted one of the boys to go with her. Then she gave the boy the car keys and asked him to drive; meanwhile she started the conversation about religion and other things, to know what was going on. Farhia also hid the passports of the boys to prevent them from travelling secretly.

Abdulkadir lamented how he, along with other parents, had taken the boys to the mosque when they were small, and now the parents had to worry when children did go to a mosque as they could not know whom they would meet there. In despair he even had gone to the mosque where the boys used to visit, and verbally threatened some of the leaders.

At the time of the fieldwork some years had already passed from the time that, according to the parents, was the scariest in their life, and the situation of the boys had calmed down; they were not that devoted and uncompromising about religion any more. One of the boys was still a pious Muslim, whereas the other brother had distanced himself from religion. Both of them had graduated and also found jobs, and Farhia and Abdulkadir did not fear that they could be influenced by radical ideas any more.

New meanings and discourses on Islam

Earlier research has shown that many Somali migrants became more religious following the events of the civil war and a new life in the diaspora (Berns-McGown, 1999). Somali mothers whom I studied for my PhD research in Finland at the end of the 1990s (Tiilikainen, 2003), described how Islam provided a kind of safe space for them: through religious practices they recreated home and continuity. In addition, a mosque was unquestionably seen as a good place to be, and they were happy about their children spending time there. Giulia Liberatore (e.g. 2016) has shown that the children of Somali migrants distance themselves from their parents' religious views and practices, which they closely link with Somali culture, and instead adopt their own reformist Islamic discourse. My recent data from Toronto, however, shows a new complexity in the perspectives of the parental generation on Islam. Like Farhia and Abdulkadir, parents want their children to identify as Muslims and practise religion, but in a 'moderate' way. Being 'too religious', which might entail, for example, stopping studies and focusing more on the afterlife than their current life in Toronto, or in the case of girls, starting to wear the *niqāb* (face veil) and wanting to marry early, was perceived negatively. In addition, potential violent radicalization worried some of the parents due to the instance, mentioned earlier in the chapter, of a small number of boys from Toronto who had disappeared some years back and travelled to Somalia to join Al-Shabaab. All in all, violent radicalism in the name of Islam was perceived very negatively and condemned, and many parents were angry that Islam had been 'hijacked' by violent groups. Many parents mentioned that they had discussed with their children the events in Somalia and in the Middle East. In addition, the parents had started to follow more what was being taught at the Qur'anic schools (held on weekends) to monitor who was teaching and what was being taught to their children.

The studied parents varied in how strongly Islam guided their actions or impacted their decisions, or how they interpreted religion. For example, while most parents seemed to hold negative views regarding mortgage or study loans, there were also those who were willing to take loans and pay interest. In one of the families the parents reasoned that they saw it actually as a necessity from an Islamic point of view to take a mortgage to ensure that the family did not need to live in an insecure neighbourhood. Some parents were active in mosques and, in addition to teachers of religion, might ask for advice and support from other people and friends whom they met there. Some parents were actively contributing to the activities of the mosque, volunteering to raise money and organize different family events and activities. Those families who were connected to mosques might take children to mosques not only for religious purposes but also, for example, to play basketball in a secure environment.

For some of the mothers, relying on religion was one of the few resources that they seemed to have, and something that they depended on for help, hope, and consolation. For example, an unemployed mother in a low-income neighbourhood explained how she woke up every night to pray for her son, to get protection for him from God. She also repeatedly and systematically read through the Qur'an to calm her own mind. In addition, sending troubled youth or children to relatives in the Horn of Africa or the Middle East was also motivated by the goal of having the child learn about Islam and take the right path in life. At the same time, parents encountered the new globally and transnationally shaped vulnerabilities in relation to Islam, that is, the threat of young people, in particular boys, being exposed to radical ideologies and joining violent extremist groups.

Regardless of the role of religion in the lives of individual interlocutors, being categorized as Muslims impacted most of them in some way or another. Some interlocutors complained that being Somali, black, and Muslim together reinforced the negative public image of the Somalis and resulted in discrimination and racism. Experiences of discrimination and racism were brought up, for example, from the school context where Canadian Somali children were not expected by their teachers or counsellors to excel or follow an academic path through high school to university, but rather be more suited to vocational training. In addition, parents felt that as a black student, it was more likely that a student would be suspended from school or referred to special education classes. At the time of the fieldwork, some of the housing complexes in neighbourhoods where many Somali families live (e.g. Dixon) were raided by the police, and interlocutors felt that the Somali communities were particularly targeted. In the media, Somalis were criminalized and stigmatized as a group (see Tiilikainen, 2015). Moreover, some adults and youths related incidents where they had been stopped at the border control, in particular if they had worn visible Muslim garments, or how they had received angry looks or comments in a public space after a terrorist attack against non-Muslims had been in the news.

Farhia and Abdulkadir tried to resolve the issues with their boys inside the family, which speaks of the mistrust of authorities as in Ayaan's case. But perhaps the bad public image of the Somalis also prevented them from contacting the authorities, and the parents rather wanted to keep the matter in the family and mosque circle. In addition, the authorities might not have been able to provide suitable support in any case. Furthermore, parents probably wanted to avoid the stigmatization of their sons as terrorists and possible measures by the authorities.

The example also reveals temporal and contextual changes in parental views on Islam. Islam as the religious tradition that they used to know in Somalia and the central source of their ethical wellbeing was contested and questioned in Canada and other non-Muslim diasporic countries by the mainstream societies, but gradually also by the new, educated generation who started to redefine the meanings of religion and search for suitable religious communities and authorities across ethnic boundaries (also Liberatore, 2016). Apart from the negotiations and tensions that evolved as part of the migration process and resettlement in a new environment of the families, the parents also recognized the threat from new violent radical groups whose propaganda and ideology tempted young people across borders. In their pursuit of security and wellbeing for their children, parents also tried to respond to these new challenges by engaging their religious tradition in different ways: for example, some parents became active in mosques and tried to help them develop and provide leisure time activities for young people in a secure environment; some monitored the Islamic teaching provided by mosques to their children more closely than before; some decided to teach Islam to their children by themselves at home in order to be sure that they were taught 'correct' Islam; some sent their children to the Horn of Africa or the Middle East for protection and to learn more about Islam; some reinterpreted Islamic juristic rulings regarding prohibition of usury and decided to take interest-based mortgages because they saw it as necessary for moving the family to a good neighbourhood and securing their wellbeing; some tried to convince their children to moderate their strict religious views and prevent them from travelling by hiding their passports; and some intensively prayed for God to protect their children. Even though Islam in the lives of the parental generation mostly remained important, including as a resource to raise children, the parents were now aware of new potential (transnational) risks related to Muslim communities, and also mosques, and tried to mitigate these risks.

Conclusion

In this chapter I approached the concept of wellbeing through experiences of everyday security, insecurity, and vulnerability as well as people's aspirations and practices to foster security in their daily lives. The data showed the continuum of violence in the lives of Canadian Somalis: Somali migrants escaped the violence of their home country to finally reach Canada, which did not prove to be the secure place that they had hoped for. Many low-income neighbourhoods where Somali families lived were insecure; racism, discrimination, criminalization, and stigmatization were frequently encountered; schools failed to accommodate and support Somali Canadian children; and even mosques were not necessarily the safe places that they used to be, that is, spaces that used to be safe and trusted in Somalia had turned alien in Canada.

In addition to the material and physical dimensions of everyday insecurity and vulnerability that Canadian Somali parents encountered, they also faced insecurity related to relationships and interactions with authorities and structures of power, in particular the police and justice system. Furthermore, the vulnerability of the Canadian Somali parents and their children was reinforced by the stigmatized public image of the community, where ethnicity, race, and religion intertwined and reinforced each other. The relationships inside immediate and extended families, including transnational kin, however, were trusted by the parental generation to deal with problems relating to raising children and youths.

It is not an accident that in both of the narratives that I presented, the young people in question were males. Boys in particular were seen to be at risk of becoming involved in gangs and criminal activities, or in militant religious groups, but also of becoming victims of profiling and racist attacks both in neighbourhoods and in public spaces. The vulnerability of black Canadian Somali youths illustrates the general vulnerability of black youth in North America where use of force by the police has targeted black residents disproportionately (e.g. Goff et al., 2016; Brunson and Miller, 2006). The data confirms that the body of a black boy is an obvious target for violence in Canada as well, and therefore, parents need to worry about them and consider how to change the stereotypical images given to them.

Canadian Somali parents "live with insecurity" (Crawford and Hutchinson, 2016, p.1188) and strive for wellbeing for themselves and their children in conditions of structural inequality, injustice, and violence. However, parents' understandings of, as well as aspirations and strategies for creating, security vary according to their situation and life cycle as well as the parents' own background, expectations, and resources. Transnational family connections and (reinterpreted) religious traditions appear as some of the resources that parents rely on when raising their children. Somali parents are not only differently resourced financially, but also in terms of educational and class background, English language skills, or their understanding of the service system. Importantly, certain groups of parents are particularly vulnerable: single parents, who in most cases are women; parents who are uneducated and unemployed; or those who are unable to work due to sickness or lack of sufficient English language skills. Single-parent families of African origin in Canada are often socioeconomically highly vulnerable (Mata, 2011, pp.38–39). In addition, parents are differently networked and connected. All these factors impact the opportunities that Canadian Somali parents have to support and protect their children.

Depending on the personal resources that parents possess, they engage schools, institutions, or authorities differently. For example, a well-educated parent who understands what is needed to succeed at school and who is able to communicate with the teachers is more likely to get a positive response when she or he approaches the school. There have also been community-driven initiatives to try to impact the existing structures, such as the Task Force on the Success of Students of Somali Descent by the Toronto District School Board, and the non-governmental organization Positive Change, which has been active in creating collaboration between the police force and the Canadian Somali community and lobbying government to improve the justice system.

The focus on lived experiences of (in)security among racialized Somali migrant families in Canada reveals a paradox: while national- and municipality-level official security practices normally aim at fostering the security of all residents, they marginalize Somali families and lead to their insecurity, especially by framing black youth – in particular black young men, many of whom are Muslims – as threats to security. In addition to police and the legal system, the media reinforces the image of Somali youth as criminals. Furthermore, at schools, Somali youth are often regarded as under-achievers, and hence upward social mobility and better future prospects such as good jobs are difficult to obtain (also Davis, 2017, p.743). For the poor Somali parents, the insecurity that they and their children encounter on a daily basis greatly undermines their wellbeing: fear of losing a child to gun violence in Canada or in a fight for an Islamist militant movement abroad were the ultimate fears that parents had.

Based on the experiences of Canadian Somali families discussed in this chapter, "the 'promise' of multiculturalism" in Canada (Davis, 2017, pp.726–732) has not succeeded in guaranteeing equal rights, security, and welfare to communities of colour. Studying these phenomena in the lives of marginalized communities through the prism of the everyday may provide new approaches to better understand the meanings of security and wellbeing as well as their linkages to the political level.

Notes

1 The data for this chapter were collected as part of 'Islam and Security Revisited: Transnational Somali Families in Finland, Canada and Somalia' research project, funded by the Academy of Finland (2012–2017). My sincere thanks go to all participants of the study, who generously provided their valuable time and help. I also want to acknowledge all those who advanced the writing of this chapter with their insightful comments, in particular Dr Mulki Al-Sharmani, Dr Sanna Mustasaari, Dr Ruba Salih, and Dr Sara Silvestri.
2 The data in Toronto was originally collected on nine families, but one family withdrew from the research after the data collection was completed and their interviews were omitted from the final data set.

Bibliography

Al-Sharmani, M., 2006. Living transnationally: Somali diasporic women in Cairo. *International Migration*, 44(1), pp.55–77.

Al-Sharmani, M., 2010. Transnational family networks in the Somali diaspora in Egypt: Women's roles and differentiated experiences. *Gender, Place and Culture*, 17 (4), pp.499–518.

Baldassar, L. and Merla, L., eds. 2014. *Transnational Families, Migration and the Circulation of Care: Understanding Mobility and Absence in Family Life.* London: Routledge.

Berns-McGown, R., 1999. *Muslims in the Diaspora: The Somali Communities of London and Toronto.* Toronto: University of Toronto Press.

Berns-McGown, R., 2013. *"I Am Canadian." Challenging Stereotypes about Young Somali Canadians.* IRPP Study No. 38. Montreal, Quebec: IRPP.

Bledsoe, C.H. and Sow, P., 2011. Back to Africa: Second chances for the children of West African immigrants. *Journal of Marriage and Family,* 73, pp.747–762.

Brown, M., 2006. In their own voices: African Canadians in Toronto share experiences of police profiling. In: F. Henry and C. Tator, eds. 2006. *Racial Profiling in Canada: Challenging the Myth of 'a Few Bad Apples'.* Toronto: University of Toronto Press, pp.151–183.

Brunson, R.K. and Miller, J., 2006. Young black men and urban policing in the United States. *British Journal of Criminology,* 46, pp.613–640.

Charron, M., 2009. *Neighbourhood Characteristics and the Distribution of Police-reported Crime in the City of Toronto.* Crime and Justice Research Paper Series. Ottawa: Statistics Canada.

Crawford, A. and Hutchinson, S., 2016. Mapping the contours of 'everyday security': Time, space and emotion. *The British Journal of Criminology,* 56, pp.1184–1202.

Davis, A., 2017. "The real Toronto": Black youth experiences and the narration of the multicultural city. *Journal of Canadian Studies,* 51(3), pp.725–748.

Goff, P.A., Lloyd, T., Geller, A., Raphael, S. and Glaser, J., 2016. *The Science of Justice: Race, Arrests, and Police Use of Force.* Los Angeles: Center for Policing Equity.

Inglehart, R.F. and Norris, P., 2011. The four horsemen of the apocalypse: Understanding human security. *Scandinavian Political Studies,* 35(1), pp.71–96.

Kubo, H., 2010. Operationalising human security: A brief review of the United Nations. In: M. McIntosh and A. Hunter, eds. 2010. *New Perspectives on Human Security.* Saltaire, UK: Greenleaf Publishing in association with GSE Research, pp.31–48.

Liberatore, G., 2016. 'For my mum it comes with the culture': Intergenerational dynamics and young Somali women's interventions within multicultural debates in Britain. *Bildhaan: An International Journal of Somali Studies,* 16, pp.49–64. Available at: http://digitalcommons.macalester.edu/bildhaan/vol16/iss1/10 [Accessed August 5, 2018].

MacDonnell, S., Embuldeniya, D., Ratanshi, F., Anderson, J., Roberts, P. and Rexe, K., 2004. *Poverty by Postal Code: The Geography of Neighbourhood Poverty, 1981–2001.* A report prepared jointly by United Way of Greater Toronto and the Canadian Council on Social Development. Toronto: United Way of Greater Toronto.

Mata, F., 2011. *Lone-parent Status Among Ethnic Groups in Canada: Data Explorations on its Prevalence, Composition and Generational Persistence Aspects.* Working Paper Series, No 11–17. Vancouver: Metropolis British Columbia, Centre of Excellence for Research on Immigration and Diversity.

Murdie, R.A., 2003. Housing affordability and Toronto's rental market: Perspectives from the housing careers of Jamaican, Polish and Somali newcomers. *Housing, Theory and Society,* 20, pp.183–196.

Nagra, B., 2017. *Securitized Citizens: Canadian Muslims' Experiences of Race Relations and Identity Formation Post–9/11.* Toronto: University of Toronto Press.

Staggers-Hakim, R., 2016. The nation's unprotected children and the ghost of Mike Brown, or the impact of national police killings on the health and social development of African American boys. *Journal of Human Behavior in the Social Environment*, 26 (3–4), pp.390–399.

TDSB, 2014. *The TDSB Task Force on Success of Students of Somali Descent Report.* Report No 12-13-2233. 22 January 2014. Toronto District School Board. Available at: https://www.ett.ca/stf/ [Accessed July 16, 2018].

Tiilikainen, M., 2003. *Arjen islam: Somalinaisten elämää Suomessa* [Everyday Islam: The life of Somali women in Finland]. Tampere: Vastapaino.

Tiilikainen, M., 2011. Failed diaspora: Experiences of *dhaqan celis* and mentally ill returnees in Somaliland. *Nordic Journal of African Studies*, 20(1), pp.71–89.

Tiilikainen, M., 2015. Looking for a safe place: Security and transnational Somali Muslim families. *Journal of Religion in Europe*, 8, pp.51–72.

Tiilikainen, M. and Koehn, P.H., 2011. Transforming the boundaries of health care: Insights from Somali migrants. *Medical Anthropology*, 30(5), pp.518–544.

White, S.C., 2008. *But What is Wellbeing? A Framework for Analysis in Social and Development Policy and Practice.* Paper for Regeneration and Wellbeing: Research into Practice, University of Bradford, 24–25 April 2008. University of Bath, Centre for Development Studies. Available at: http://staff.bath.ac.uk/ecsscw/But_what_is_Wellbeing.pdf [Accessed August 7, 2018].

White, S.C., 2010. Analysing wellbeing: A framework for development practice. *Development in Practice*, 20(2), pp.158–172.

Williams, P.D., 2008. Security studies. An introduction. In: P.D. Williams, ed. 2008. *Security Studies: An Introduction*. Abingdon, Oxon: Routledge, pp.1–12.

10 Childhood, wellbeing, and transnational migrant families

Conceptual and methodological issues

Ann Phoenix

Introduction

Since the beginning of the 21st century, the concepts of 'wellbeing' and 'transnational families' have become part of research consciousness as well as everyday discourse so that there is now a range of studies on both. The proliferation of work on wellbeing has resulted from recognition that wellbeing, happiness, and outcomes for children, families, and society are interlinked. It follows from this that there are likely to be particular issues of wellbeing for 'transnational families'. Indeed, as intimate life, relationships, and families have been increasingly opened up to scrutiny, it has been recognized that migration status differentiates the experiences and everyday practices of families. Yet, while both 'wellbeing' and 'transnational families' have gained traction, there are relatively few studies that explicitly address the wellbeing of transnational families (Mazzucato and Schans, 2011; Mazzucato, et al., 2015), particularly from the perspectives of their various members. This may be because wellbeing is frequently employed in individualizing ways that do not address the impact of sociostructural issues on family wellbeing (Dreby, 2015). It is clear, however, that differences among families and children, including inequalities, are central to children's wellbeing in their families. If this criticism is to be taken seriously, a holistic understanding of family wellbeing requires engagement with the ways in which different family members are simultaneously positioned in multiple social categories of, for example, nation, generation, and gender, as well as social class and racialization.

This chapter makes a contribution to thinking simultaneously about wellbeing and transnational families, two categories that are rendered elusive because they are both extensive and encompassing. Wellbeing, in particular, is subject to contentious debate about its conceptualization and methodologies (White, 2016) and in the relatively rare studies where wellbeing and transnational families are brought together, methodological debate is often also at play (Mazzucato and Schans, 2011) because the explanations generated and understandings produced depend on the data and analyses generated. This chapter, therefore, considers the conceptual and methodological issues raised in studying the wellbeing of transnational families. In order to do so, it draws on the concept of intersectionality, which is concerned with the ways in which people are multiply positioned. The chapter suggests that intersectionality should thus be central to considerations of wellbeing by presenting examples of how the intersections of gender, social class, racialization, and sexuality impact childhood and hence (transnational) family wellbeing, focusing particularly on children in such families. The chapter is divided into three sections. The first discusses contemporary conceptualizations of wellbeing. It includes examination of both family relations and the ways in which families are sociostructurally positioned. The second section employs the concept of intersectionality to engage with the issue of wellbeing for transnational families, particularly in relation to children and young people from minority ethnic groups. The final section discusses methodological issues that need to be considered in order to take thinking about the wellbeing of transnational families forward. It presents two examples to illuminate these issues and to propose some fruitful methodological approaches. The chapter argues for a multidisciplinary perspective in the study of the wellbeing of transnational families, taking into account the viewpoints and experiences of the particular family members involved.

Theorizing wellbeing

A particular impetus for concern with family wellbeing was the publication in 2007 of the UNICEF quantitative comparison of children's happiness and wellbeing in 21 affluent countries. In the UNICEF domains (material; health and safety; education; peer and family relationships; behaviours and risks; and subjective wellbeing) the UK scored very low. This result was shocking and puzzling for many policy makers and researchers in Britain. Internationally, it fuelled many analyses and studies of childhood and family wellbeing, including UNICEF's publication of a qualitative research comparison of Spain, Sweden, and the UK that also showed that children's lives were qualitatively worse in the UK than in Spain and Sweden (Ipsos MORI and Nairn, 2011).

In the years since the publication of the 2007 UNICEF report, wellbeing has become commonplace and there are now thousands of studies on wellbeing, most of which are quantitative attempts either to refine the domains that should be included in wellbeing scales and/or linking particular domains with outcomes. The debate generated since the UNICEF (2007) report served to popularize the term 'wellbeing' and it is now a trope for the conditions considered necessary to ensure that children maximize their potential, can live happy, successful lives, and contribute to society. This appears straightforward, but definitions of wellbeing have been much debated as the term has become commonplace. In 2008, Ereaut and Whiting explained that, despite its ubiquity, there is no straightforward agreement about what constitutes 'wellbeing'.

> 'Wellbeing' is a ubiquitous term, occurring frequently and widely in public discourse. It is ... not yet present in the unprompted discourse of parents and children and indeed is not well understood by these groups. ... Within academic science, it is often taken for granted as something that 'is', and which simply needs investigating. ... some studies, for example, draw on the positive psychology movement and might characterize wellbeing as "positive and sustainable characteristics which enable individuals and organizations to thrive and flourish". ... Within the science discourse, however, there are also more critical approaches ... [that do] not accept wellbeing as a 'thing' that needs research to uncover its essential nature, but as a social and cultural *construction* (Ereaut and Whiting, 2008).

Since the term 'wellbeing' is in everyday usage and appears incontrovertibly positive, it might be expected that its popularity in academic work and policy is also accepted as necessarily good. Wellbeing indices, for example, have been adopted by the Royal Kingdom of Bhutan instead of economic indicators, and the then UK Prime Minister, David Cameron, introduced a Happiness Index in 2012, although economic indicators such as Gross Domestic Product are still recorded in the UK (Bentley, 2012). However, as White (2010) suggests, wellbeing is always a political process grounded in place and time. A major criticism of the ways in which wellbeing is frequently studied (with its links to happiness studies and the ways in which it is picked up in policy) is that it individualizes and depoliticizes children's (and adults') lives and oversimplifies international comparisons (Morrow and Mayall, 2010; Manderson, 2005). As a result, it both focuses on economic indicators and neglects the crucial role of economic inequalities, although there is ample evidence that economic inequality in societies is associated with poor wellbeing (Wilkinson and Pickett, 2009). It is one reason that Gross Domestic Product is not a satisfactory proxy for wellbeing. Schwanen and Atkinson (2014, p.100) point out that, while wellbeing can help academics and policymakers understand how life can be made better for individuals and communities, it can also "become a cover for the promotion of potentially oppressive norms and practices".

Despite the lack of consensus about what constitutes wellbeing, there is general agreement that 'wellbeing' has to be viewed as multidimensional, consisting of physical, economic, social, emotional, and psychological dimensions. An influential review of wellbeing by the UK New Economics Foundation at the beginning of the 21st century concluded that it is linked to a range of desirable health, social, and educational outcomes, including optimal development in childhood and over the life course (Marks and Shah, 2004). Wellbeing is also a dynamic state, rather than a static achievement, so that it varies in different contexts and changes over time. It is enhanced when people can "... develop their potential, work productively and creatively, build strong and positive relationships with others, and contribute to their community" (Jenkins, et al., 2008, p.10). Findings such as these are encapsulated in the five 'postcards' devised by the New Economics Foundation (2008), each with a slogan condensing the factors identified as central to wellbeing for anybody, namely: connect, be active, take notice, keep learning and give (i.e., make a contribution). Schwanen and Atkinson (2014) argue that consistently conceptualizing wellbeing in terms of multiplicity reduces the limitations of the term and their negative implications for the most vulnerable in society. From a review of the literature, Statham and Chase succinctly summarize the research findings on children's wellbeing as follows:

> There is some emerging consensus that childhood wellbeing is multidimensional, should include dimensions of physical, emotional and social wellbeing; should focus on the immediate lives of children but also consider their future lives; and should incorporate some subjective as well as objective measures (Statham and Chase, 2010, p.2).

In pointing out that childhood wellbeing should focus on children in the here and now, Statham and Chase's summary fits with what has been called the 'new' sociology of childhood over the last 30 years. One crucial insight from the sociology of childhood was that, in order to understand childhood and children's lives, researchers should focus on children's current lives, rather than viewing them only as adults in the making (James and James, 2012). It is, therefore, important not only to focus on children's deficits, what they cannot (yet) do and what is wrong in their lives, but also on what they can, and actually do, do (Pollard and Lee, 2003). Statham and Chase's (2010) summary also fits with developmental psychology notions that children's current lives are important to their future prospects. In recognition of this, 'wellbecoming' has increasingly been recognized as conceptually important, with education and learning, not surprisingly, being viewed as important routes to wellbeing. Underpinning all the dimensions Statham and Chase identify is an economic dimension in that economic inequality is associated with poor wellbeing for society as a whole as well as for individuals (Ballas, Dorling and Shaw, 2007; Wilkinson and Pickett, 2009). The immediate and future lives of children are necessarily dependent on the socioeconomic circumstances in which they live.

In the above extract, Statham and Chase (2010) also point out the importance of subjective wellbeing. The name comes from the subdiscipline of positive psychology and is an umbrella term to encompass the overall evaluations people make of their experiences and lives. These are affective, cognitive, embodied, and socioeconomic (Diener, 2013) and include self-acceptance, environmental mastery, purpose in life, personal growth, positive relations with others, and autonomy (Haworth and Hart, 2007). It is widely agreed that objective measures of wellbeing are not in themselves sufficient for understanding outcomes or the development of policy. This is because findings developed from scalar measures of domains of wellbeing do not engage with the ways in which people themselves feel about their experiences and their personal approach to psychological wellbeing impacts on their quality of life and life satisfaction and outcomes (Ryff, et al., 2006). Both subjective and 'objective' wellbeing are important for outcomes in that people sometimes like to do things that damage their wellbeing or wellbecoming. If, for example, people have no positive evaluations of their experiences and lives, they are unlikely to thrive. In addition, children, as well as adults, have subjective understandings of what contributes to their wellbeing. In a qualitative Australian study, Fattore, Mason and Watson (2009) found that 8–15-year-olds understood wellbeing in relation to their significant relationships and their emotional lives. They believed that it included a positive sense of self, having some agency and control in everyday life and security and safety. From quantitative analyses, Bradshaw (2016) also found that children viewed a sense of freedom and relationships with their families as most important to their subjective wellbeing.

The centrality of relationships to wellbeing partly accounts for why issues of wellbeing are linked to notions of resilience, which is also currently a common trope for good outcomes. While it is frequently treated as an individual characteristic, recent theorizing grounded in research suggests that it is the case neither that resilience inheres in individuals nor that environments are risky or protective in themselves. Rather it is an interplay between both factors. Some contexts and experiences enable resilience for some people, but not others (Rutter, 2006). Adversity affects people in different ways with the result that what is apparently a similar environment and the same events can lead to different outcomes and reactions. It is of course difficult to establish that environments are similar since an important development in family psychology is the recognition that even siblings with the same parents live in 'non-shared environments' because, for example, they are born in different years that may constitute different family or societal periods; they may look different; meet different people; and show different characteristics with the result that people react to them in different ways (Asbury, et al., 2003; Mullineaux, et al., 2009). It is for such reasons that some people have relatively good outcomes despite bad experiences, while others have relatively poor outcomes from apparently less disadvantageous circumstances. The picture is even more nuanced in that people may be resilient to some difficult experiences but not others, and they may be resilient in some outcomes (e.g. education), but not others (e.g. relationships or jobs). The same experience can, therefore, produce different findings in different domains (Rutter, 2006). Resilience is, therefore, about the ways in which people can cope with adversity and risk experiences or overcome them. In other words, it is about relative resistance to risk experiences. Relationships are important to resilience (and to wellbeing) in that who it is that provides help and support at particular times can make important differences in how people deal with circumstances (Hauser, Allen and Golden, 2009). Thus, a lifespan perspective is important in that whether or not people overcome stress or adversity may partly depend on whether they have had previous exposure to risks in controlled circumstances, rather than having been protected from all risks and adversity. Rutter (2006) points out that exposure to some risk and adversity in circumstances where children are protected from the worst impacts can 'steel' them to deal with problems (Rutter, 2006). Equally, overcoming adversity depends on experiences after adverse events have occurred and whether experiences following adversity help ameliorate negative effects or reinforce them. The factors that facilitate resilience may thus include personal agency, coping strategies, socioeconomic contexts and the nature of environment and relational contexts. This multidimensional perspective explains why some things work in some situations and not in others and why a single strategy is unlikely to work in every circumstance. In practice, those working on wellbeing sometimes shift focus between different domains and so different ways of understanding it (Hone, et al., 2014). As White (2016) suggests, this plurality is a strength, with the concomitant weakness that it is frequently not clear how wellbeing is being conceptualized.

The above discussion of the conceptualization of wellbeing raises important issues for a consideration of transnational families and wellbeing. First, it is important to take a multidimensional perspective that brings together physical, material (including socioeconomic), emotional, and social dimensions, and to recognize the interlinking of subjective and 'objective' perspectives. A multidimensional approach requires a dynamic rather than a static view of wellbeing. Relationality is an important part of this perspective, so that families have to be viewed as central to the wellbeing of all their members, including children, over the lifespan. It is, however, important to study families in ways that do not individualize, decontextualize, and depoliticize people's lives while over-simplifying international comparisons (Morrow and Mayall, 2010; White, 2017). A focus on 'wellbecoming' means that children and young people's learning as well as the quality of their lives and experiences are central to wellbeing (Statham and Chase, 2010). Yet difference and inequality are frequently left silent in work on wellbeing, particularly in relation to children. Using the concept of intersectionality, the next section will examine the issue of difference and inequality in relation to wellbeing in the case of transnational families.

Transnational families, intersectionality, and wellbeing

Before engaging with the wellbeing of transnational families through the lens of intersectionality, this section begins by outlining prevalent academic understanding of the characteristics of transnational families. By definition, transnational families are spread across nation-states so that family and household are not co-resident unities (Goulbourne, et al., 2010). In order to be categorized as transnational families, however, family members need to share a sense of collectivity (Bryceson and Vuorela, 2002). They are often characterized by complex care arrangements that shape this sense of collective belonging across international boundaries. The research available indicates that transnational families face a range of issues relevant to their positioning as children, mothers, and fathers. Hondagneu-Sotelo and Avila (1997), who coined the term 'transnational motherhood', suggested that women's geographical separation from their children can produce a sense of liminality, ambiguity, and indeterminacy of identity: a sense of simultaneously 'being here and there'. This is partly because it is often very difficult for mothers to develop new lifestyles in a new country while ensuring that their children are well cared for in other countries (Lutz, 2008). Fathers have been largely neglected in research on transnational families, although some research is now being done (Sørensen and Vammen, 2014; Souralová and Fialová, 2017), but relatively little is known about their experiences of being part of transnational families. However, the burgeoning work done on transnational families in general points out that it is generally mothers who take the responsibility for making arrangements for their children abroad as well as working to earn money to support them and enable family reunion (Budginaite and Juozeliuniene, 2018). This is borne out in a study of Filipino/a 'children of migration', where Parreñas (2005) found that the mothers' hard work provided material comforts that their children very much appreciated, even though they were often particularly sad about their mothers' absence.

It is possible for transnational families to maintain shared imaginaries and narratives of belonging through contact and visits in either direction (Yeoh, Huang and Lam, 2005) and through 'virtual intimacies' (Wilding, 2006). They are thus sometimes able to maintain the simultaneity of family members' lives across transnational space through shared activities, routines, and institutions (Levitt and Glick Schiller, 2004). This geographically separated simultaneity takes effort, resources, and organization to maintain and so is emotionally, cognitively, and financially costly (Orellana, et al., 2001). Transnational families thus have to negotiate transnational circuits of emotion, material goods, and financial support. Wolf (2002) coined the term 'emotional transnationalism' to capture the emotional ties that are evoked, despite migration and geographical separation. The work of emotional (and often economic) maintenance across national borders often falls to women (Skrbiš, 2008). Children's emotions are less explored and there is a dearth of research on transnational relations other than parent–child.

The above-mentioned complex and layered dimensions of transnational family lives underline the importance of the theoretical concept of intersectionality in arriving at a nuanced understanding of the wellbeing of transnational family members and particularly that of children.

Intersectionality has come to be recognized as fruitful for analysing and explaining the complexity and plurality of contemporary life. The term was coined by Kimberlé Crenshaw (1989) to account, theoretically, for what she perceived as the systematic invisibility of black women in US legal processes. Crenshaw provided examples of how black women's experiences of discrimination are distorted when analysts focus only on a single category of social inequality (e.g. 'femaleness' or 'blackness'). She argued that black women's positioning and the discrimination to which they are subjected is "greater than the sum of racism and sexism" (Crenshaw, 1989, p.140). In other words, simple additive models cannot account for the complexity that arises from the fact that social categories never operate in isolation. The simultaneity of categories such as gender and racialization (Brah and Phoenix, 2004; Collins and Bilge, 2016) means that while not all the possible categories of difference and inequality are relevant in every context, it is important to analyse the multiple social categories that are relevant to understanding any particular issue, such as the wellbeing of transnational families. Cho, Crenshaw and McCall suggest that social categories have to be viewed "... not as distinct but always permeated by other categories, fluid and changing, always in the process of being created by dynamics of power ..." (Cho, Crenshaw and McCall, 2013, p.795). Since social categories are not fixed, but permeate and mutually constitute each other, it follows that any individual category is also dynamic and changing, rather than fixed. The dynamism and mutual constitution of categories means that any one social category is only meaningful in relation to other social categories. In other words, categories have to be seen as decentralized in that there is no central fixed meaning to a category. For example, what it means to be a 'transnational family' is only meaningful in relation to families that are constructed as not transnational and meanings within the category will vary with the categories that intersect with international family status such as age, generation, gender, social class, and nation. Thus, in order to approach an understanding of children's wellbeing in transnational families it is helpful to consider what is currently known about how children's wellbeing is differentiated by the social categories to which they belong.

It has long been established that there are intersectional inequalities in how children from different ethnicized groups perform in schools in different countries (Gillborn, 2008). Gross, Gottburgsen and Phoenix (2016, p.51) suggest that: "Education remains one of the most important determinants of social inequalities across generations and the life course and educational systems are the main places for generating these disparities."

Empirical education research identifies particular social groups that are especially at risk of being losers in various educational systems. Being male, being of migrant status, and belonging to lower social classes are factors that have repeatedly been found to be disadvantageous for the attainment of educational qualifications. However, by themselves, none of the axes of inequality are sufficient to fully explain educational disparities. Instead, they operate simultaneously and are mutually constitutive (Gillborn and Mirza, 2000). The concept of intersectionality helpfully emphasizes this simultaneity. From an intersectional point of view, social inequality is not only determined multidimensionally along different axes of inequality – such as gender, migration, socioeconomic background, age, handicaps, etc. – but also emerges particularly in the intersection of these axes as they mutually reinforce each other within social contexts such as the family, school, or the labour market.

It is not only educational attainment that differs by racialized / ethnicized / gendered / classed / sexuality intersections (Gillborn, 2008), but also the ways in which pupils are constructed by teachers and other pupils is intersectionally differentiated so that the 'ideal pupil' in Minority World contexts has long been constructed as white, male, middle class, and heterosexual (Walkerdine, 1988; Archer, 2011). Classrooms provide possibilities and constraints for 'who students can be' (Youdell, 2006). For example, from an ethnographic study of one US school, Ferguson (2000) found that the cultural images and racial myths in the school produced a racialized / gendered hierarchy where the school institutional practices were couched in universal language, but maintained a racial order. White boys who 'act out' were viewed as 'naughty', while black boys who did so were adultified as criminals in the making.

Various studies have also found complex intersections of social class, racialization, and gender in children's friendships. For example, in a study conducted by Neal and Vincent (2013); Iqbal, Neal and Vincent (2017), the friendships of 8–9-year-old children in 'super-diverse' London boroughs were shown to involve complex "entrenchments around similarity" (Iqbal, Neal and Vincent, 2017, p.128) and interactions across difference where racialization was sometimes made salient in informal segregation. Children and young people are very well aware of how they are positioned in terms of status. This has been repeatedly shown in relation to consumption and socioeconomic status (e.g. Croghan, et al., 2006) and in terms of racialization (Howarth, 2002; Hughey and Jackson, 2017). This has implications for how children treat each other within and across intersectional categories. For example, in a study of 16–18-year-old Somali Muslim girls in a London sixth form college, some of whom were migrants, Aisha Phoenix (2011) found that they attempted to avoid social exclusion through creative claims to 'new ethnicities' by attempting to be 'cool', or popular by copying the disaffected behaviour of students perceived to possess 'vernacular prestige' (Labov, 1972). Some perceived truanting from school and being disruptive in class as an important way to 'fit in', gain higher status, and 'be the centre of attention'. They considered that truanting also served a further function, to avoid being bullied, while competing for popularity with the popular girls (who were white). From their own reports, the girls were different at home than they were at school. At school their wellbeing was fractured by intersections of racialization, gender, ethnicity, and Muslim identity and they sought to avoid the exclusion they were subjected to by virtue of being Muslim by downplaying their religious identity. As they got older, the Somali Muslim girls reported that they were better able to deal with the embarrassment caused by their intersectional positioning, as in the following example.

Rahma: All my friends were like "Rahma, I pray that a Somali girl that doesn't speak English [laughs] comes and you have to teach her" [laughs] and I was thinking what! Before I used to get vexed about it and stuff like that, but now … if I see someone who doesn't know Somali I won't, I won't hesitate to help them, but when I was in secondary school or something I was really shallow and I was like you know just so childish and I wouldn't.

Facilitator: You wouldn't have wanted to help someone who didn't speak English?

Rahma: Maybe I'd be like embarrassed, 'cos like you know when you're in school and all of that bitchiness and stuff (Focus Group 2). (Phoenix, 2011, p.323)

Similar patterns are found in other countries. For example, Gilliam and Gulløv (2017) found that Danish Muslim boys (although less so girls) were considered to be properly Muslim boys only if they made trouble and did not behave properly at school. It is not just students who position each other in intersectional racialized / religious / gendered positions; teachers also do so. Teachers have been found to stereotype ethnic minority parents and families in negative ways in Denmark (Gitz-Johansen, 2003; Gilliam, 2016) and in the UK, where, for example, black middle-class parents report that they have to carefully negotiate the low expectations teachers hold about their child's capabilities and they have to make concerted efforts to avoid this (Rollock, et al., 2014). So, while middle-class status does help them deal with discrimination, the pervasive dynamics of racial stereotypes means that being middle class does not guarantee black families protection against racism.

The implications of these patterns of findings for an understanding of wellbeing (particularly in the case of transnational families) is that, alongside analysing national differences, it is also important to consider how racialization, ethnicity, gender, and social class intersect in school and family lives to produce patterns of wellbeing and wellbecoming. The complex patterns of attainment and everyday practices at school are differentiated by the social categories in which children and other family members are positioned. Since young people consider that they are positioned differently at home and school, it is clearly important for considerations of wellbeing to include the ways in which different family members are socially positioned in diverse contexts, their own perspectives, and the differences between them.

Methodological issues in building conceptualizations of wellbeing for children in transnational families

The question of how the wellbeing of members of transnational families can usefully be studied is both important and relatively open. Mazzucato and Schans (2011) suggest that it is important to combine quantitative and qualitative methods in order to get a more holistic picture. There are, however, more fundamental issues to be considered about the methods best suited to studying wellbeing. Some of these issues arise from the diversity of ways in which wellbeing is conceptualized into domains. This has led various researchers to suggest that there is a need for standardization of measures and a great deal of energy has been expended in attempts to improve measurements of wellbeing (Dolan and Metcalfe, 2012). The concern with refining measurement, however, is founded on the assumption that scales and other quantitative measures are sufficient to underpin reliable understandings of wellbeing. Yet, Ed Diener, who is a pioneering theorist of subjective wellbeing says that there is currently insufficient research evidence to make policy application straightforward and that the plethora of measures available often make "simplifying assumptions that could potentially create biases and errors in a national index of well-being" (Diener, Lucas and Schimmack, 2009, p.11). White and Jha (2014) also point out that while wellbeing measures are designed to give a holistic humanistic focus to public policy, these measures are highly quantitative and decontextualized. It is not that White and Jha are opposed to quantitative work in this area since, for example, White, Gaines and Jha (2012) welcome the attention that some reports bring to the global issue of subjective wellbeing and, in 2014, they themselves devised a scale of inner wellbeing. The issue is rather that their extensive research in India and various countries on the African continent, together with their collaborations with researchers working in International Development on other continents, leads them to recognize that such scales do not exhaust people's subjective understandings of their lives and wellbeing.

In the introduction to an edited collection that discusses new and helpful ways of thinking about wellbeing, White (2016) suggests that what the contributors bring together is a shift away from conceptualizing wellbeing (what wellbeing is) to exploring how accounts of wellbeing are produced. In other words, methods produce ways of seeing. This is a crucial point. White (2016) points out that the contributors' analyses resist the reification of wellbeing as a 'real thing' that people may or may not 'have'. This perspective fits with that on resilience discussed above. It is not an absolute characteristic that people do or do not have. Equally, it is not possible to bring about one's own wellbeing through force of will, as implied by approaches that individualize wellbeing. Instead, the volume, White explains, shows that it is important to examine what is claimed in research, how research is undertaken, and where and with whom the research takes place. Place and cultural and socioeconomic context are all important to understanding wellbeing. It is therefore too simplistic to be methodologically dogmatic by prescribing either quantitative or qualitative approaches or even mixed methods as a panacea for current methodological shortcomings in the wellbeing literature since the methods used have to be appropriate for answering the particular research question addressed. White's (2016) edited collection is particularly helpful in showing how bringing together multidisciplinary and methodologically diverse research on different places (but with consistent epistemological, ontological, and axiological perspectives) can illuminate plural 'cultures of wellbeing'.

This section takes for granted the need for disciplinary and methodological pluralism in research on wellbeing so that no one study has to bear the burden of addressing all the issues necessary to a consideration of wellbeing, but all have to contextualize their own findings in order to contribute to producing holistic understandings.

The section examines, specifically, two examples to illustrate how engagement with the experiences of children in transnational families can aid understandings of the wellbeing of transnational families, showing the importance of focusing on subjective perspectives without asking about wellbeing per se, and analysing the impact of intersectional positioning, including of place. It argues that a holistic understanding of wellbeing requires a focus on negotiations of relationality and racism as transnational families forge their family practices in particular contexts.

The selected examples also show how different sources of material on wellbeing can provide fruitful analyses.

Everyday wellbeing and transnational families

The first example makes the case for analysing wellbeing in cultural analyses of events reported in the media. It shows how transnational families negotiate family practices in new ways in the context of the policy of the post-9/11 anti-terrorist agenda in the USA. It is a newspaper report of an incident where, on September 14, 2015, a 14-year-old Muslim schoolboy Ahmed Mohamed, reputed for his interest in engineering, was arrested after taking a clock he had made by himself to his school, MacArthur High School in Irving, Texas. Far from being praised for his ingenuity, Ahmed's English teacher told the principal and he was questioned by five police officers, pictured handcuffed and taken to the police station without his parents, on the grounds that he had brought in a hoax bomb. He was suspended from school. When the event was made public, Ahmed was invited to places such as Facebook headquarters, Twitter, and the White House. The family received a great deal of support from members of the public, including money from crowd funding, but were also subjected to upsetting vitriolic and threatening communications. The family pursued unsuccessful lawsuits against the City of Irving and the Irving School district as well as Fox television studios. Although his parents are Sudanese, they moved the whole family to Qatar, where Ahmed received a scholarship to continue his education.

The above example clearly does not constitute a research interview or self-completion scales. Nonetheless, it allows a cultural reading that exemplifies issues important to the wellbeing of transnational families. In terms of wellbeing, this everyday example shows how contingent wellbeing is on the local context. The increase in Islamophobia in many 'Western' countries with Muslim minorities that has been reported since 9/11 has the potential to disrupt what appears to have been the achievement of a settled life in the USA and, to underline that, at least for some, the family were ascribed an outsider and unwelcome status on the basis of racialization and religion. Their wellbeing was disrupted and the children's future prospects threatened. As White

(2016) suggests, this example can only be understood if the local context is made central to analyses. A further analytic point is that wellbeing can encompass contradictory elements in that this frightening and upsetting episode also produced invitations and opportunities to meet powerful people that would not have been forthcoming but for Ahmed's infamy. His future prospects, and so his 'wellbecoming', were therefore both potentially damaged and enhanced by this episode. As is evident in the transnational family literature, the impetus to search for a better life, particularly for children, is not one that is acted on once and for all. Ahmed's parents moved the family again, leaving behind extended family members in the USA, as well as in Sudan and indeed, they spent the summer after Ahmed's first year in a Qatari school in the USA in order to see family members. That search for a better life was clearly not just economic. Intersectionally, this episode arises from intersections of Ahmed's racialized positioning in religion and no doubt gender as well as his family's migration status and that intersectionality is visible from the various media reports.

The second example comes from a study of childhood language brokering, where children interpret and translate for their parents and others and so take on responsibilities in situations in which adults would normally be in control. From her longitudinal research on childhood language brokers, Orellana (2009) suggests that the indirect work of children as language brokers helps support and sustain their parents as workers and so make significant contribution to institutions (schools, healthcare, etc.) and to society. The following example comes from a narrative interview study of 40 adults looking back on their childhoods as language brokers.[1] Husniyah, in her twenties, is part of a nuclear family that has migrated from Syria, initially leaving her father as well as their extended family behind. Her father joined them after some time.

> Husniyah: When we were newly arrived and none of us spoke Swedish, translators usually addressed my mother when translating, even if the topic was about school and us kids. I didn't need to take responsibility and my mom handled the information. After a while I had to tell my mom what had happened in school and what the teachers told us to prepare for the next day. This was my first encounter with translating for my parents and I found it quite amusing. I was also rather proud of myself for knowing things that my parents didn't. At the same time, I didn't want people to know that my parents didn't understand Swedish or that their language skill was poor. To me, it was kind of a family secret that I usually enjoyed but did not want to reveal to others ...
>
> So, whenever I got a letter that I didn't understand I was reminded about my lack of skill in the Swedish language. In the beginning I thought that it all depended on my language skill, but after a while I understood that at my age (about 11–12 years) I wasn't supposed to

know anything about taxes, company rules, and so on. And sometimes even if I understood all the words, I [did not] discern the meaning because I lacked a context in which to situate them, and I had to ask my parents to give me more information so I might be able to get the whole picture. I remember feeling that my family and I were marginalized because we lived in a society where we didn't know all the rules or all the words and we didn't know what people wanted to say to us when they sent us letters. I felt bad for being able to read better than my parents but still not being good enough ...

In outlining her career as a language broker, Husniyah explains how it starts and continues to its end, when she refuses to continue language brokering because her father, frustrated at not being able to communicate and unhappy in Sweden, is frequently critical of her language brokering work. She is both initially captured by the practice of language brokering and then lost from it. The method of narrative interviewing is a helpful way to get at Husniyah's subjective understanding of her experiences. Her account shows that she identified the contradictory nature of language brokering and wellbeing. Her narrative suggests that she is initially amused and proud to know what her parents did not, but, simultaneously, wanted to keep her language brokering a family secret. While she does not say so, her desire to keep this secret suggests that she had learned about the power relations stratified in language, recognizing that parents who speak Arabic and not Swedish are devalued in Swedish society. As with the example from Ahmed above, this method is also able to show the situatedness of wellbeing. It also shows the temporality and dynamism of language brokering in that the whole career of language brokering is visible. The analysis of Husniyah's narrative also shows that she considers herself to be exercising agency in various ways, not only in doing language brokering, but also in keeping language brokering private, presumably to avoid stigma, and in eventually refusing to do any more language brokering. In keeping with the work of Andresen et al. (2017) on child wellbeing and poverty, this method is also able to show the ways in which Husniyah, and other child language brokers, take responsibility for their parents. Generation, age, and language visibly intersect with migration status in this narrative. However, ethnicity and racialization are not brought into being in this account and, since both would seem relevant here, they would have to be analysed in other ways. Overall, the narrative method that generated the extract above is able to indicate the situated, plural, and dynamic nature of wellbeing for children in transnational families, as well as the way in which Husniyah herself constructs her life and experience. It is less clear from this method, however, what the issues would be for her 'wellbecoming', although Orellana (2009) concludes that language brokering enables children to develop many skills that their peers do not. It would seem, however, that Husniyah draws on her relationships to craft resilience in context.

Conclusion

The above consideration of the conceptual and methodological issues raised in studying the wellbeing of transnational families has drawn on the concept of intersectionality to argue that childhood wellbeing is always intersectional and thus psychosocial and permeated by inequalities. The methods used above are not usually used by those studying wellbeing. However, examples presented above show that children develop complex understandings of positioning and potential 'wellbecoming'. These would not necessarily be the understandings of wellbeing that adults or many wellbeing researchers would favour. However, the examples fit with White's (2016) notion that wellbeing is understood differently in different cultures, is situated in place, and that it is important to use methods that allow researchers to listen to participants' subjective perspectives rather than simply using reductionist measures of subjective wellbeing (White, 2010; White, Gaines and Jha, 2012). The notion of 'relational wellbeing' (White, 2016) becomes evident in the analysis of what children and young people say about their lives (or adults say about their childhood experiences).

The examples above make two further contributions to studying and understanding wellbeing as it relates to children in transnational families. First it shows that it is possible to illuminate concerns that have an impact on wellbeing from participants' talk about other issues. Wright (2012) has also shown that deploying wellbeing theory in an interview study can help to broaden analyses of how people's understandings and expectations of wellbeing change as they move across borders and that interviews can allow holistic understandings of wellbeing by showing the dynamic interplay between domains of wellbeing. Second, it has shown that it is possible to understand wellbeing from analyses of cultural products such as newspaper reports as long as the accounts of particular events and so on are analysed as situated in place, culture, and intersectional positioning and it is recognized that the subjective element is missing or partial in such reports. For children, it is also possible to gain some insights into issues of wellbecoming, as in the example of Rahma and Ahmed above. As White (2016) advocates, it is important to recognize the shortcomings of any methods such as those outlined above, which do not remove the necessity of using other methods including quantitative methods, to address other issues. However, taking an intersectional perspective on the study of wellbeing helps illuminate the importance of recognizing that children's wellbeing is necessarily constrained by their positioning in relation, for example, to racism, racialization, religion, gender, and nation. In other words, wellbeing is necessarily political, particularly as operationalized in policy measures.

Note

1 The study was an ESRC Professorial Fellowship (ESRC number: RES-051–27–0181-A) awarded to Ann Phoenix as part of a larger study of adult retrospective narratives of their 'non-normative' childhood experiences. It consisted of three projects: (i) serial migrants who came from the Caribbean to rejoin their parents in

the UK, (ii) members of visibly ethnically different households, (iii) childhood language brokers who interpreted and/or translated for their parents in childhood. The extract above comes from the third project. Forty adult language brokers (27 women and 13 men) were interviewed individually in five countries and three group discussions were held, two in the UK and one in the USA.

Bibliography

Andresen, S., Fegter, S., Hurrelmann, K. and Schneekloth, U., 2017. *Well-being, Poverty and Justice from a Child's Perspective: 3rd World Vision Children Study*. Cham, Switzerland: Springer.

Archer, L., 2011. Constructing minority ethnic middle-class identity: An exploratory study with parents, pupils and young professionals. *Sociology*, 45(1), pp.134–151.

Asbury, K., Dunn, J.F., Pike, A. and Plomin, R. (2003). Nonshared environmental influences on individual differences in early behavioral development: A monozygotic twin differences study. *Child development*, 74(3), pp.933–943.

Ballas, D., Dorling, D. and Shaw, M., 2007. Social inequality, health, and well-being. In: J. Haworth and G. Hart, eds. 2007. *Well-being: Individual, Community, and Social Perspectives*. London: Palgrave Macmillan, pp.163–186.

Bentley, D., 2012. 'First annual results of David Cameron's happiness index published'. *The Independent*, 24 July 2012. Available at: http://www.independent.co.uk/news/uk/politics/first-annual-results-of-david-camerons-happiness-index-p ublished-7972861.html [Accessed January 4, 2018].

Bradshaw, J. ed., 2016. *The Wellbeing of Children in the UK*. Bristol: Policy Press.

Brah, A. and Phoenix, A., 2004. Ain't I a woman? Revisiting intersectionality. *Journal of International Women's Studies*, 5(3), pp.75–86.

Bryceson, D. and Vuorela, U., 2002. *The Transnational Family: New European Frontiers and Global Networks*. Oxford: Berg.

Budginaite, I., and Juozeliuniene, I., 2018. How transnational mothering is seen to be 'troubling': Contesting and reframing mothering. *Sociological Research Online*, 23(1), pp.262–281.

Cho, S., Crenshaw, K. and McCall, L., 2013. Toward a field of intersectionality studies: Theory, applications, and praxis. *Signs: Journal of Women in Culture and Society*, 38(4), pp.785–810.

Collins, P.H. and Bilge, S. 2016. *Intersectionality*. New York: John Wiley and Sons.

Crenshaw, K., 1989. Demarginalizing the intersection of race and sex: A black feminist critique of antidiscrimination doctrine, feminist theory and antiracist politics. *University of Chicago Legal Forum*, 1, Article 8. Available at: http://chicagoun bound.uchicago.edu/uclf/vol1989/iss1/8 [Accessed January 2, 2018].

Croghan, R., Griffin, C., Hunter, J. and Phoenix, A., 2006. Style failure: Consumption, identity and social exclusion. *Journal of youth studies*, 9(4), pp.463–478.

Diener, E., 2013. The remarkable changes in the science of subjective well-being. *Perspectives on Psychological Science*, 8(6), pp.663–666.

Diener, E., Lucas, R. and Schimmack, U., 2009. *Well-being for Public Policy*. Oxford: Oxford University Press.

Dolan, P. and Metcalfe, R., 2012. Measuring subjective wellbeing: Recommendations on measures for use by national governments. *Journal of Social Policy*, 41(2), pp.409–427.

Dreby, J., 2015. US immigration policy and family separation: The consequences for children's well-being. *Social Science and Medicine*, 132, pp.245–251.

Ereaut, G. and Whiting, R., 2008. *What do we Mean by 'Wellbeing'? And why Might it Matter?* Research Report No DCSF-RW073. Available at: http://dera.ioe.ac.uk/8572/1/dcsf-rw073%20v2.pdf [Accessed December 17, 2017].

Fattore, T., Mason, J. and Watson, E., 2009. When children are asked about their well-being: Towards a framework for guiding policy. *Child Indicators Research*, 2(1), pp.57–77.

Ferguson, A., 2000. *Bad Boys: Public Schools in the Making of Black Masculinity.* Ann Arbor, MI: University of Michigan Press.

Gillborn, D., 2008. *Racism and Education: Coincidence or Conspiracy?* London: Routledge.

Gillborn, D. and Mirza, H.S., 2000. *Educational Inequality: Mapping Race, Class and Gender: A Synthesis of Research Evidence.* London: OFSTED.

Gilliam, L., 2016. The paradox of civilizing: Civilizing offensives and counter-cultural forms among ethnic minority boys in the Danish school. Conference paper: American Anthropological Association 114th Annual Conference, Denver, Colorado, 18–22 November 2015.

Gilliam, L. and Gulløv, E. eds. 2017. *Children of the Welfare State: Civilising Practices in Schools, Childcare and Families.* London: Pluto Press.

Gitz-Johansen, T., 2003. Representations of ethnicity: How teachers speak about ethnic minority students. In: D. Beach, T. Gordon and E. Lahelma, eds. 2003. *Democratic Education: Ethnographic Challenges.* London: Tufnell Press, pp.66–79.

Goulbourne, H., Reynolds, T., Solomos, J. and Zontini, E., 2010. *Transnational Families: Ethnicities, Identities and Social Capital.* London: Routledge.

Gross, C., Gottburgsen, A. and Phoenix, A., 2016. Education systems and intersectionality. In: A. Hadjar and C. Gross, eds. 2016. *Education Systems and Inequalities: International Comparisons.* Bristol: Policy Press, pp.51–72.

Hauser, S.T., Allen, J.P. and Golden, E., 2009. *Out of the Woods: Tales of Resilient Teens.* Cambridge, MA: Harvard University Press.

Haworth, J. and Hart, G. eds. 2007. *Well-being: Individual, Community and Social Perspectives.* London: Palgrave Macmillan.

Hondagneu-Sotelo, P. and Avila, E., 1997. "I'm here, but I'm there": The meanings of Latina transnational motherhood. *Gender and Society*, 11(5), pp.548–571.

Hone, L.C., Jarden, A., Schofield, G.M. and Duncan, S., 2014. Measuring flourishing: The impact of operational definitions on the prevalence of high levels of wellbeing. *International Journal of Wellbeing*, 4(1), pp.62–90.

Howarth, C., 2002. 'So, you're from Brixton?': The struggle for recognition and esteem in a stigmatized community. *Ethnicities*, 2(2), pp.237–260.

Hughey, M.W. and Jackson, C.A., 2017. The dimensions of racialization and the inner-city school. *The Annals of the American Academy of Political and Social Science*, 673(1), pp.312–329.

Ipsos MORI and Nairn, A., 2011. *Children's Well-being in UK, Sweden and Spain: The Role of Inequality and Materialism.* London: UNICEF. Available at: https://www.unicef.es/sites/unicef.es/files/IPSOS_UNICEF_ChildWellBeingreport.pdf [Accessed January 10, 2018].

Iqbal, H., Neal, S. and Vincent, C., 2017. Children's friendships in super-diverse localities: Encounters with social and ethnic difference. *Childhood*, 24(1), pp.128–142.

James, A. and James, A., 2012. *Key Concepts in Childhood Studies.* London: Sage.

Jenkins, R., Meltzer, H., Jones, P.B., Brugha, T., Bebbington, P., Farrell, M. and Crepaz-Keay, D.K., 2008. *Foresight Mental Capital and Wellbeing Project. Mental health: Future challenges.* London: The Government Office for Science.

Labov, W., 1972. *Language in the Inner City: Studies in the Black English Vernacular.* Philadelphia: University of Pennsylvania Press.

Levitt, P. and Glick Schiller, N., 2004. Conceptualizing simultaneity: A transnational social field perspective on society. *International Migration Review*, 38(3), pp.1002–1039.

Lutz, H. ed. 2008. *Migration and Domestic Work: A European Perspective on a Global Theme.* Farnham: Ashgate.

Manderson, L., 2005. Introduction: The social context of wellbeing. In: L. Manderson, ed. 2005. *Rethinking Wellbeing: Essays on Health, Disability and Disadvantage.* Perth: Curtin University Press for API Network, pp.1–25.

Marks, N. and Shah, H., 2004. A well-being manifesto for a flourishing society. *Journal of Public Mental Health*, 3(4), pp.9–15.

Mazzucato, V. and Schans, D., 2011. Transnational families and the wellbeing of children: Conceptual and methodological challenges. *Journal of Marriage and Family*, 73(4), pp.704–712.

Mazzucato, V., Schans, D., Caarls, K. and Beauchemin, C., 2015. Transnational families between Africa and Europe. *International Migration Review*, 49(1), pp.142–172.

Morrow, V. and Mayall, B., 2010. Measuring children's well-being: Some problems and possibilities. In: A. Morgan, M. Davies and E. Ziglio, eds. 2010. *Health Assets in a Global Context: Theory, Methods, Action.* New York: Springer, pp.145–165.

Mullineaux, P.Y., Deater-Deckard, K., Petrill, S.A. and Thompson, L.A., 2009. Parenting and child behaviour problems: A longitudinal analysis of non-shared environment. *Infant and Child Development*, 18(2), pp.133–148.

Neal, S. and Vincent, C., 2013. Multiculture, middle class competencies and friendship practices in super-diverse geographies. *Social and Cultural Geography*, 14(8), pp.909–929.

New Economics Foundation, 2008. *Five Ways to Wellbeing: The Postcards* (Steps we can all take to improve our personal wellbeing), 21 October 2008. London: NEF. Available at: http://neweconomics.org/2008/10/five-ways-to-wellbeing-the-postcards/ [Accessed December 12, 2017].

Orellana, M.F., 2009. *Translating childhoods: Immigrant youth, language, and culture.* New Brunswick, NJ: Rutgers University Press.

Orellana, M.F., Thorne, B., Chee, A. and Lam, E.E.S., 2001. Transnational childhoods: The participation of children in processes of family migration. *Social Problems*, 48(4), pp.572–591.

Parreñas, R.S., 2005. *Children of Global Migration: Transnational Families and Gendered Woes.* Stanford, CA: Stanford University Press.

Phoenix, A., 2011. Somali young women and hierarchies of belonging. *Young*, 19(3), pp.313–331.

Pollard, E.L. and Lee, P.D., 2003. Child well-being: A systematic review of the literature. *Social Indicators Research*, 61(1), pp.59–78.

Rollock, N., Gillborn, D., Vincent, C. and Ball, S.J., 2014. *The Colour of Class: The Educational Strategies of the Black Middle Classes.* London: Routledge.

Rutter, M., 2006. Implications of resilience concepts for scientific understanding. *Annals of the New York Academy of Sciences*, 1094(1), pp.1–12.

Ryff, C.D., Love, G.D., Urry, H.L., Muller, D., Rosenkranz, M.A., Friedman, E.M., Davidson, R.J. and Singer, B., 2006. Psychological well-being and ill-being: Do they have distinct or mirrored biological correlates? *Psychotherapy and psychosomatics*, 75(2), pp.85–95.

Schwanen, T. and Atkinson, S., 2014. Geographies of wellbeing: An introduction. *The Geographical Journal*, 181(2), pp.98–101.

Skrbiš, Z., 2008. Transnational families: Theorising migration, emotions and belonging. *Journal of intercultural studies*, 29(3), pp.231–246.

Sørensen, N.N. and Vammen, I.M., 2014. Who cares? Transnational families in debates on migration and development. *New Diversities*, 16(2), 89–108.

Souralová, A. and Fialová, H., 2017. Where have all the fathers gone? Remarks on feminist research on transnational fatherhood. *NORMA: International Journal for Masculinity Studies*, 12(2), pp.159–174.

Statham, J. and Chase, E., 2010. *Childhood Wellbeing: A Brief Overview*. London: DfE Childhood Wellbeing Research Centre. Available at: http://www.cwrc.ac.uk/resour ces/documents/CWRC_State_of_Play_briefing_paper_for_DFE_website4Aug2010_(2). pdf [Accessed January 10, 2018].

UNICEF Innocenti Research Centre, 2007. *Child Poverty in Perspective: An Overview of Child Well-being in Rich Countries*. Florence: Innocenti Report Card 07/19. Available at: https://www.unicef-irc.org/publications/pdf/rc7_eng.pdf [Accessed January 10, 2018].

Walkerdine, V., 1988. *The Mastery of Reason: Cognitive Development and the Production of Rationality*. London: Taylor and Francis/Routledge.

White, S., 2010. Analysing wellbeing: A framework for development practice. *Development in Practice*, 20(2), pp.158–172.

White, S., 2016. Introduction: The many faces of wellbeing. In: S. White, ed. 2016. *Cultures of Wellbeing: Method, Place, Policy*. Basingstoke: Palgrave Macmillan, pp.1–44.

White, S., 2017. Relational wellbeing: Re-centring the politics of happiness, policy and the self. *Policy and Politics*, 45(2), pp.121–136.

White, S.C., Gaines, S.O. and Jha, S., 2012. Beyond subjective well-being: A critical review of the Stiglitz report approach to subjective perspectives on quality of life. *Journal of International Development*, 24(6), pp.63–76.

White, S.C., Gaines, S.O. and Jha, S., 2014. Inner wellbeing: Concept and validation of a new approach to subjective perceptions of wellbeing – India. *Social Indicators Research*, 119(2), pp.723–746.

White, S.C. and Jha, S., 2014. The ethical imperative of qualitative methods: Developing measures of subjective dimensions of well-being in Zambia and India. *Ethics and Social Welfare*, 8(3), pp.262–276.

Wilding, R., 2006. 'Virtual' intimacies? Families communicating across transnational contexts. *Global networks*, 6(2), pp.125–142.

Wilkinson, R.G. and Pickett, K., 2009. *The Spirit Level: Why More Equal Societies Almost Always Do Better*. London: Allen Lane.

Wolf, D.L., 2002. There's no place like 'home': Emotional transnationalism and the struggles of second-generation Filipinos. In: P. Levitt and M.C. Waters, eds. 2002. *The Changing Face of Home: The Transnational Lives of the Second Generation*. New York: Russell Sage Foundation, pp.255–294.

Wright, K., 2012. Constructing human wellbeing across spatial boundaries: Negotiating meanings in transnational migration. *Global Networks*, 12(4), pp.467–484.

Yeoh, B.S., Huang, S. and Lam, T., 2005. Transnationalizing the 'Asian' family: Imaginaries, intimacies and strategic intents. *Global networks*, 5(4), pp.307–315.

Youdell, D., 2006. *Impossible Bodies, Impossible Selves: Exclusions and Student Subjectivities*. New York: Springer.

Glossary

Arabic terms

al-usra	the family
da'wā	promoting Islamic faith and teachings
ḥadīth	(lit., report, account, statement). A report recounting what Prophet Muhammad said, practised, approved of or disapproved. A ḥadīth consists of: 1) the chain of narrators who transmitted the report (*isnād*) and, 2) the content of the report (*matn*)
halāl	permitted according to Islamic theology
harām	forbidden or sinful according to Islamic theology
ibda' bi-man ta'ūl	begin with those whom you financially maintain (i.e. your dependents)
ijāb	the act of the bride's (or her guardian's on her behalf) offer of marriage to the groom when concluding an Islamic marriage contract
istikhāra prayer	prayer conducted for the purpose of asking for God's guidance when a Muslim needs to make an important decision and is unsure which path to take
mahr	dower, a legal obligation of the groom due to the bride in Islamic jurisprudence
mawada	affection
nikāḥ	the act of concluding a marriage in Islamic jurisprudence
nikāh 'urfi	a 'customary' Muslim marriage contract not officially registered with state authorities
niqāb	face veil
qiwāmah	a principle in Islamic jurisprudence that obligates husbands to provide for and act as the guardian of their wives
qubūl	the groom's acceptance in answer to the bride's or her guardian's *ijāb* when concluding an Islamic marriage contract
rahma	compassion
sharī'a	(lit., water source; the way, the path). Understood in Islamic theology as the totality of God's will / path / message, comprised of multiple dimensions (theological, ethical, spiritual, and legal)

shumūlīya	the condition of being comprehensive and holistic
talāq	unilateral divorce initiated by the husband in an Islamic marriage, through an act of pronouncement, often extra-judicially
'urfi	customary
wali	guardian of a dependent (e.g. son or daughter) in Islamic jurisprudence charged with managing the affairs of the dependent
wastīya	moderation
zinā	illicit sexual relationship, i.e., taking place outside of marriage, according to Islamic jurisprudence

Somali terms

buufis	mental distress
gaal	non-Muslim
fadhi-ku-dirir	sitting in cafés with other Somalis to engage in heated discussions about home-country politics
khat	a plant (*Catha edulis*) native to East Africa and Yemen that releases a stimulant when its narcotic leaves are chewed

Index